BETWEEN THE WARS

Marie Laurençin—'Woman with Fan'
(Reproduced by permission of Gustav Kahnweiler, Esq., and Everett, Morgan & Grundy).

BETWEEN THE WARS

by

James Laver

HOUGHTON MIFFLIN COMPANY
Boston, The Riverside Press, Cambridge
1961

FIRST PUBLISHED IN 1961 BY
VISTA BOOKS; LONGACRE PRESS
161–6 FLEET STREET, LONDON E.C.4
PRINTED IN GREAT BRITAIN BY
MORRISON AND GIBB LTD
LONDON AND EDINBURGH

INTRODUCTION

AFTER *Victorian Vista* and *Edwardian Promenade* it seemed logical to continue the series with a study of the period *Between the Wars*, constructed very much on the same plan. The method employed in the two previous volumes was to concentrate on trifles, in the belief that the surface-pattern can sometimes reveal the depths. War and politics were alike eschewed, unless they could be shown to have influenced the shape of a chair or the cut of a coat. It was assumed that the Victorians and the Edwardians were able to live their lives almost untouched by foreign wars and revolutions.

Unfortunately (and it is indeed unfortunate in more ways than one) this non-political approach is impossible for the period *Between the Wars*. This was a time when politics and foreign affairs impinged on everybody's life. Revolution was no longer something that happened in South America, or even in France. It was something that might happen *here*, at any moment. We were compelled to be part of Europe and to share in world upheavals, whether we liked it or not.

This book, therefore, is much more concerned with public events than either of its predecessors, for public events had become part of private life. No longer was it possible to content oneself with the mere symbols of an age: a paper-lace Valentine or an Edwardian menu. Even the social history of the period is written in headlines. It would be idle to deny that the present volume cannot, in the nature of things, be as *pretty* as the two that preceded it. Even the illustrations, whatever their documentary value, cannot pretend to charm.

There is also the fact that, at least for those of us who have reached middle age, the theme of *Between the Wars* is contemporary history. Distance no longer lends enchantment to the view. This is the period

3

we have lived through. Many of us *remember* the General Strike; most of us were involved in the Second World War.

The clothes and interior decorations have no 'period flavour': they are merely 'old-fashioned'. They fall into that 'Gap in Appreciation' which follows every style. Even the mechanical contrivances which have developed so rapidly in our era have not had time to slip into the perspective of history. There are, so far as one knows, no collectors of early 'wireless' sets. We have societies for preserving primitive steam locomotives, but none, as yet, for salvaging early flying machines. We do not even think them quaint; we think them clumsy.

Perhaps later generations will be of a different opinion. Perhaps they will forget the frivolities, the frustrations, the anxieties, the guilt-obsessions of those strange years from 1918 to 1939, and find only romance in the story of an abdicating King, and a quaint old-world charm in Dr. Summerskill's hats. Meanwhile it is hoped that the present volume will serve to remind older readers of their own ardours and endurances, and to paint, for younger ones, a picture of what life in England was like *Between the Wars*.

J. L.

4

ACKNOWLEDGEMENTS

THE PUBLISHERS and Editor gratefully acknowledge permission given by the following for the quotations used:

Mr Richard Aldington (*Death of a Hero*); Messrs George Allen & Unwin (*Down the Fairway* by Robert T. Jones, Jnr. and O. B. Keeler, and *The Twenties* by John Montgomery); Messrs Barrie & Rockliff (*Berlin: The Eagle and the Bear* by John Mander); Messrs B. T. Batsford (*Soccer* by Denzil Batchelor, *Our Times* by Vivian Ogilvie and *Movies for the Million* by Gilbert Seldes); Mr H. L. Beales (*Memoirs of the Unemployed* by H. L. Beales and R. S. Lambert); Messrs Ernest Benn (*Housing* by Harry Burnes and *The Great Delusion* by Neon); Bookman Associates Inc. (*Marriage, Morals and Sex in America* by Sidney Ditzion); Messrs Jonathan Cape (*The Necessity of Communism* by John Middleton Murry, and *Twenty-Five* and *Cry Havoc* by Beverley Nichols); Messrs Jonathan Cape and Duell, Sloan & Pearce Inc. (*England's Crisis* by André Siegfried); Messrs Cassell & Co. and Houghton Mifflin Co. (*The Second World War* by Winston Churchill); Messrs Chatto & Windus (*The Buried Day* by C. Day Lewis, *Flying* by Claude Grahame-White, *These Hurrying Years* by Gerald Heard and *Disenchantment* by C. E. Montague); Mr Noël Coward and Messrs William Heinemann ('Débutantes', 'Dance Little Lady' and 'A narrow strip of sand . . .' from *Play Parade*); Messrs. J. M. Dent & Sons (*Can Governments Cure Unemployment?* by Norman Angell and Harold Wright); Messrs J. M. Dent & Sons and E. P. Dutton & Co. Inc. (*A History of Golf* by Robert Browning, © 1955 by E. P. Dutton & Co. Inc.); Messrs J. M. Dent & Sons and the estate of Cicely Hamilton (*Modern England*); E.P. Dutton & Co. Inc. (*Her Name Was Wallis Warfield* by Edwina H. Wilson); Messrs Elek Books (*Madness After Midnight* by Jack Glicco); Messrs Faber & Faber ('I remember Spain' from *Collected Poems 1949* by Louis MacNeice); Messrs Faber & Faber and Random House Inc. ('Moving through the silent crowd . . .' from *Collected Poems 1955 — Poems by Stephen Spender —* and lines from 'Not palaces, an era's crown' from *Collected Poems 1928-53* by Stephen Spender, *both* © 1934 by The Modern Library Inc. *Look Stranger* and 'What's your proposal?' from *Collected Shorter Poems 1950* by W. H. Auden); Messrs Victor Gollancz and Columbia University Press (*Communism and British Intellectuals* by Neal Wood); Editions Bernard Grasset (*Une Mélodie Silencieuse* by René Schwob, © Editions Bernard Grasset); Mrs Philip Guedalla (*The Hundredth Year* by Philip Guedalla); the estate of Cicely Hamilton (*Modern Germanies*); Messrs Hamish Hamilton (*After All* by Sir Norman Angell); Messrs Harper & Brothers (*Only Yesterday*, © 1931 by Frederick Lewis Allen); Messrs George Harrap & Co. (*Taste and Fashion* by James Laver); Messrs William Heinemann (*I Believed*

6

CONTENTS

LIST OF ILLUSTRATIONS

9

52. Diana Fishwick, Palm Beach, Florida, 1933.

53. *Left:* Walter Hagen in play, 1920.
Right: The Prince of Wales playing golf at Biarritz, 1924.

60. A crystal set for 7/6. Radio Exhibition, White City, 1924.

61. Rudolph Valentino lying in state in the Campbell Funeral Parlour, New York, 1926.

64. Marlene Dietrich in *The Blue Angel.*

65. Greta Garbo, before the days of fame.

80. The R.101 riding at its mooring mast, Cardington, 1930.

81. The wreck of the R.101, near Beauvais, France. October 7th, 1930.

84. H. G. Hawker at Hendon with his 80 h.p. Sopwith machine.

85. *Above:* First England–Australia Flight, 1919. Vickers Vimy bomber with crew.
Below: The Vickers Vimy in which Alcock and Brown flew the Atlantic in 1919.

92. Charles Lindbergh after crossing the Atlantic solo, 1927.

93. Amy Johnson after her solo flight to Australia, 1930.

96. The Charleston: Bee Jackson, World Champion, c. 1925.

97. Henry Lamb—*Lytton Strachey* (Reproduced by permission of the Executors of Henry Lamb and The Tate Gallery).

100. Jack Buchanan and Lily Elsie, Daly's Theatre, London, 1922.

101. *Above:* Elsa Lanchester in her 'Seven Dials' Club.
Below: Mrs. Kate Meyrick: reception on her release from Holloway Prison, 1930.

10

108. Revolution in Underwear. Black and coral ribbon-threaded cami-knickers from Paris, 1926.

109. Fred and Adele Astaire dancing on the roof of the Savoy Hotel, London, 1922.

112. Noël Coward and Lilian Braithwaite in *The Vortex*.

113. *Left:* Iris and Daphne Grenfell at the 'Baby' Party, 1929.
Right: Mrs. Armstrong Jones (later Countess of Rosse) at the Austrian Legation Period Ball, 1934.
Below: A Débutante's Swimming Party, 1932.
(Photographs on this page are reproduced by permission of *The Sketch*.)

116. The Hon. David Herbert, Lady Plunket and Walter Crisham: 'Gods, Goddesses and Muses mobilised for Charity', 1935. (Reproduced by permission of *The Sketch*.)

117. Mrs. Poppet Jackson (formerly Miss Poppet John) in the costume worn at Mr. Cecil Beaton's *Fête Champêtre*, 1937. (Reproduced by permission of *The Sketch*.)

124. Super 'Oxford Bags', 1926 (Reproduced by permission of the L.N.A.).

125. L. S. Lowry—*Street Scene* (Reproduced by permission of Howard Spring, Esq.).

128. The General Strike, 1926: An armoured car escorting food convoys.

129. George Lansbury speaking at a Means Test Rally in Trafalgar Square, London.

144. Eldorado Night Club, Berlin: Four of the 'ladies' are men.

145. *Above:* Hitler taking the salute at a parade of Brown Shirts, early 'thirties.
Below: Hitler taking the salute at a military parade, mid 'thirties.

148. 'I am a Jew but I *will* not grumble about the Nazis.'

149. Hitler addressing 20,000 Nazis at the Sportspalast, Berlin, 1938.

156. Sports costume and walking costume, 1926.

157. Bathing costumes at Deauville, 1926.

160. Highlights of summer at Haslemere (Reproduced by permission of Léon).

161. Eden Roc, Cap d'Antibes, 1932 (Reproduced by permission of *The Sketch*).

176. Policemen arresting a demonstrator against the march of Mosley's Fascists in the East End of London, 1936.

177. Sir Oswald Mosley giving the Fascist salute.

192. Mr. Victor Gollancz, inventor of 'The Left Book Club'.

193. Intellectuals of the 'thirties: W. H. Auden, Cecil Day Lewis and Stephen Spender. This photograph, taken in 1949, is believed to be the only one of all three together.

196. *Above:* King Edward VIII and his brothers in procession from King's Cross Station to Westminster Hall, January, 1936.
Below: Funeral procession of King George V passing through Windsor, January, 1936.

197. King George V lying in state in Westminster Hall, 1936.

204. Mr. and Mrs. Stanley Baldwin, 1935.

205. King Edward VIII with Mrs. Simpson at Ascot, 1935.

208. *Above:* Newspaper placards, December, 1936.
Below: A scene at Marble Arch, Hyde Park, London. December, 1936.

12

13

CHAPTER I

THE AFTERMATH

'THE WAR TO END WAR' had been brought to a successful conclusion, and few people realized how much of self-delusion there is in such a phrase:

' "The war to end war" appears to have been fought more than once. Chateaubriand, at any rate, believed he had lived through it and saw its final episode in Waterloo. "Napoleon," he wrote in his *Memoirs*, "has closed the era of the past. War can never again engross the interest of humanity — he made it on too grand a scale, a scale that can never be equalled. He shut behind him, once for all, the gates of the temple of Janus and heaped against them so great a pile of dead that never again can they reopen." '

Cicely Hamilton, 'Modern England', 1938

¶ Certainly everybody in 1918 was tired of conflict, and even of victory celebrations, just as they had been in 1815:

> 'We've had enough of fleets and camps,
> Guns, glories, odes, gazettes.
> Triumphal arches, coloured lamps,
> Huzzas and epaulettes.
> We could not bear upon our heads
> Another leaf of bay.
> That wretched Bonaparte's dead.
> Yes! take the sword away!'

William M. Praed

¶ Mr. Lloyd George had promised the returning soldiers 'a Land fit for Heroes to live in'. In case the awkward question of paying for the War should be raised he had also promised to 'squeeze Germany till the pips squeak'. Few people seemed yet to have realized that wars can never be paid for out of 'reparations' and that lands fit not for

15

heroes but just for ordinary men and women are not so easily built. The soldiers were so glad to be back that for the moment everything seemed rosy:

Charles F. G. Masterman, 'England After War', 1922 'It is certain that the larger movements of social unrest amongst the workers in Britain were at the beginning fomented, not by or among the men who fought abroad, but by and among the men who stayed at home. It was the great centres of home industry which were exempted from the conscription who first agitated the nation with truculent demands for the betterment of their conditions. The railwaymen, the coal-miners, the dock-labourers, the workers in the munition cities such as Glasgow, were the leaders in this revolt. No prominent part in this revolt was taken by the travellers who had returned. They were mostly, as discharged soldiers and sailors, for the moment at least, returned to a world where they were very contented to find security and any place reserved for them at all; very content, indeed, to find themselves alive. Later there have been signs that this numbness is passing away, and passing away even now, not as the truculent demand of the returned hero, but because that hero has been shelled out of the lair which he thought secure by the coming of unemployment, as once he was shelled out of the dug-out by the enemy's guns.'

¶ For some time after the conclusion of hostilities an artificial boom continued. Business was brisk, for there was still some money about, and the supply of consumer goods still insufficient to meet the demand. Why should such a happy state of affairs not go on for ever?

Charles F. G. Masterman, 'England After War', 1922 'But some year and a half after the war, the whole thing came to an end, like the sudden stopping of a clock. Through world reactions over which they had no control, who live in courts and streets where the sun never rises, the inhabitants of these secluded regions suddenly found that no one had any need for their services. They all fell in a heap into the abyss.'

¶ Great Britain had suffered a social upheaval the like of which had perhaps never been seen in her history since the Black Death:

Charles F. G. Masterman, 'England After War', 1922 'It is difficult rightly to estimate the effect upon the future of Britain of the gigantic migration which tore men from the fields or from town and office stool, and sent them out by millions beyond the sea to risk

16

Victory celebrations in London, November, 1918.

Homes for Heroes.

their lives in every corner of the world. In France each citizen had passed through the disturbing and unifying influence of the two years' conscription in times of peace. France had still close at hand the bitter memories of foreign invasion. And France was for the most part fighting during the war on the soil, and in defence of the soil, of its own sacred land. The French armies were also largely peasant armies, recruited from the owners of the soil and their children, accepting the necessity for the defence of their own fields and homes. But in Britain none of these conditions occurred. Men volunteered or were pressed into the armies and shipped over the sea in millions who otherwise would never have seen the sea or visited foreign lands or left their native town. They owned no piece of land in which they fought. They had owned no portion of the land from which they had gone. They went out into the great adventure of all the world. They served in France and Italy, in Gallipoli and Salonica, in Egypt and Palestine and India and Mesopotamia, in the frosty Caucasus and the White Sea. And at the end they came home also in millions again, also without owning any piece of their own land, to take up the thread of life which had been so rudely snapped by service in a struggle they had always previously regarded as incredible. A friend of mine heard fragments of conversation between a bus conductor and a passenger, while the vehicle was held up by the passing of a regiment of Guards. The conductor had fought through the war and become a Sergeant-Major: "But that's not to say that I liked it." In reply to some patriotic platitude he burst out fiercely: "I don't see that it *is* my country. I don't own a thing in it." '

¶ There was, however, one gleam of light — Women now had the Vote:

'Peeresses in their own right were not dealt with in this Act, and *Ray Strachey,* although in 1922 the Viscountess Rhondda secured a judgment from *'The Cause', 1928* the Committee on Privileges that she was qualified to take her seat in the House of Lords, this decision was subsequently reversed. In the same year that the Act was passed, however, the first woman appeared in the House of Commons, when the Viscountess Astor was returned as a Conservative for the Sutton Division of Plymouth at a by-election made necessary by her husband's accession to a Peerage. This event was hailed all over the country, and indeed all over the world, as a great achievement; and although there were still a few sulky and old-fashioned M.P's who shook their heads, and went out of their way to be politely disagreeable, her reception in the House was better than had been feared. For a time, of course, it was attended with a blaze of publicity. Everything she did or said was reported and exaggerated, and it was fortunate indeed for the movement that she was not only courageous, but also able and witty. Inside the House she speedily won for herself a unique position; and outside she became the symbol of hope to people whom she could never meet. Hundreds of letters poured in upon her daily from every part of the kingdom. "You, Lady Astor, being a woman and a mother yourself, will understand what we feel . . ." And understand she did. In a very short time she was identified in the public mind with all the social reforms which are dear to ordinary women, as well as being known everywhere as the champion of women's equal rights in every aspect of life.'

¶ But what was the good of 'Women's Rights' if you couldn't even find a house to live in?

Norman Angell and Harold Wright, 'Can Governments Cure Unemployment?', 1931 'Immense efforts have been made since the war to grapple with the housing problem, and enormous numbers of houses have been built. Nevertheless the problem has not been solved. Even the crude demand for houses has not yet been met . . . [and] the slum problem remains as acute as ever . . . it was stated a few weeks ago in the House of Lords that about a hundred thousand people were at present living in London basements under unhealthy conditions. The rate of mortality among those who live in these places is ten times as heavy as it is in Hampstead. The basements have in many cases been condemned by the sanitary authorities, but nothing happens. Where are the hundred thousand people to go? In about every London borough families of six or seven living, eating, sleeping, doing all their daily domestic tasks in a single room, are common. In Manchester, where overcrowding is said to be below the average for urban districts, an investigation recently conducted in a street containing seventy-one houses revealed that in twenty-two out of the seventy-one the overcrowding was such that separate bedroom accommodation for growing boys and girls was impossible.'

¶ The slums indeed were very far from being abolished.

Mrs. C. S. Peel, O.B.E., 'Life's Enchanted Cup', 1933 'One family which I visited lived in an odd little house consisting of one bedroom, one ground-floor room, and a basement kitchen opening into a high-walled yard, more like a tank than a yard, and

18

from which almost all light was obscured by surrounding buildings which pressed right up against it. In these quarters lived a respectable hard-working man, a kind, good hard-working mother and seven children. There had been nine, but the eldest boy had been killed in the War ("Oh, he was a good lad to me", sighed the mother) and the eldest girl, aged seventeen, was out in service.

'In the bedroom the bugs were crawling on the walls and dropping on to the beds. "We have tried everything," our hostess explained, "but as fast as we get 'em down, they come in fresh from houses on either side."

'Father, mother and the two youngest children slept in this room. Three girls slept in the ground-floor room and the two boys in the kitchen. The mother took in washing. It was a hot June day when we visited her, and the kitchen was an inferno of heat, and thick with steam. The children were just coming home for their dinner, which they would eat there. All the clothes had to be dried in the house, for if hung in the yard, they became black with smuts. At twelve-thirty on this summer morning, gas was burning in the kitchen for the only window was a mere slit just above the pavement and obscured by dirt. It could not be opened except after everyone had gone to bed, for while any children were about, and they played in the streets until late at night in that neighbourhood, they would lie on their stomachs and throw dust and stones and garbage into the kitchen.

'The "Sanitary Lady" told me that the children of this family were sickly, but admirably brought up, and that every week on her afternoon out the eldest girl came to lend her mother a hand with the ironing and to bring a few sweets for the little ones.'

¶ The big Government housing project proved a disastrous failure:

'The Addison Scheme gave the opportunity for an interesting experiment in the direction of reducing the cost of the building materials required for the erection of working-class houses. There is no mystery about what happened . . . In the criticism so unsparingly cast upon Dr. Addison's administration, too little allowance is made for his war experience. Called in to provide munitions, when munitions whatever they cost had to be found, he did find them, and moreover greatly reduced their cost. After the war he was charged to produce houses as he had produced shells and he went at it with the same energy. Unfortunately for him he took the expression Homes

Harry Burnes, 'Housing', 1923

for Heroes a little too seriously and thought it meant Homes for Heroes at any cost, forgetting that peace is not war, that while she may have her victories not less renowned than war, they cannot be allowed to be as expensive. In his eagerness to be assured that his houses should not have to wait for materials, his Department of Building Materials Supplies was set to work buying materials up in advance. I think it is true that in the earlier days the prices paid were less than the market price, but unfortunately it was largely the prices paid by the Department of Building Materials Supplies that later put up the price . . . The experience so gained has been an expensive one, but may yet be profitable if it teaches us what not to do when we are embarked on a great and continuous housing programme.'

¶ The Middle Classes had their difficulties too:

Mrs. C. S. Peel, O.B.E., 'Life's Enchanted Cup', 1933   'London is a striking witness to the changes which have taken place in the life of the educated classes. With few exceptions great houses have become clubs, institutions, offices; their former owners can no longer afford their upkeep. The roomy houses in which Victorian and Edwardian families lived have been divided into upper and lower parts, reconstructed to form flats, or turned into boarding houses, private hotels or hostels. Young people of good position live in reconstructed mews and many girls who would in pre-War days have married into a nice little house, and kept a nice little household, live in a minute flat or upper part and afford, perhaps, a nurse, and themselves act as cook and house parlourmaid, with or without the assistance of a "daily". In my youth there were charwomen but the "daily" is a new invention.'

¶ The same acute commentator gives us some interesting notes on price-levels:

Mrs. C. S. Peel, O.B.E., 'Life's Enchanted Cup', 1933   'Until 1912 or '13, when prices began to rise slightly, it was possible for a competent housewife, even in a servant-keeping house, if the cook was willing to do her part, to provide an early cup of tea, a breakfast dish and the usual toast, butter and marmalade, an 11 o'clock refresher for the maids, a substantial luncheon which was also the nursery and servants' dinner, a simple tea, and a three-course dinner for eight people, two of whom dined late, for 10s. per head per week; the 10s. to include the cost of food and cleaning materials only. To

20

The Big Three in Paris, 1919: Clemenceau, Woodrow Wilson and Lloyd George.

Lloyd George addressing a meeting at Lampeter station, Wales, 1919.

Woodrow Wilson at bay.

keep within this limit it was necessary to buy all provisions to advantage and to use them to advantage.

'In a two-to-four-servant middle-class household (including a nurse) the standard of living expected by the maids was not as high as it is now.

'During the War the cost of food rose by 129 per cent above 1914 prices, and in 1920, the year of the highest prices, to 191 per cent above 1914 prices. At the time that I write these words — March, 1933 — it is again possible — given clever management — to provide plain food of the kind to which middle-class people are now accustomed at the 10s. rate.'

¶ For the more thoughtful of the returning warriors, the disillusionment was complete.

' "The freedom of Europe", "The war to end war", "The overthrow of militarism", "The cause of civilization" — most people believe so little now in anything or anyone that they would find it hard to understand the simplicity and intensity of faith with which these phrases were once taken among our troops, or the certitude felt by hundreds of thousands of men who are now dead that if they were killed their monument would be a new Europe not soured or soiled with the hates and greeds of the old. That the old spirit of Prussia might not infest our world any more; that they or, if not they, their sons might breathe a new, cleaner air they had willingly hung themselves up to rot on the uncut wire at Loos or wriggled to death, slow hour by slow hour, in the cold filth at Broodseinde. Now all was done that man could do, and all was done in vain . . . had failed — had won the fight and lost the prize; the garland of the war was withered before it was gained. The lost years, the broken youth, the dead friends, the women's overshadowed lives at home, the agony and bloody sweat — all had gone to darken the stains which most of us had thought to scour out of the world that our children would live in. Many men felt, and said to each other, that they had been fooled. They had believed that their country was backing them. They had thought, as they marched into Germany, "Now we shall show old Fritz how you treat a man when you've thrashed him." They would let him into the English secret, the tip that the power and glory are not to the bully. As some of them looked at the melancholy performance which followed, our Press and our politicians parading at Paris in moral *pickelhauben*

C. E. Montague,
'Disenchantment',
(republished) 1940

21

and doing the Prussianist goose-step by way of *pas de triomphe*, they could not but say in dismay to themselves: "This is our doing. We cannot wish the war unwon, and yet — if we had shirked, poor old England, for all we know, might not have come to this pass. So we come home draggle-tailed, sick of the mess that we were unwittingly helping to make when we tried to do well." '

¶ Some of those who had been through the War turned with fury on those who had made it, or at least made it possible. They had come to believe that the War which had carried away so many of the young had been entirely the fault of the old men, the pompous, platitudinous politicians who (such was the theory) had sat comfortably at home while the casualty lists lengthened and the heap of 'riddled corpses round Bapaume' grew higher and higher. The mood in which Rupert Brooke had set out contrasted strongly with the mood in which Siegfried Sassoon had come home. The world of idealism had been destroyed and instead there was a 'Waste Land', a kind of lunar landscape like that shown in the canvases which Paul Nash had brought back from the Front.

No one expressed this feeling more bitterly than Richard Aldington. He makes one of his characters express shame at having survived the holocaust, when so many good men had died:

Richard Aldington,
'Death of a Hero',
1929
' "What am I? O God, nothing, less than nothing, a husk, a leaving, a half-chewed morsel on the plate, a regret . . . What right have I to live? Is it five million, is it ten million, is it twenty million? What does the exact count matter? There they are, and we are responsible. Tortures of hell, we are responsible! When I meet an unmaimed man of my generation, I want to shout at him: 'How did you escape? How did you dodge it? What dirty trick did you play? Why are you not dead, trickster?'

' "You the war dead, I think you died in vain, I think you died for nothing, for a blast of wind, a blather, a humbug, a newspaper stunt, a politician's ramp. But at least you died . . .

' "And the women? Oh, don't let's talk about the women. They were splendid, wonderful. Such devotion, such devotion! How they comforted the troops! Oh, wonderful, beyond all praise! They got the vote for it, you know. Oh, wonderful! Steel-true and blade-straight. Yes, indeed, wonderful, wonderful! What ever should we have done without them? White feathers, and all that, you know.

Oh, the women were marvellous. You can always rely upon the women to come up to scratch you know. Yes, indeed. What would the country be without them? So splendid, such an example." '

¶ The hysterical bitterness expressed by Aldington's hero was, perhaps, exceptional, but disillusionment was general enough. And if the young were disillusioned with the conduct of the world by the old, the old were certainly disillusioned by the mood of the returning warriors.

' "Our splendid troops" were to come home — oh very soon — purged and ennobled by slaughter and lice, and were to beget a race of even nobler fellows to go and do likewise. We were to have a great revival of religion, for people's thoughts were now turned from frivolities to great and serious themes.'

Richard Aldington, 'Death of a Hero', 1929

¶ Certainly the great Religious Revival failed to materialize:

'The B.E.F. were in general irreligious: they had reduced morality to the single virtue of loyalty. The Seven Deadly Sins of Pride, Envy, Lust, Avarice, Intemperance, Anger and Sloth were venial so long as a man was courageous and a reasonably trustworthy comrade. God as an all-wise Providence was dead; blind Chance succeeded to the Throne.'

Gerald Heard, 'These Hurrying Years', 1934

¶ Another social commentator noted, sadly:

'It may be something of the disillusionment of middle age, but I cannot help thinking that twenty years ago the younger men, clergy and laymen, were preaching a gospel with vigour and sincerity which today finds no advocates. I remember the days of the Christian Social Union, with the extraordinary wisdom and genius of Bishop Westcott at the head of it, and with Scott Holland and Gilbert Chesterton and myself and others conducting "crusades" in the great cities of England, where we would fill the largest halls, in say, the railway sheds at Derby, or Saint George's Hall at Bradford, or the great Public Hall at Leeds; in which, although our doctrines scared the local clergy out of their wits, the packed audiences of the common people heard us gladly. But the thing appears at the moment dead, and our efforts expended in vain. And those who still remember the good times, when so much of the Church that was alive with names

Charles F. G. Masterman, 'England After War', 1922

like Stanton and Dolling was on the side of the poor, must feel some sadness in gazing over the desolation of an organization which does indeed do an enormous amount of efficient and good work, but which cannot at the moment claim to present any vision capable of combating the prevailing materialism.

'Shortly after the war, a report was issued, signed by members of all the religious bodies, of the experience of chaplains in dealing with the ordinary adult male soldier during the war. The report, if pessimistic, had at least the merits of candour. The general testimony was that, with occasional distinguished exception, this great mass of British male young adult life was facing death and being killed without any of the conviction of a spiritual existence, a dominating Providence, or a future life, which have been entertained unchallenged for nearly two thousand years. It was not the war which had made this change. It was the war which had revealed this change: England, according to these testimonies, was no longer Christian, and become pagan; and the great majority of the male population of England had completely ceased to believe in the faith of the forefathers.'

¶ Such idealism as there was was centred round the idea of the League of Nations, yet it was very far, as yet, from having imposed tranquillity on a troubled world. Peace had been signed but '*les guerres de la paix*' continued to rage. There was a Greek war in Asia Minor. D'Annunzio was still in occupation of Fiume and was defying the 'Powers' to get him out. The Bolsheviks were advancing into Siberia, the French occupied Frankfort. There was shooting in Amritsa, street-fighting in Berlin, and, of course, 'trouble' in Ireland where the Sinn Feiners had just made the unfortunate discovery that there is no answer to terrorism.

The League of Nations had been largely Woodrow Wilson's own idea. At least it was he, and he alone, who had imposed it on the Peace Conference, and got the Allies to accept it.

Frederick Lewis Allen, 'Only Yesterday', 1931
'The European diplomats wanted to leave the discussion of the League until after the territorial and military settlements had been made, but he forced them to put the League first. Sitting as chairman of the commission appointed to draw up the League Covenant, he brought out a preliminary draft which met, as he supposed, the powerful objections to it made by men at home like Taft and Root and Lodge.'

¶ On July 10th, 1919, back in Washington, he laid the Treaty of Versailles before the Senate, and in his speech he said:

' "The stage is set, the destiny disclosed. It has come about by no *Frederick* plan of our conceiving, but by the hand of God who led us into the *Lewis Allen,* way. We cannot turn back. We can only go forward, with lifted eyes *1931* and freshened spirit to follow the vision. It was of this that we dreamed at our birth. America shall in truth show the way." '

Eloquent words, but the Senate refused to be convinced:

'Woodrow Wilson decided to play his last desperate card. He would go to the people. He would win them to his cause, making a speaking trip through the West . . .

'His nerves frayed by continuous overwork and by the thought of possible failure of all he had given his heart and strength for, he was like a man possessed. He could think of nothing but the Treaty and the League. He cared for nothing but to bring them through to victory. And so, despite all that those about him could say, he left Washington on September 3rd to undergo the even greater strain of a speaking trip — the preparation and delivery of one or even two speeches a day in huge sweltering auditoriums (and without amplifiers to ease the strain on his voice); the automobile processions through city after city (during which he had to stand up in his car and continuously wave his hat to the crowds); the swarms of reporters, the hand-shaking, the glare of publicity, and the restless sleep of one who travels night in and night out on a swaying train . . .

'The expected surge of public opinion toward Wilson's cause failed to materialize. The Senate went right on discussing reservations. On September 24th, the first test vote went against the President 43 to 40.

'On the night of the next day Wilson came to the end of his strength . . . A few days later a cerebral thrombosis partially paralysed his left side. Another act of the tragedy had come to an end. He had given all he had to the cause and it had not been enough.'

¶ On November 19th, 1919, the Treaty was defeated. Wilson still hoped that the election of 1920 would enable him to reverse this decision. But it was not to be. The anti-League Republican candidate William Gamaliel Harding was swept into office with a majority of seven million votes. Wilson lived on for three years, a broken man.

Those in other countries who believed in the League were naturally

25

distressed by the American reaction, but there were many who gave it lip-service who had no real interest in it, even then:

Charles F. G. Masterman, 'England After War', 1922 'While the "League of Nations Union" exists, and is run by passionate idealists, and holds great meetings, and has no reputable enemies, there is no general uprising in its defence or interest in its doings. The editor of a great newspaper told me that, in all his articles descriptive of the League's activity, he always had to put headlines, and if possible the first few sentences, without mention of the League. Otherwise he knew the article would go unread. Its very conception is (by the majority) damned with faint praise. Its action — when it can be galvanized to action — is subjected to bitter criticism, exactly similar to that of the action of each individual nation, when that decision is disliked by its critics.'

¶ Among intellectuals the belief in progress had received a rude jar, and their growing scepticism was expressed in incisive phrases by that remarkable cleric, the Dean of St. Paul's.

W. R. Inge, 'Outspoken Essays' (2nd series), 1922 'The belief in Progress, not as an ideal but as an indisputable fact, not as a task for humanity but as a law of nature, has been the working faith of the West for about a hundred and fifty years . . .

'There is much to support the belief that there is a struggle for existence among ideas, and that those tend to prevail which correspond with the changing needs of humanity. It does not necessarily follow that the ideas which prevail are better morally, or even truer to the law of Nature, than those which fail . . .

'For this reason, we must cut down our hopes for our nation, for Europe, and for humanity at large, to a very modest and humble aspiration. We have no millenium to look forward to . . .'

¶ It is little wonder that he was called 'the Gloomy Dean', especially when he offended the Left by declaring that:

W. R. Inge, 'The End of an Age', 1948 'We must face a progressive deterioration in the quality of our people if we encourage those who are at the bottom of the social ladder to multiply at the expense of those who are able to pay their way as useful citizens. We in our overcrowded island must expect a terrible fate if we are ever at the mercy of an enemy strong enough to cut off our supplies of the necessities of life. That we escaped this disaster with a margin of a few weeks in the first Great War is common knowledge. We have accustomed ourselves to a standard of living which we are not earning and which was won for us while we held a privileged position as the workshop of the world, a position which we have lost and can never recover.'

¶ An acute foreign critic makes the same point:

'Old England has been living in a fool's paradise, fondly imagining that she could still rely on the spirit and methods of the nineteenth century. Such reforms as have been attempted are insignificant; at any rate, up to the War no serious efforts were made to transform coal mining, the metal industry, or textiles — the three bases on which exports and prosperity were founded. England is like a venerable mansion which though well and solidly built, has for years lacked repairs both in and out . . . *André Siegfried, 'England's Crisis', 1931*

'The British people as a whole have not yet realized the gravity of the situation, and as their optimism is a mixture of patriotism and lethargy, it can hardly be undermined . . . With the present decade passes the era of unrivalled British supremacy, marked in history by two great milestones, 1815 and 1914.'

¶ The British people were facing problems they had never had to face before:

'The after-war summer was over. The insatiable markets were satiated: the idiocies of the Versailles Treaty were destroying any hopes of prosperity in Europe: the hashish dreams of the new rich vanished and left a headache. In November 1919 there had been 353,000 ex-soldiers unemployed and the nation had been scandalized. By March 1921 the registered unemployed numbered 1,664,000; and in May the coal stoppage had brought the total to over 2,500,000 exclusive of the miners themselves. Even at the end of the year, when the miners were back at work, unemployment was barely under 2,000,000. It then fell gradually, to 1,400,000 at the end of 1922 and about 1,200,000 a year later. Until 1939 it hardly ever fell below a million. *G. D. H. Cole and Raymond Postgate, 'The Common People', 1946*

'Neither the Lloyd George Government nor the official Labour movement had any remedy for this colossal disaster. The Government merely cut expenditure wildly, throwing more and more men on to the labour market.'

¶ Cutting expenditure was both difficult and unpopular:

*John Montgomery,
'The Twenties', 1957* 'Unemployment and the trade depression led in February 1922 to the "Geddes Axe", a report by the Geddes Economy Committee which recommended cuts of over £75,000,000 in national expenditure. The Air Force estimates were to be cut by £5,500,000 and the Army by £20,000,000. The Navy protested at their proposed cut of £21,000,000, education costs were to be reduced by £18,000,000, war pensions by £3,500,000 but the working classes remained unimpressed by the plan, in spite of Lord Inchcape's declaration that the country was facing bankruptcy. Eventually the government accepted cuts of £64,000,000, the proposed naval reductions were halved, and the saving on education was reduced to £6,500,000.'

¶ The trade unions were accused of preferring high wages and the dole to lower wages with full employment.

*André Siegfried,
'England's Crisis',
1931* 'The trade unions . . . prefer high wages with unemployment to lower wages with the unemployed reabsorbed, for lower wages mean a reduction in the standard of living. In a word, England would rather support indefinitely a million unemployed than reduce wages . . . To all intents and purposes, unemployment is accepted and supported, until it has now become a permanent characteristic of modern England.'

¶ The economists blamed the workers for not working hard enough:

*André Siegfried,
'England's Crisis',
1931* 'There has been a decided decline in the output of labour. There is no doubt about the excellent qualities of honesty, loyalty and decent living, as well as the skill of the British workman, but the fact remains that he has been accustomed to and still clings to a wage level which is no longer compatible with the depressed state of industry . . .
'The English workman spends freely, chiefly because he is not clever at organizing his life. His wife is also somewhat lacking in *savoir-faire*. She does not take a keen delight in shopping economically, nor does she pride herself on her cooking. She is honest and loyal, but slipshod, and her household often lives on tinned goods and prepared food . . . she requires higher wages to maintain a very ordinary standard . . . This English standard of living means, to a certain extent, the right to live shiftlessly without exertion, and at the same time to be well paid for doing so.'

28

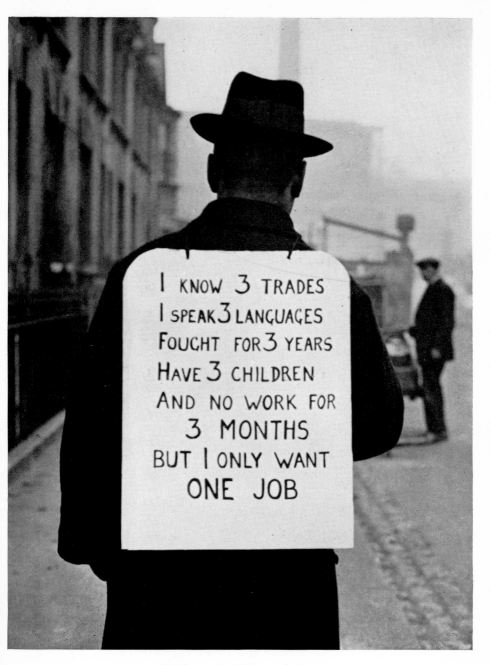

The Depression: Trying to find work.

'The Gloomy Dean': Dr. W. R. Inge, Dean of St. Paul's.

'The Cambridge Economist': John Maynard Keynes, later Lord Keynes.

¶ Many of those in work were convinced that if they worked to full capacity they would be doing someone else out of a job. But,

'If men continue to hold the view that production according to capacity is economically and morally wrong, disaster seems certain. Other countries are producing and whatever may be our political theories, the fact remains that the efforts of these other countries threaten our remaining markets. Sheffield has justly been famous for its tools. She has sold them everywhere and her qualities and prices were such that effective competition against her was difficult. She no longer enjoys immunity; countries which formerly purchased, now manufacture, and manufacture for export as well as for use. France was a purchaser: today she is a competitor, and if in Great Britain the doctrine of indifferent production is maintained, France, controlling the Ruhr and the Saar, will have something like a walk-over.' *W. A. Appleton, 'Unemployment', 1923*

¶ There was a tendency in England to blame the foreigner for our troubles.

'One cannot help remarking that England usually looks abroad first for the causes of her difficulties — always they are the fault of someone else. If only this culprit or that would reform then England might be able to regain her prosperity. It is magnificent, the way she can preach a service to the rest of the world, expose their weaknesses, and point out their duties . . . Her instinct is to try to restore the conditions which suited her, instead of revising her own standards and adapting them to a world in which they are now out of place . . . *André Siegfried, 'England's Crisis', 1931*

'If one suggests that English wages are too high for competition — very well, let the Continental nations raise theirs; that the English working day is too short — reduce your own; that the English standard of living is pretentious — renounce your measly economy, civilize yourselves, be like us, learn how to live! . . .

'The purely British causes of the economic depression are complex, but they can be summed up in a single sentence: English manufacturing costs are among the highest in the world. If this situation continues, any economic structure based on exports is faced with inevitable ruin.'

¶ We can all see now that England's return to the Gold Standard after the War was a mistake. Foreign observers were convinced of it even at the time:

*André Siegfried,
'England's Crisis',
1931*
'We are, therefore, forced to the conclusion that though England alone, among the European belligerents, saved her currency by intense budgetory energy and fiscal patriotism, the effort involved has proved too great a strain. She is bearing a load of debt that is too heavy; she is actually paying her creditors twenty shillings in the pound, while France is paying hers only twenty centimes in the franc.'

¶ Englishmen were apt to look at it from another angle. Why couldn't those blasted foreigners keep their currencies stable?

*W. A. Appleton,
'Unemployment',
1923*
'We are beginning to understand how difficult it is to maintain an even rate of employment if we suffer from varying rates of exchange. The manufacturer, forced with difficult and financially dangerous calculations concerning costs of raw materials and labour and transit, and worried about selling prices in countries where currency values are continually changing, may well hesitate. Those who ask him to continue operations and manufacture under such circumstances ask him to risk reserves and to invite bankruptcy . . .'

¶ In England the pound was still 'worth' twenty shillings, only, unfortunately, the twenty shillings did not purchase as much as they used to. Orthodox Finance had triumphed, but at disastrous cost:

*Norman Angell and
Harold Wright, 'Can
Governments Cure
Unemployment?',
1931*
'The return to gold in 1925 was a victory of finance, the City, over industry — the workers as well as the employers. It was something more. It was the abandonment of "conscious control" for automatic control, *laissez-faire*. So long as we were on a paper currency our money could, in some measure at least, be managed with a view to business needs. As soon as it was linked to gold we were at the mercy, in a monetary sense, of the behaviour of that metal in international circumstances — particularly American circumstances — beyond our control. If "social control" and "conscious planning" is of the essence of Socialism, as I assume it is, Labour should have opposed that return tooth and nail, their interests were at one with the interests of industry . . . The real alignment was not "Worker *v.* Capitalist", it was "Industrial Workers and Employer *v.* Banker, Financier, and Bondholder". The conflict of interest as presented normally by the Marxian here is simply fantastic misrepresentation. The grouping of real interest is not the Marxian grouping at all.

30

'It is noteworthy, by the way, that the most striking protests against this folly did not come from Marxian economists nor from the Labour Movement. They came from a "Capitalist" Cambridge economist.'

The modern reader will hardly need to be told that the name of the 'Capitalist Cambridge economist' was John Maynard Keynes.

CHAPTER II

GENTLEMEN AND PLAYERS

CRICKET is supposed to be a peculiarly English game. For those who delight in it (i.e. the English, the Australians, the South Africans and the West Indians) it is a religion; for those who do not (i.e. the Americans, the Canadians and the rest of the world) it is as boring as it is incomprehensible. Poor wretches! They just do not understand:

Neville Cardus,
'Days in the Sun',
1924

'Cricket is more than a game. For one thing it is part of summer. How many of us have gone home after watching cricket and taken with us no impression more likeable than that we have seen during the day the sun climb up the sky, pause over us for a while in beneficent noon heat, and then descend towards evening while the field turned a softer and softer green? The leisureliness of cricket, the room in it for graces and amenities deliciously irrelevant? — all these make for the poetry of cricket; yes, and make for the urbane Charles Lamb prose of cricket. And it is these graces of cricket that the literature of the game has not attended to amply enough in recent days; we have made, perhaps, overmuch of the technique of cricket. In the first year of the game after the war the cry was: "Speed up cricket!" *The Times* came out with an ingenious suggestion involving the banishment of the left-handed batsmen because he interferes with bustle. But we are finding out, at last, that the summer game is not as other games; that the rhythm of it may be as lazy as June's and yet enchant us . . .

'And because cricket frequently takes a placid course the crowd has liberty for self-expression. Think of it — twenty thousand men (and some women), most of them certain to possess a share of the more or less shabby worries that afflict the race nowadays — they will sit in the air, throughout the long day, attending on a game that can

Test Match Crowd. The Oval, Adelaide, Australia.

Lords: Eton and Harrow, 1931.

No Play Today.

charm but can hardly inebriate! The foreigner may well gasp at the spectacle of Lord's on a Saturday afternoon in June.'

¶ However, even those who delight in it most are apt to complain that, like many good things, cricket is not what it used to be:

'When we went on with cricket again in 1919, after the war, bowling was so poor that batsmen were under little compulsion to learn the difficult art of scoring from a good attack. To get a decent number of runs a batsman needed simply to stop the occasional dangerous ball that came his way; he could fatten his score from the long-hops and half-volleys. As he could depend on a constant supply of indifferent-length stuff, he required to take no risks with the occasional good bowling sent him, and it is no difficult matter for a batsman on a first-class wicket to stop an average good ball so long as he is not compelled to try to score from it. How different it was from this in the 1904–1912 period! . . .
'Among batsmen of today it is difficult to think of any save Hobbs, Woolley, Hendren and Mead who have command of the wide range of strokes possessed by . . . those cricketers of 1910 . . .
'The low condition of English batsmanship in 1919 and 1920 was noted by many an old judge of the game, but their warnings were unheeded. "Jeremiahs!" said the batsmen, who then turned again to their half-volleys. But their fool's paradise was about to crash down and dusty disillusion rise up from the wreckage on our cricket fields. The Australians came in 1921 and forthwith smote our bowling hip and thigh.'

Neville Cardus, 'Days in the Sun', 1924

¶ The same excellent writer shares with us his disquiet at the attitude to cricket of the young men at the universities in the early 'twenties:

'At Lord's during the last two or three University matches old men have walked about the field moaning to one another that young men nowadays are not as young as young men used to be. "Why don't these boys hit the ball?" asked the old men. "Why don't they play as we played when youth was hot in our blood?"'

Neville Cardus, 'Days in the Sun', 1924

¶ Cardus was inclined to put it all down to Freud:

'Cricket is a living art and so it is expressive of the Time Spirit: young men, maybe, are today different in mood and mind from young

Neville Cardus, 'Days in the Sun', 1924

c

men of the roaring times of old . . . Are not Freud and the psychological novelists the fashion there at the moment? . . . The trouble with
university cricket just now is that introspection disturbs the game
over-much: it has the tentativeness which is the mark of the subtle
mind . . .

'There is about the batsmanship of these young men that self-
effacing sameness which happens in any activity as soon as style is
looked on as something possessing a fixed character . . . There has
always been a tendency for cricketers to think too narrowly upon the
meaning of style . . . But, as a fact, there is no single style in cricket
which is *the* style. The style is the man — one simply has to drag in
Buffon's commonplace thought once more. All these batsmen were
stylists — MacLaren, Ranjitsinhji, Spooner, Trumper, R. A. Duff,
Shrewsbury, Lucas and Walter Read. And not one of them played his
game after the manner of the others. They all expressed in cricket
themselves, their own private and immortal souls, using bats as great
artists use fiddles, paintbrushes and pianos.'

¶ Well, if *aficionados* of the bull-ring can describe the style of their
favourite *toreros* as baroque or neo-classical why should not cricket
enthusiasts be granted a similar licence? 'Cricket', said Sir James
Barrie, 'is not so much a game as a way of life.'

Another Scot, the witty author of *England, Their England*,
gives us a picture of the reaction in this country when the news
from the Antipodes came through that the M.C.C. team which
J. W. H. T. Douglas took to Australia in 1920 had been disastrously
defeated:

A. G. Macdonell,
'England, Their
England', 1933
'One morning at about 9 o'clock, Donald got a most painful
fright . . . For in the King's Road (Chelsea) stood three newspaper
boys, with long, gloomy faces and not even the heart to cry their
wares . . . Queues of men were standing in front of the boys, digging
into their pockets for coins, snatching at the papers, and then stumb-
ling away with ashen faces and quivering lips. Donald, almost numb
with the cold of sheer panic, took his place in the queue. The man in
front of him held out a shilling and would not even wait for the change.
He grabbed the *Star*, glanced at it, exclaimed "Oh, God!" and reeled
drunkenly away, cannoning into passers-by and bumping into a shop
window, his eyes devouring the stop-press news as he went. Donald
only just succeeded in retaining his native prudence sufficiently to

34

present a penny rather than a shilling, and drew aside with his paper from the jostling crowd.

'There was no difficulty about discovering what the *Star* was trying to convey. There was the giant headline — IS ENGLAND DOOMED? — splashed right across the page, and under it the smaller amplifying headlines, and even they were half an inch high:

DEVASTATING ATTACK AT MELBOURNE
HOBBS OUT FIRST BALL: HEARNE 9, WOOLLEY 0
ENGLAND'S APPALLING DEBACLE
CAN HENDREN SAVE US?

'In the Underground at Sloane Square Station an elderly man in a top-hat and black, velvet-collared overcoat, with an elegant long white moustache, and carrying a rolled-up silk umbrella, said fiercely to Donald, "It all comes of treating it as a game. We don't take things seriously enough in this country, sir, damnation take it all", and he stepped heavily upon the toes of a humble clerkly looking person behind him.

'Donald slipped away to another part of the train and read the sad story of England's shame in the Second Test Match against Australia at Melbourne.'

¶ However! By the time the English team went to Australia again in 1924–25, a decisive success over South Africa had removed the feeling of inferiority. But apart from the bowling of Maurice Tate the English attack was not outstanding . . . Hobbs, Sutcliffe and Tate were now recognized as the world's three outstanding cricketers . . .

'In 1925 everyone in Britain interested in sport — which meant nearly everybody — was asking, "Will Jack Hobbs do it?" He had made 226 runs at Scarborough, 215 at Birmingham, and altogether 125 centuries in first-class cricket. Now enthusiasts were wondering if he would beat the record of 126 centuries held by W. G. Grace. When he eventually did so, at Taunton, he received the congratulations of the King and the whole country . . .

John Montgomery,
'The Twenties', 1957

'In 1926 the tide turned in England's favour, and Australia lost to England . . . It was at The Oval in the last match of the series that Australia at last met defeat — for the first time for fourteen years. Hobbs and Sutcliffe, batting in rain on a wet wicket, were the heroes of the hour. England had at last won the Ashes.'

35

¶ Perhaps the climate had something to do with it:

Don Bradman,
'Farewell to Cricket',
1950
'After the hard Australian wickets and our warm sunshine, the cold and damp weather of England provided unusual and often unpleasant conditions. I found it difficult for instance to adjust myself to the idea of wearing a sweater, blazer and overcoat before a roaring fire awaiting my turn to bat . . .

'During a later match at Oxford, the Press referred to a heat wave, but seven of our team turned out against the University in sweaters. Perhaps this only tends to indicate the difficulties which confront English players when they visit Australia.'

¶ Bradman made his début against the English team under Chapman which sailed to Australia in 1928, but he was dropped for a time and did not emerge again until later. The most formidable English batsman was Walter Hammond and the most formidable bowler Larwood. England won all four matches; but the Australians had their revenge in 1930 when they visited England and won back the Ashes 2–1, thanks chiefly to their fast googly bowling. The excitement aroused by these matches, however, was as nothing to the sensational happenings of 1932–33 when an English team under Douglas Jardine visited Australia. The controversies which resulted shook the Empire to its foundations:

Don Bradman,
'Farewell to Cricket',
1950
'The last thing I want to do at the close of my career is to revive unpleasant memories. However, I would be failing in my duty if I did not record my impressions of something which very nearly brought about a cessation of Test cricket between England and Australia, especially as I was one of the central figures.

'Jardine, who captained England in that series, wrote a book defending his theory. So did Larwood. The defence could have impressed the jury not at all, for body-line is now outlawed . . .

'Now what exactly was body-line bowling? It was really short-pitched fast bowling directed towards the batsman's body with a supporting leg-side field . . . This is how Wally Hammond defined it:—

1. Delivered by a speed merchant
2. Bumped so as to fly high above the wicket
3. Delivered straight at the batsman
4. Bowled with a leg-side field of six to eight men

36

'Of course the protagonists of body-line always claimed that it was leg-theory — an entirely fallacious claim.

'Warwick Armstrong, Fred Root and others bowled leg-theory. Nobody was in the slightest danger therefrom.

'With body-line it was different. The risk of actual physical danger to the batsman became his chief consideration.'

¶ Jardine explains:

'Most people are familiar with off-theory. In off-theory it is the off stump which is attacked, when the bowler's margin of error will be limited to the off-side for the sufficiently obvious reason that nearly all his fieldsmen are stationed on that side of the wicket. Off-theory bowling can be exceedingly dull for players and spectators alike . . . *D. R. Jardine, 'In Quest of the Ashes', 1933*

'Now, in leg-theory it is the leg stump which is the object of the bowler's attack, and since the majority of his fieldsmen are employed in various positions on the leg-side, the margin of error in this case must be limited to a few inches outside the leg stump . . .

'I would not suggest that leg-theory, if bowled by a hefty lad of eighteen to a fourteen-year-old on a bumpy park pitch, might not legitimately be described as "rather strong meat", but, in these circumstances, any fast bowling might be so described, and the same term might also be applied to shots such as the leg glance or the late cut.'

¶ Bradman has an answer to this:

'If body-line is allowed in first-class cricket, it must be allowed in *all* forms of cricket. One bowler cannot have a monopoly of a theory. For this reason, I . . . quote Larwood from his book. "If it really was body-line, bowling would be really dangerous to the batsmen." ' *Don Bradman, 'Farewell to Cricket', 1950*

¶ Sir Pelham Warner had, long before, expressed his views on body-line bowling, even before the actual term had been invented. Commenting on a match at The Oval between Yorkshire and Surrey he wrote:

'Bowes must alter his tactics. Bowes bowled with five men on the on-side and sent down several very short-pitched balls which repeatedly bounced head-high and more. Now that is not bowling; indeed it is *'Morning Post', August 22nd, 1932* not cricket; and if all the fast bowlers were to adopt his methods M.C.C. would be compelled to step in and penalize the bowler who bowled the ball less than half-way up the pitch.'

¶ Matters came to a head during the M.C.C. tour in Australia in 1932–33. The English captain was Douglas Jardine, the fast bowler H. Larwood.

Don Bradman,
'Farewell to Cricket',
1950

'Walter Hammond . . . made no secret of the development of the theory when he wrote on the subject. According to him "body-line" was born in the grill room of the Piccadilly Hotel, London, where Jardine, Arthur Carr, Voce and Larwood worked out the idea. Hammond claims that P. G. H. Fender had suggested to Jardine that he should adopt these tactics. "Jardine", says Hammond, "spent some days painstakingly analysing all the scoring diagrams which Ferguson, the famous M.C.C. scorer, had made of the Australian batsmen's Test innings." It was after this meeting, according to Hammond, that Jardine went to see F. R. Foster . . .

'F. R. Foster . . . gave an interview to the Press and said: "Before Jardine left England he came frequently to my flat in the St. James *(sic)* and secured from me my leg-theory field placings. I had no hint that these would be used for body-line bowling. I would like all my old friends in Australian cricket to know that I am sorry that my experience and my advice were put to such unworthy uses . . ."

'From my own talks with members of the M.C.C. team, I understand that this theory was discussed in detail on the way out to Australia, a fact which Jardine does not deny.

'I think readers will be able to judge what type of bowling it was, and furthermore that I was to be the principal target . . .'

¶ Jardine, however, says:

D. R. Jardine,
'In Quest of the
Ashes', 1933

'I am sorry to disappoint anyone who has imagined that the leg-theory was evolved with the help of midnight oil and iced towels, simply and solely for the purpose of combating Bradman's effectiveness as a scoring machine. However highly Bradman may have been rated, this view is exaggerated.'

¶ The Australian crowd, as might have been expected, reacted strongly to the English captain's tactics, so strongly indeed that Jardine was moved to the acid comment:

38

'Cricket is a game for eleven a side. During the recent tour of the M.C.C. in Australia this short, simple and self-evident fact seems to have been largely forgotten or ignored.

D. R. Jardine, 'In Quest of the Ashes', 1933

'The behaviour or misbehaviour of crowds and the Press reactions thereto the world over lead inevitably to the main question:

' "Are Test Matches between England and Australia to continue, and, if so, are they really worth while?" . . .

'The arena, hitherto sacred to eleven players on either side, has been invaded by newspapers, broadcasters, and spectators. Well may this prove to be the death knell of cricket . . .

'It is not cricket (however), but Test Match cricket which is at the crossroads. For it is all too common and too easy to attach to Test Matches an importance which is out of all proportion to their true worth.'

¶ The body-line bowling controversy reached such a pitch that it almost looked, at one moment, as if Australia would break away from the Commonwealth. However, in the end, the M.C.C. itself came down against it. At a joint meeting of the Advisory County Cricket Committee and the Board of Control of Test Matches at home, held at Lord's in November 1933, it was decided that any form of bowling 'which is obviously a direct attack by the bowler upon the batsman' was contrary to the spirit of the game.

But let us leave these world-shaking matters to consider another ball-game slightly less esoteric.

The 'twenties saw the rise of a comparatively new game to popular favour, to such popular favour indeed that 'Wimbledon' became as much a feature of the Season as Ascot or the Derby. It had become clear, even before the 1914–18 war that the old Worple Road site was inadequate and the present courts replaced them in 1922 at a cost of almost £140,000. The new Centre Courts provided accommodation for 15,000 spectators and 'No. 1 Court' for another 6,500. The once despised Lawn Tennis (long referred to by old-fashioned schoolmasters as 'pat-ball') had indeed arrived.

'Real' tennis[1] had, of course, been known for centuries. As long ago as 1396 a man was prosecuted for allowing his friend to play 'le tenesse' in his house. This implied no prejudice against tennis as such, but against all games which did not train men in archery and

[1] The 'real' fanatics will not allow one to speak of 'real tennis'. It is simply 'tennis' and 'lawn tennis' is a mere bastard derivative.

39

other warlike accomplishments. Gradually, however, the game made its way, at least among the aristocracy. Henry VIII was, as everyone knows, an enthusiastic player. So, as everybody does not know, was Charles II.

But lawn tennis, which was at first given the pedantic name of Sphairistike, did not come into existence until the early 1870's. It was taken up at Prince's Club where, 'away on an extra lawn on the London side of the ground — away from the cricket, away from the mock ice and the real ices — away from the skirts and the bugle-embroidered bodies,[1] from the colour, the costumes, and the fashionable crowd, they are playing "Sphairistike" or "lawn tennis".'

The spread and development of the game has been admirably set forth in Lord Aberdare's *The Story of Tennis*. It is sufficient for us to note that in 1875 some ground at Wimbledon which had been used for croquet since 1869 was set aside for lawn tennis. The first Wimbledon Lawn Tennis Championship meeting was held in 1877. Two hundred spectators paid a shilling each and the club made a profit of £10. Three years later the event attracted thirteen hundred spectators and the profits rose to £300. It is interesting to note that Miss Lottie Dod (who died in 1960) made her first appearance in 1887 at the age of fifteen, and dominated the Ladies' Singles for seven years.

It is not our purpose to write a history of tennis. Let us take up the thread immediately after the First World War:

Lord Aberdare, 'The Story of Tennis', 1959   'Among the men, Americans were prominent in the early post-war years. They had had the opportunity of continuing to practise while others were involved in war, and they had produced some fine players, outstanding among them "Big Bill" Tilden, who had been rejected for military service owing to "first degree flat feet" and "Little Bill" Johnson . . .

'Tilden came to Wimbledon in 1920 and was the first American to win the championship. He was without doubt one of the finest tennis players of all time and his record speaks for itself. He was at his peak from 1920 to 1925, in which period he won the American Singles championship six years in succession, won Wimbledon both times he competed, and won fifteen Davis Cup Singles without a defeat. He had in unique degree all the qualities that go to make a great player — speed and stamina, a good eye and a good sense of timing, all the strokes in the game and a fighting spirit determined to win . . .

[1] We would say 'bodices'.

40

'In 1923 the top of the middle finger of his right hand had to be amputated after he had cut it on the top netting. He modified his game by dint of hard practice to suit his altered grip. His temperament endowed him with great personality on the courts; his self-confidence gave him an air of conceit and his concentration resulted in some unpleasantness with linesmen and ball boys. But he was a great showman as well as a great player . . .'

¶ But even the most brilliant and determined players cannot go on for ever.

'The Wimbledon of 1927 was remarkable in many ways: for the failure of Tilden . . . the amazing win of Cochet in the Singles, and also for the first triumph of Helen Wills in the Ladies' championship. *H. W. Austin, 'Lawn Tennis Bits and Pieces', 1930*

'It was Cochet's first victory, and perhaps no man has ever come through successfully so stormy a passage or ever had luck so very much on his side . . . His vicissitudes began in the round before the semi-final when he was two sets to love down against Hunter. Crowds flocked to No. 1 Court to see what promised to be a sensational victory. But the imperturbable Cochet was only giving . . . the crowd a thrill. In the last three sets Cochet was covering the court with amazing speed and as usual without visible movement . . . When Hunter saw his hopes of victory receding he sent for Tilden to spur him on. Tilden, his ever faithful supporter, did his utmost but all in vain. The issue of the last three sets was never in doubt.

'But Tilden in the next round was himself to fall before the racket of Hunter's conqueror in a match that lives in lawn tennis history as one of the most remarkable and inexplicable of all time. For perhaps three sets Tilden played what is perhaps the finest tennis that has ever been seen. The controlled speed of his every shot was superb. His cannon-ball services were invisible, his returns of Cochet's services untakable. Cochet was a child in the master's hand. Tilden bestrode the court like a Colossus, the master of his craft . . . And then the miraculous occurred. The master hand faltered and Cochet won.

'Tilden's collapse has never and will never be explained. He himself cannot explain it, and if he cannot who can? . . .

'After the match Tilden was asked time and time again, "What happened?"

' "Nothing", he replied, "the other man came on."

'I admired him for that.'

41

¶ Other formidable Frenchmen, besides Cochet, invaded England in the 'twenties: Jean Borotra, René Lacoste and Jacques Brugnon. But the French player who most completely captured the public imagination was a woman: Suzanne Lenglen.

H. W. Austin, 'Lawn Tennis Bits and Pieces', 1930

'In 1919 she flashed like a meteor into the sky, only to disappear in 1926 as quickly as she had arisen. During those seven years her vivid personality had held spectators spellbound, she had fascinated them by her grace and the ease with which she played. She proved herself supreme in ladies' lawn tennis, a player without a peer. So great was her personality that huge crowds flocked to see her play the easiest matches. The mention of her name was sufficient to fill the Centre Court . . .

'During the seven years that she reigned supreme, Mlle Lenglen was nearly always the centre of a storm. Controversies raged round her. Secretaries were kept on tenterhooks by her vagaries. Clubs, expecting her to play in their tournaments, built large stands to accommodate spectators and she did not come to draw the crowd. Few, if any, ever knew what her next move would be. Eventually the tennis public, ever fickle in their hero worship, began to grow tired of their idol. They had raised her on a pedestal; they were now prepared to cast her down. The crisis arrived at this Wimbledon of 1926 — Mlle Lenglen kept the Queen of England waiting. She retired from the Singles and was beaten in the Doubles. After Wimbledon she joined the ranks of professionals and passed for ever out of amateur tennis.

'Suzanne, through her unorthodox behaviour, her tantrums and hysterics, has often been accused of lack of sportsmanship. But, although this in a sense is true (and undoubtedly she did lack something of the sporting spirit that is the essence of all games), I personally defend her. To my mind she was, at any rate in matters connected with lawn tennis, a being above ordinary mortals; one that had strayed into the sporting world to show us something that was far beyond the possibility of attainment by men of common clay. She was not a sportswoman at all, that is to say, a person of brawn and muscle, energy and sweat. Neither was she merely a skilful manipulator of a racket. She was more than this. She was an artist — highly strung, delicately attuned, sensitive. And just as geniuses in the realms of art had and have faults (often the outcome of their temperament) allied to their genius, so had Suzanne. But through her artistic temperament she brought to the game something more than the game itself holds, lifting it to a higher sphere. As well as consummate skill, she possessed arresting personality and unrivalled and exquisite grace, and although her face was far from beautiful, that something in her make-up which made her supreme among lawn tennis players as Pavlova among dancers . . . Suzanne brought to the tennis world something that it had never previously possessed, may never possess again. Her gift was priceless. Can we not therefore forget and forgive her her faults?'

'As striking as her successes at Wimbledon were her revolutionary fashions in clothes. Like a previous great champion, Lottie Dod, Suzanne acquired strength and pace of shot by practising with men, and for playing a man's type of game she needed freedom of movement. Off came the suspender belt, and she supported her stockings by means of garters above the knee; off came the petticoat and she wore only a short pleated skirt; off came the long sleeves and she wore a neat short-sleeved vest. Her first appearance at Wimbledon caused much comment, but the practical success of her outfit led to its adoption by others. Each new fashion of dress which she introduced was closely followed and widely copied. In her first championship she had worn a white hat, but on subsequent occasions she wore a brightly coloured bandeau which was outstandingly popular until challenged by Miss Helen Wills's eyeshade in 1924.' *Lord Aberdare, 'The Story of Tennis', 1959*

¶ The great Suzanne herself offered sartorial advice to her followers:

'If you wish to look neat in court, never wear a coloured skirt, always a white one. French ideas of dress differ somewhat from English. I will briefly detail what I consider the ideal dress: a simple *piqué* dress, or one of drill or white linen, made in the old Grecian style, and fastened at the waist with a ribbon or leather belt. The sleeves should be short. A simple pair of canvas "gym" shoes are best.' *Suzanne Lenglen, 'Lawn Tennis for Girls', 1922*

¶ The evolution of an accepted costume for tennis is so much bound up with the history of ordinary feminine dress at this period that a few words of elucidation may be necessary:

'In 1919 the game was played in a long, very full skirt, a woollen jumper, and a hat . . . Suzanne Lenglen was one of the first to wear a shorter skirt, and her success contributed to establish this new mode; but as late as 1921 we find tennis being played in an ordinary summer frock, quite long and with sleeves . . . *James Laver, 'Taste and Fashion', 1937*

43

'For the next five or six years the skirts of day dresses grew steadily shorter and shorter, and the tennis skirt naturally followed a mode so consonant with its own purposes. By 1927 it was knee-length, worn with a V-neck blouse without sleeves . . . Stockings were still worn, but the extreme fineness of stockings which came in about this period rendered them unsuitable for so strenuous a game as tennis, and so it became the fashion to wear short socks over the stockings. It was not until 1931 that Mrs. Fearnley-Whittingstall, playing at Forest Hills in the United States of America, appeared on the courts with bare legs. She wore on this occasion short socks rolled over the top of the shoe, a short pleated skirt, and a short-waisted woollen jumper. In spite of some opposition the stockingless mode triumphed, because it enabled women to abandon any type of corset or other support for the suspenders which stockings made necessary . . .

'What had seemed the natural evolution of tennis costumes was, however, seriously interrupted at the end of the 'twenties by the reversion of ordinary clothes to long skirts. Tennis skirts immediately followed suit, and by 1931, the year of Mrs. Fearnley-Whittingstall's startling innovation in the matter of stockings, they had already returned to half-way down the calf. So strong was the reaction against the ordinary modes of the late 'twenties that the short skirt became impossible even on the tennis court, and some other solution had to be found; for it was inconceivable that women should return for that extremely vigorous game to the hampering folds of cloth which they had endured earlier in the century.

'In April 1931 Señorita de Alvarez played in divided skirts which came to slightly below the knee, and two years later Miss Alice Marble, of San Francisco, appeared in shorts above the knee. For some time the designers of tennis costumes were undecided, and even in 1934 quite long skirts were offered to the tennis-playing public. Shorts, however, were growing in popularity, and received great impetus from the example, once more, of Mrs. Fearnley-Whittingstall, and also of Miss Kathleen Stammers, whose extreme elegance in these garments induced a host of other women to follow her example . . .

'In 1935 a new kind of pleated shorts was introduced, which looked, at a distance, like a very short skirt . . . It seems possible that women's tennis costumes has at last crystallized into a uniform.'

¶ And now we come to Golf. Much ink has been spilt on the question of its origin, but apart from an epic account of its being played by the

44

Ulster hero Cachullain, the consensus of opinion seems to give the credit, if credit it be, to Scotland:

'Of the history of golf prior to the famous Act of Parliament of 1457 in which we find it coupled with football as one of the two great national sports of Scotland, nothing certain is known. As a similar Act of the previous reign, passed in 1424, refers to football but not to golf, it has been conjectured that the rise of golf to popular favour must have taken place during the intervening quarter of a century, but its origin is lost in the mists of antiquity.'

*Robert Browning,
'A History of Golf',
1955*

¶ Let us jump to more recent times:

'The modern history of golf begins with the formation of the first Golf Clubs in the middle of the eighteenth century . . . Courses in those days were wholly natural; the only green-keepers were the rabbits.'

*Robert Browning,
'A History of Golf',
1955*

¶ Clubs were formed at Leith and St. Andrews and, oddly enough, at Blackheath; but many years were to elapse before golf made much progress in England. In Scotland Leith was increasingly eclipsed by St. Andrews, and it was at the latter place that eighteen holes first became the recognized round. It was not until the middle of the nineteenth century that the first championships were inaugurated. Gradually the English began to take an interest, the annual match between Oxford and Cambridge being started in 1878.

The 'father of English golf' was Balfour, who once declared that his ideal in life was 'to read a lot, write a little, play plenty of golf, and have nothing to worry about'. His example 'set the seal on golf as the sport of busy men'.

In America golf had been played by Scottish officers in New York during the War of Independence, but it was not until a hundred years later that clubs began to be formed. In 1888 it is recorded that 'when a club was broken it was necessary to send to Scotland for the head or shaft as the case might be'. But America made rapid strides and it was here that the rubber-covered ball was first produced at the beginning of the present century. Americans also began to win championships. They introduced new methods by means of more scientific approach to the 'swing', to stance and to the method of holding the club:

Robert Browning,
'A History of Golf',
1955
'In all departments of the game American science modified the conception of good style, but in the matter of holing out they brought about a complete revolution of method. The man who taught the world how to putt was Walter Hagen. He raised the standard of the short game to such a degree that, as Archie Compton once said to me, "the rest of us had to do the same or quit!" At first the accepted explanation was that British inferiority near the pin was due simply to the fact that our players did not practise enough. But this was by no means true of all of them . . . The trouble was that they had no scientific method . . . It was left to the Americans to evolve a method that is to a limited extent foolproof, the idea of straight-line putting . . .

'Along with these improved methods of execution, American keenness introduced new standards of achievement . . .

'Add to this the intense competition of the U.S. tournament season — the Gold Dust Circuit — had made their professionals "tournament tough" to a degree unequalled in any other country. The late Lord Castlerosse used to tell a story of the coolness of Walter Hagen in this respect. On one occasion when he was studying the line of a more than missable putt to secure first prize in a big tournament, a stray dog darted up, seized the ball in its teeth, and made off with it. The spot was immediately marked, the dog pursued, the ball recovered and replaced, and Hagen duly holed the putt. A friend who came forward to congratulate him expressed his relief, saying: "I was afraid you'd be upset by that dashed cur making off with your ball." "Why should I be upset?" retorted Walter. "It was the same putt, wasn't it?" '

¶ The improvement of performance had been made possible only by what is called 'golf architecture', i.e. the construction of links specially prepared. First-class courses began to be built up all over the world in answer to the golf boom which was in full blast before the First World War. That conflict of course, threw things back a bit:

Robert Browning,
'A History of Golf',
1955
'The impact of the First World War was more severely felt in Great Britain than in the United States, where the new stars were just coming along. Nevertheless, the first season after the war found British golfers still sitting on top of the world. Vardon and Ray paid a return visit to the States in 1920, and this time it was Ray's turn to carry off the U.S. Open . . . The victory of Ted Ray . . . helped to make history, for it produced "the Oath of Inverness" by which a small band of American professionals bound themselves to go over year

46

after year to the British Championship until they had squared the account by bringing it to America. They did not have long to wait, for in 1921, at St. Andrews, "Jock" Hutchinson won the British title after a tie with Roger Wethered, then a young man of twenty-two, who had captained Oxford in the previous year . . . The true beginning of American triumphs was Walter Hagen's great win at Sandwich in 1922 . . . It is true that Arthur Havers won back the Championship at Troon in the following year, with Hagen a stroke behind him, but after that for ten lean years the Open Championship trophy made the journey across the Atlantic with monotonous regularity. Walter Hagen was the winner on four occasions, "Emperor" Bobby Jones on three, But it was Hagen who started the landslide.'

¶ There was a time when Hagen and Bobby Jones seemed to dominate the world of golf:

'Golf is a very queer game. I started the year 1926 with one glorious licking and closed it with another. And it was the biggest golf year I'll ever have. Walter Hagen gave me the first drubbing . . . He was national professional champion; I was national amateur champion; we liked to play against each other.'

Robert T. Jones Jnr. and O. B. Keeler, 'Down the Fairway', 1930

¶ Bobby Jones was certainly an astonishing phenomenon:

'About one person in every ten million might have an interesting autobiography to put out at the age of twenty-five. Bobby Jones in this respect is one among ten millions . . . for he was almost a seasoned competitor, a competitor meeting and beating champions, at the age of fourteen . . . At the age of twenty-five . . . he had won almost every championship known to golf . . . he had won the United States Open twice, from the best professionals and the best amateurs. He had won the British Open. He had won the Amateur Championship of the United States twice. For a period of five years he had never finished lower than second place in United States Open Championships, facing the best golfers in the game.'

Robert T. Jones Jnr. and O. B. Keeler, 'Down the Fairway', 1930

¶ The American dominance was brought to an end by the victory of Henry Cotton in the Open Championship at Sandwich in 1934. Meanwhile the ladies were proving almost as good at golf as the men — almost, but not quite:

Robert Browning,
'A History of Golf',
1955

'Even when Miss [Joyce] Wethered was at the height of her powers
. . . the family estimate was that the handicap difference between her
and her hard-hitting brother Roger varied from two to seven strokes
according to the nature of the course; for distance counts . . . and it
is still true that length is the chief factor in the difference between the
standard of women's golf and men's . . .

'In the years between the wars we had a regular series of "Men *v.*
Women" Test Matches at Stoke Poges. The women's team was almost
invariably the more representative, most of their players being of
international class occasionally strengthened by the inclusion of
distinguished visitors from overseas, while the men were not much
more than a good London side. But over a considerable period of
years the men fairly demonstrated their ability to concede the girls
eight or nine strokes per round.'

¶ Royalty itself, reviving the old practice of the Scottish kings, began
to take a hand in the game. The Captain of the Royal and Ancient for
1922–23 was the Prince of Wales:

J. B. Salmond,
*'The Story of the
R. & A.'*, 1956

'[The] Royal Captain, wearing Highland dress, arrived in St.
Andrews from Balmoral on 26th September, 1922 . . . Next morning
some seven thousand people watched through the mist and the rain
while Andrew Kirkaldy, wearing his Tel-el-Kebir Medal, teed up the
royal ball, and, when the Prince exclaimed to him, "This is an awful
job", replied: "Keep your eye on the ball." It is not known whether
the Prince did so, but the drive was not a very good one . . . The
Prince himself had a practice round over the New Course in the
morning . . . A large gallery accompanied the match, and at one hole
the new Captain lifted a very large divot, which Andrew Kirkaldy
did not replace, being too much occupied in telling his "mon" just
what had gone wrong. A spectator was about to replace the turf, when
he was pushed aside by a very excited lady who seized the piece of
living grass, rammed it into her handbag, and rushed on after the
players. In what garden that divot rests and flourishes, I do not know,
or whether the bed where it grows has a nice little label stuck on it
to tell of the circumstances.'

¶ In 1930 the Duke of York (later King George VI) performed a
similar function and 'this time the royal drive was a good one'.

48

Suzanne Lenglen at Wimbledon, 1922.

H. Cochet and J. Borotra, Wimbledon, 1927.

It will be noticed that no less than seven thousand people watched the Prince of Wales drive off, but this figure has often been exceeded in Championship matches. And these large figures have made possible a spectacular increase in the amount of prize-money:

'After the First World War, when Hagen won his first British Open, his prize was no more than £75. By 1931 the total had been increased to £500, of which £100 went to the winner, but it remained at this figure until after the Second World War, when it was increased to £1,000 . . . [Nowadays] in a normal year in the States a hundred and fifty regular tournament professionals are contending in thirty-seven big events for a total prize-money of around $750,000.'

Robert Browning,
'A History of Golf',
1955

¶ And now let us turn to a sport in which much larger sums are involved: football.

'It can rarely have been the case that a game has been so closely bound up with the life of a nation as football is with English life today. Hundreds of thousands of men and boys play it, in one form or another; millions of both sexes watch it every week during the season; millions more "go in for the pools". To the great majority of these football is one of the prime interests of life, sometimes an all-consuming interest, without which life would literally be scarcely worth living.'

Morris Marples,
'A History of
Football', 1954

¶ The game in question is, of course, Association Football — Soccer. Mr. Marples gives a learned account of the remote origins of football, its connection with Shrovetide rituals, its prohibition in the fourteenth century (because it interfered with the practice of archery). But it was not until the mid-nineteenth century that the games we know (Soccer and Rugger) took definite shape. They did so in the Public Schools.

'The Rugby variety of football was . . . well on the way to becoming the accepted public school game by 1860. If all had come into line, the history of football might have been very different . . . Eton chose to practise its two peculiar varieties of the game in splendid isolation . . . Harrow and Winchester similarly refused to surrender the particular type of game to which they had grown accustomed . . . Those schools which adopted the isolationist policy naturally had very little influence on the future course of events. But two schools in particular not only favoured a non-handling game, and refused to fall into line with the majority, but also declined to withdraw into a private world of their own.'

Morris Marples,
'A History of
Football', 1954

D

49

¶ Both varieties of the game spread from the schools to the universities. The Football Association came into being in 1867, and by the end of the decade 'Soccer' had spread to towns and villages all over the country. Mr. Marples tells us that:

Morris Marples, 'A History of Football', 1954 'The earliest football clubs had mostly been started by old public school boys, or at any rate by members of the middle classes . . . But the next twenty years brought a remarkable change. There was now a new football public consisting of the artisans, the factory workers and the rapidly increasing thousands of blackcoated workers who crowded the industrial towns, and it was mostly among these that the new clubs were formed in the 'seventies and 'eighties. To this period belong many of the famous Association Football clubs of today . . . Very few of those which came into existence after 1870 sprang from the middle classes . . . [Moreover] as the social origin of the players changed, and the centre of the game moved north, the number of those who watched matches rather than playing them began rapidly to increase . . . the football crowds of the 'eighties were already large enough to become a problem to the authorities: 27,000 people saw the Cup-tie between Aston Villa and Preston North End in 1888; 45,000 attended the Cup Final in 1893; 80,000 was the average over the next ten years, reaching a climax with the huge total of 110,820 at the Final of 1901.'

¶ By that time, Soccer had become a professional game. The Cup Final of 1885 was the last in which an amateur side competed. The first club to charge for admission was Aston Villa in 1874 — and the gate money amounted to 5s. 3d.!

Morris Marples, 'A History of Football', 1954 'Even in 1882 Newcastle United only took 7s. 11d. at their first match. The tremendous change that occurred during the last quarter of the century may be gauged, when we compare with these figures the total of £14,329 14s. 2d. taken by Aston Villa at a single match in 1904 . . .

'Association Football in fact had become such a money-making proposition that it could more properly be described as an industry than a sport . . . [It] had become a form of entertainment, and the more skilfully it was done the better pleased were the spectators. Whatever middle-class critics might say, the man in the street had no doubt whatever about his approval of professionalism and showed it by turning up in tens of thousands to watch professional football.'

50

¶ The crowds were enormous before the First World War; after it, they were prodigious:

'All sporting events drew large crowds, but in April 1923 the authorities were unprepared for the 160,000 people who wanted to see the Cup Final at Wembley. The new stadium had been built to hold 125,000 and the extra 35,000 people overflowed on to the football pitch and held up the game. Nearly three thousand policemen found themselves unable to deal with the situation, for this was before the time of wireless loudspeakers. When the King arrived in his car the pitch was completely covered with people, and many thousands more were pushing and fighting to get into the stadium. Eventually, a policeman mounted on a grey horse persuaded people to stand back along the touch-lines, and the game started nearly an hour late. A thousand people were injured in the stampede and hundreds were knocked down.'

John Montgomery, 'The Twenties', 1957

¶ The victors on that occasion were Bolton Wanderers:

'The side of the post-war decade was Bolton. They were a fair League side (third in 1921 and again in 1925) but as Cup fighters they put up a record that still remains to be eclipsed. They appeared at Wembley in three Finals between 1923 and 1929; and they won every one of them . . .
'They came to Wembley (in 1923) to win the first Cup Final in that fixture's final home before the biggest crowd ever assembled in Europe (and perhaps in the world) to watch an afternoon's sport. The famous ground had been given less than a year to take shape out of a patch of hillside on which the foundations of a monument which was to rival the Eiffel Tower had once been laid by Sir Edward Watkin.
'In 300 working days the new stadium was made to look ship-shape. A quarter of a million tons of clay was moved at a cost of £750,000. Twenty-five thousand tons of concrete and fifteen hundred tons of steel were assembled. Near enough to the site of "Watkin's Folly" the new colossal amphitheatre began to soar . . . And at last, by April 28th, 1923, the ground was ready, the half-millionth rivet was hammered in its place, the last lick of paint was dry; and there was the crowd pouring in to watch the first Wembley Cup Final, between Bolton Wanderers and West Ham United.
'Only it didn't just pour in. It swept in like a tidal wave, through

Denzil Batchelor, 'Soccer', 1954

51

the turnstiles and across the barriers, over the palings and above the palisades. Perhaps there were a quarter of a million people there, less than half of them with tickets.'

¶ Football had indeed become big business. Star players became national figures and the club managers men of power. One of the most striking among the latter was Herbert Chapman who was brought in to manage Arsenal in 1925. Another great organizer of victory was Major Frank Buckley:

Denzil Batchelor, 'Soccer', 1954
'This remarkable manager had begun as a £3-a-week player and had won his international cap while on the books of Derby County. He came to Wolverhampton as manager in 1927, to find the club facing an overdraft. He stayed at Molineux for eighteen years . . . and when he left had the satisfaction of knowing that there was a £50,000 credit in the bank.

'He did more than achieve a profit. His plan, carried out to the last particular, was to make stars and sell them. He sold stars during his stay at Wolverhampton, to the tune of £160,000 — it was said that when his team travelled to away matches by bus there was a placard on the windows: "Stop me and Buy One." Buckley built new stands with the money he made, rather than buy new stars. Between 1935 and 1939 he took over £110,000 in transfer fees and only spent £42,000 on new stock.'

¶ But Soccer was no longer merely a British game:

Morris Marples, 'A History of Football', 1954
'Association Football has become the game of young men of every colour in every quarter of the globe. It had spread to the continent from the British Isles soon after the forming of the Association, and the first international matches, with Germany, Austria and Bohemia, took place in 1896. By 1904 so many countries had adopted the game that an International Federation of Association Football was formed, of which all the western nations, except Spain and Portugal, were members. At that date many Englishmen, perhaps most Englishmen, tended to adopt a somewhat superior and self-satisfied attitude towards foreign footballers. We were very happy to teach the foreigners our game, indeed who but an Englishman could teach it? — such was the general feeling — but it was not to be expected that the foreigners would ever play it very well . . . It soon became clear, to the surprise

Diana Fishwick, Palm Beach, Florida, 1933.

Walter Hagen in play, 1920.   *The Prince of Wales playing golf at Biarritz, 1924*

of many Englishmen, that foreigners could play football as well as they could themselves, and indeed very often much better. Though England had won the International football tournament at the Olympic Games of 1908 and 1912, and it might have seemed pre-ordained that she should always win it, things were very different after the First World War. Belgium won in 1920, and Uruguay in 1924. An adjustment of ideas became necessary.'

¶ Some critics were inclined to think that a slight change in the rules of the game was responsible for the British decline:

'On June 13th, 1925, at its meeting in Paris the International Board changed the offside law. If — apart from a few exceptions — a player did not have at least three opponents between himself and their goal-line, he was offside: but from then onwards two opponents were to be sufficient to make him offside.

*Willy Meisl,
'Soccer Revolution',
1955*

'What might have appeared to the layman a slight revision in the Laws of the Game turned out to be the crack of a shot that started an avalanche. It revolutionized Soccer as we then knew it, quickly brought about the "safety-first" game, and with that the slow, but soon unmistakable downslide and deterioration of British football.

'Looking at it now we may almost discover some divine gesture in this, because when the literally *good old* offside rule was changed, this was done by the British *for* the British. At least, that was how it was meant. As a matter of fact, more than a million British, and many a million foreign amateur footballers, had been quite happy with the law as it stood. Many professional sides also had no complaints, but there was a large number of them whose directors had got the jitters. The balance sheets of some limited companies, popularly known as football clubs, acquired a more and more anæmic look when the boom after World War One was over and the turnstiles had begun to click rather sluggishly . . .

'In their opinion this (the offside law) had all of a sudden begun to favour defence and to emasculate attack. How otherwise could one explain the fact that goals had become scarce? And goals were the life-blood of the soccer business; basically the crowd paid only to see goals . . . Spectators did not go to a football match to watch free-kick after free-kick for offside. They wanted to see kicks in the opposite direction — at goal! They were out for thrills, and where can you harvest thrills in the soccer fields? Close to the goalmouth. The

53

biggest thrill of all is the ball in the net, or at least on its way there, and in Britain goals were becoming rarer and rarer . . .

'The directors triumphed. The little difference worked like a vitamin injection into the turnstiles. They clicked much livelier — for a time. As so often with new patent medicines, the miracle cure wears off and what remains is the old ailment — only worse. The tiny alteration turned the game upside down and all but killed it.

'In its 1948–49 *Year Book* the F.A. published a very instructive graph which showed how goal production soared for a few years after 1926. Then goals became fewer and fewer. The First Division enjoyed a short come-back, then goal production dropped off again. The "safety-first" games had overtaken the effect of the changed offside rule. Once more the forwards were the fools and the defence dominated.'

¶ But why were foreign nations not affected in the same way. Willy Meisl explains:

Willy Meisl, 'Soccer Revolution', 1955 'The British were bent on "safety-first", on preventing the opponent from scoring goals. The Continentals were out to score goals. Most schoolboys good at arithmetic will tell me that it amounts to the same whether I win by scoring goals, or by giving away fewer to the opponent.

'In football I challenge this axiom. Though it may be the same mathematically, it makes all the difference to the soul of soccer . . .

'A generation of "safety-first" football created a "safety-first" mentality, just as the existence of that "unassailable fortress" created a "Maginot Line" mentality (read complex) in the French nation. In soccer as in politics and warfare "safety-first" meant surrendering the initiative, choosing the passive rôle. This must lead to decadence and weakening.'

¶ So one can't keep politics out of sport! This became increasingly obvious as the years went by:

Morris Marples, 'A History of Football', 1954 'One is bound to ask whether all this international sport has really promoted understanding and friendship between the nations . . . Englishmen are prone to regard all sport, and particularly football, as a means of making friends . . . But other nations have not always adopted this cheerful, and, one must admit, adolescent attitude, and

54

during the last twenty years in particular sport has become involved with politics . . . In Fascist Italy and Nazi Germany the sportsman who competed against foreigners was regarded as a champion on whose performance the national prestige depended. If he won, it was treated as a triumph, and hailed as proof of national superiority. If he lost, he was disgraced, even punished or fined. The members of an Italian team which lost a European cup-tie were actually fined £25 each by the State, and, to underline his supreme responsibility, the captain was fined £40.'

¶ The same spirit still persists in 'certain quarters'.

'More recently we have seen another demonstration of what happens when sport gets mixed up with an exaggerated nationalism. The Russian team, known as the Moscow Dynamos, which visited this country in 1945, had a magnificent opportunity of promoting friendship between their country and ours. The time was ripe. Everyone was eager to welcome them — in fact, 258,000 saw the four matches. They themselves were great players, whom Englishmen were ready to admire for their own sakes. When the Russian captain on landing declared "We are ambassadors of sport", it seemed indeed that sport was once more coming into its own as the supreme maker of friendships. But it soon became obvious that the cliché meant nothing, and that the Russians did not intend to be friendly; or rather it was their official policy not to be friendly, for the individual players had little chance to show what they thought or felt. Misunderstandings were deliberately staged: our arrangements, our play, our rules were criticized: our hospitality was rejected. Everything was clearly done with a view to propaganda at home, and in short the purpose of the visit soon turned out to be purely political.'

Morris Marples
'A History of Football', 1954

¶ It is all rather sad! Perhaps we made a mistake in teaching the rest of the world to play games.

CHAPTER III

CERTAIN MECHANICAL CONTRIVANCES

IF A TYPICAL EDWARDIAN had been put to sleep at the end of his epoch and re-awakened in the early 'twenties, what would have impressed him most? Not motor cars, for they already existed, and although there were more of them about they were still the privilege of the rich and there had been no drastic alteration in design. Not the aeroplane, for in spite of the service it had given in the First World War, it was still a 'kite', similar to those he might have seen.

No, the two things which would have astonished him most were the radio ('the wireless' as it was still called) and the cinema, or at least the stature to which it had grown.

Radio is now so much a part of our lives that the present editor has been met with stares of incredulity by the young when he tells them that, on leave from France in the final year of the War, he sat in the lounge of Brown's Hotel in Dover Street and listened to a performance of *Yes, Uncle,* then running in London; but not a broadcast performance; a performance transmitted by telephone. Earphones, connected to the theatre by telephone, were hung round the walls and one could take the apparatus down from its hook, adjust it to one's ears and listen to a rather faint and squeaky voice singing

> 'Henry VIII was a lad in his day,
> He had several wives — yes, he was a bit gay;
> He founded the Metropole, Brighton, they say:
> Really? would you believe it?'

Wall telephones of this kind were, in 1918, considered the very height of modernity. The idea that the ether would one day be crammed with voices to which one had only to 'tune in' had not yet occurred to anyone.

Wireless *telegraphy,* of course, had long been known, for it was in

56

1899 that Marconi had transmitted a message in Morse across the English Channel. Since 1904 it had been possible, by the development of Ambrose Fleming's thermionic valve, to transmit not only signals but actual sounds, but years were to elapse before much came of it. The Irish Republic was proclaimed by wireless (not by signals but by actual speech) at Easter 1916, and the news was picked up by ships at sea and published in American newspapers. But the very idea of using 'the wireless' as a means of transmitting performances was still far in the future.

'Cultural and educational opportunities for adults came from lectures, reading, and evening institutes . . . In villages a sing-song in the village hall or the pub, perhaps some remnant of old-time country dancing on the green, maybe a lecture by the vicar on his travels in Switzerland, sufficed as recreation for rural communities who still lived close to the soil . . .

Leslie Baily,
'Scrapbook for the
Twenties', 1959

'Into this traditional scene "the wireless" crept almost unnoticed. The Marconi Company's experiments in 1919 with transatlantic telephony . . . were heard by a small number of "wireless experimenters", as listeners were then called. My own first receiving licence was not a printed form bought at the post office. It was a typewritten letter begging to convey the authority of the Postmaster-General for "the installation and use of a station for receiving wireless signals for experimental purposes". In 1921 there were in Great Britain six thousand such licensed experimenters. Ours was a technical hobby, even more esoteric than stamp-collecting, until it began to dawn on people that there was more in it than met the ear.

'All that met the ear at first was this sort of thing: "MZX calling . . . MZX calling . . . This is the Marconi valve transmitter at Chelmsford, England, testing on a wave-length of 2,800 metres. How are our signals coming in today? Can you hear us clearly? I will now recite to you my collection of British railway stations for test purposes . . ."

'The voice was that of Mr. W. T. Ditcham . . . The broadcasts of 1920 being technical tests, no importance lay in *what* he said; technicians jiggling with valves and circuits were only interested in how clearly and strongly the voice might be projected through the air. So Mr. Ditcham, engineer-cum-announcer, amused himself with his improvised recitations, but after a time (as he said many years later in *Scrapbook*): "One got very tired of railway stations and 'Mary had a little lamb' so we looked round for local talent. Mr. Edward Cooper, who worked in the Marconi factory at Chelmsford, had a good tenor voice, and Miss Winifred Sayer was another local amateur singer — these two we invited to broadcast and they were the first artists in this country to do so." '

¶ The *Daily Mail* sponsored a broadcast from Chelmsford by Dame Nellie Melba, and boasted that her voice had been heard 'within a radius of a thousand miles'.

Vivian Ogilvie,
'Our Times', 1953 'Those early transmissions from Britain's first broadcasting station were discontinued after a while. A mighty wail went up from the listeners, and in response broadcasting began again in 1922. Big business saw opportunities in this new craze and the manufacturers of apparatus approached the Government for permission to run programmes. Thus the British Broadcasting Company, Ltd., was established in 1922, the principal shareholders being the six largest manufacturers of equipment. A daily service of wireless programmes began on November 14th and the Company received a licence to be the one and only broadcasting organization in the country . . .

'The venture was an instantaneous success far beyond anything that had been dreamed of. Within a year several hundred thousand listeners had taken out licences and by the end of the fourth year the number had risen to nearly two million. At that point the Company's career ended, for the Government decided that the nation's monopoly broadcasting organization ought not to be left in private hands. The State bought out the shareholders and on January 1st, 1927, a public corporation under Royal Charter took over the function of broadcasting, with the staff and material equipment of the old company and, thanks to linguistic chance, the by now familiar initials.'

¶ The same author gives us a personal reminiscence of the early, tentative days:

Vivian Ogilvie,
Our Times', 1953 'I remember the first time I heard the wireless. It was at our village institute in Wedmore, Somerset. A couple of men came to give a demonstration to us giggling yokels. The quality of sound was poor. Every now and then something would go wrong. There would be a sudden fading or the intrusion of shrieks, howls and splutterings . . . It was not a very impressive performance. It was only remarkable that it should have been done at all. As we left the hall the older

people wagged their heads sagely and declared that nothing would come of it.'

¶ Another commentator on the 'twenties remembers that

'Although the first sets were crude and reception was unreliable these difficulties were soon overcome. Headphones and the cat's whisker gave way in time to loudspeakers, and batteries to power from the mains. At first long poles were erected at the end of gardens, or on roof-tops, to hold elaborate aerials. "Listening in" was a solemn ritual, like watching television in later years. Crystal sets and head-phones could be bought for only a few shillings, and a complete set for under ten shillings. The wireless set was accepted as a feature of the average house, and soon the coils, wires, loudspeaker and controls of the primitive sets were combined into one box or cabinet. Indoor aerials were installed in attics . . .

'Schoolboys were among the keenest of the amateurs. When the Prince of Wales visited Mill Hill School, he said, "I was interested the other day to hear that Mill Hill had got America. I think this school is among the first of the schools to wireless the Atlantic, and I congratulate you."

'To others the "magic box" remained a mystery. When the Arch-bishop of Canterbury heard a wireless set for the first time, in March 1923, he asked if it were necessary to leave a window open in order to hear the programmes.'

John Montgomery, 'The Twenties', 1957

¶ The establishment of the British Broadcasting *Corporation* meant a new and heavy responsibility for someone, and, fortunately, the man was at hand to assume it:

'At nine o'clock in the morning of December the 30th, 1922, a very tall Scotsman walked into the B.B.C. doorway in London. The liftman showed him up to an office . . . no one there . . . a chair, a table, a telephone, an empty desk . . . The tall man, whose name was John Reith, was left there alone. The newly appointed Managing Director of the B.B.C. had arrived.'

Percy Edgar, in 'Scrapbook for 1922'

¶ John Reith was a very remarkable man in more ways than one:

'From the earliest days Mr. Reith insisted on the announcers wearing evening dress. A man of strong religious conviction, he was determined

John Montgomery, 'The Twenties', 1957

59

that broadcasting should be conducted as a national service, with definite standards, and not used for entertainment alone. He wanted the service to reach the greatest possible number of homes, and to provide "all that is best in every department of human knowledge, endeavour and advancement".'

¶ In America things at first moved equally slowly:

Frederick Lewis Allen, 'Only Yesterday', 1931

'The first broadcasting station had been opened in East Pittsburgh on November 2nd, 1920 — a date which schoolchildren may some day have to learn — to carry the Harding-Cox election returns. This was station KDKA, operated by the Westinghouse Company. For a time, however, this new revolution in communication and public entertainment made slow headway — Auditors were few. Amateur wireless operators objected to the stream of music — mostly from phonograph records — which issued from the Westinghouse station and interfered with their important business . . .

'Experiment proceeded, however; other radio stations were opened, market reports were thrown on the air, Dr. Van Etten of Pittsburgh permitted the services at Calvary Church to be broadcasted, the University of Wisconsin gave radio concerts, and politicians spouted into the strange instruments and wondered if anybody was really listening. Yet when Dempsey fought Carpentier in July, 1921, and three men at the ringside told the story of the slaughter into telephone transmitters to be relayed by air to eighty points throughout the country, their enterprise was reported in an obscure corner of the *New York Times* as an achievement in "wireless telephony" . . . The great awakening had not yet come.

'That winter, however — the winter of 1921–22 — it came with a rush. Soon everybody was talking, not about wireless telephony, but about radio. A San Francisco paper described the discovery that millions were making: "There is radio music in the air, every night, everywhere. Anybody can hear it at home on a receiving set, which any boy can put up in an hour." In February President Harding had an outfit installed in his study, and the Dixmoor Golf Club announced that it would install a "telephone" to enable golfers to hear Church services. In April, passengers on a Lackawanna train heard a radio concert, and Lieutenant Maynard broke all records for modernizing Christianity by broadcasting an Easter sermon from an airplane. Newspapers brought out radio sections and thousands of hitherto

60

A crystal set for 7/6. Radio Exhibition, White City, 1924.

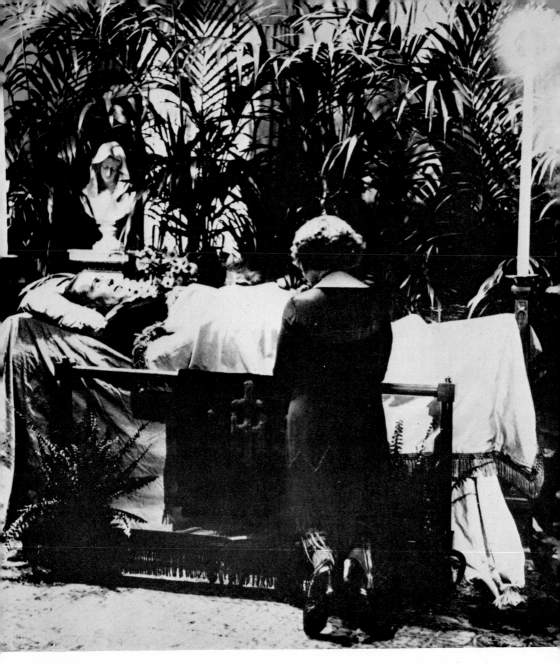

Rudolph Valentino lying in state in the Campbell Funeral Parlour, New York, 1926.

utterly unmechanical people puzzled over articles about regenerative circuits, sodion tubes, Grimes reflex circuits, crystal detectors and neutrodynes. And every other man you met on the street buttonholed you to tell you how he had sat up until two o'clock the night before, with earphones clamped to his head, and had actually *heard Havana*.'

¶ Some astute politicians were already beginning to realize the importance of the new weapon which 'the wireless' had put into their hands:

'During the Election campaign Stanley Baldwin went to the micro- *Vivian Ogilvie,* phone and very simply gave a "fireside talk". He was the first political *'Our Times', 1953* leader to understand the subtle use of the microphone. A week before his broadcast he took the trouble to go to Savoy Hill to obtain advice how to put it over. Ramsay MacDonald insisted on broadcasting *his* speech direct from a public meeting at Glasgow, despite a warning from Reith that the two techniques were utterly different. By comparison with Stan's pipe-sucking chat Ramsay Mac sounded like a street-corner ranter. Baldwin's quietly spoken plea for a "sane, common sense Government, not carried away by revolutionary theories or hare-brained schemes", went straight to the heart and home.'

¶ Unfortunately it was not only men like Stanley Baldwin who were able to make use of the new medium. But in the mid 'twenties hardly anyone in England had even heard of Adolf Hitler.

The other 'mechanical contrivance' which came to full stature in the 'twenties was, of course, the cinema.

'When the war ended, a large proportion of the population of *Vivian Ogilvie,* Britain was going to the cinema at least once a week. Chaplin and *'Our Times', 1953* Mary Pickford were at the head of an ever-lengthening galaxy of stars who became the darlings of a world-wide public. World-wide it was, for until speech was added the film was a truly universal medium. Captions were kept down to the minimum needed for following the story and they could be translated into any language.'

¶ The operative word in this passage is the word 'stars'. Who were the 'stars'?

'Up to 1909, film actors, in striking contrast to stage actors, had *Egon Larsen,* been anonymous, the reason being that the producing companies *'Spotlight on Films', 1950*

61

wished to avoid paying big salaries. An anonymous player, they thought, had no justification for demanding excessive fees, and had to take what the company offered him, just like any unknown stage actor. Mary Pickford, for instance, had been thrilling thousands of cinema-goers week after week in her heart-rending films before she was given a name, and that was not her own — not at first, anyway. For in England the exhibitors, faced with the problem of advertising the news that another film with "that girl" was being shown, invented a name for her — Dorothy Nicholson. Love-letters and marriage offers were sent to Miss Nicholson, but they never reached Mary Pickford, as no one in England knew her real name; and Mary herself had no idea that she had become England's sweetheart under an alias.

'Carl Laemmle, the biggest independent producer, broke with that system of anonymity . . . There is no doubt that in those days the liquidation of the system of anonymity was a good thing. Soon, however, the star system developed so excessively that it became a millstone around the neck of all who tried to make the film a serious art . . .

'It was a sleepy little village, south of Los Angeles, called Hollywood, which Laemmle selected as his new home . . .

'Perhaps it was the star system that broke down the last barrier between the film and the public. The personal interest in film people made the new form of entertainment really popular. Mary Pickford, as "Little Mary", was the first star whose name became known all the world over . . . [She] won her fame as the glorified working-class girl. Her golden curls cast a glamorous shimmer on her dirty rags. She was always poor, but loving, true, virtuous, and cheerful.'

¶ America's impact on the world through the medium of the film had begun:

Egon Larsen,
'Spotlight on Films',
1950

'In 1914 America made more than half the world's films. The other half was supplied by a few European countries, mainly France and Italy . . . The strain of war was too much for a young industry in the countries which had to put all their strength into the national effort . . . Thus by 1917 America supplied almost 100 per cent of the world's film requirements, a monopoly which meant a new gold rush to Hollywood, with enormous jumps in star salaries and the building of million-dollar cinema palaces all over the country . . .

'One of the first personifications of the successful screen hero was Douglas Fairbanks . . . There was no man in the audience who hesitated to identify himself with this knight of the screen, escaping from his own humdrum life into gallant adventures. With the female part of the audience, however, Rudolph Valentino was even more popular. Millions of women would have given anything to be in the shoes of the heroines he swept off their feet. The close-ups brought them excitingly near that man with the handsome, slightly oriental face, and few were discriminating enough to mind that he wasn't a good actor at all. When he died prematurely a number of girls committed suicide, and indescribable scenes took place at his funeral.'

¶ The ballyhoo occasioned by his death certainly touched a new high:

'Towards the season's end there was a striking demonstration of what astute press-agentry could do to make a national sensation. A young man named Rudolph Alfonzo Raffaelle Pierre Filibert Guglielmi di Valentina d'Antonguella died in New York at the age of thirty-one. The love-making of Rudolph Valentino (as he had understandably preferred to call himself) had quickened the pulses of innumerable motion-picture addicts; with his sideburns and his passionate air, "the sheik" had set the standard for masculine sex appeal. But his lying-in-state in an undertaker's establishment on Broadway would hardly have attracted a crowd which stretched through eleven blocks if his manager had not arranged the scenes of grief with uncanny skill, and if Harry C. Klemfuss, the undertaker's press agent, had not provided the newspapers with everything they could desire — such as photographs, distributed in advance, of the chamber where the actor's body would lie, and posed photographs of the funeral cortège. (One of these latter pictures . . . was on the streets in one newspaper before the funeral procession started.) With such practical assistance, the Press gave itself to the affair so whole-heartedly that mobs rioted about the undertaker's and scores of people were injured. Sweet are the uses of publicity: Valentino had been heavily in debt when he died, but his posthumous films, according to his manager's subsequent testimony, turned the debt into a $600,000 balance to the credit of his estate.'

Frederick Lewis Allen, 'Only Yesterday', 1931

¶ Parallel with the career of men like Rudolph Valentino was the rise of 'the vamp':

Gilbert Seldes,
'Movies for the
Million', 1937 'The vampire type of which Miss Theda Bara was the most effective example is actually the popularization of the courtesan as people imagine she lived in the wicked French novels. It was not considered fitting that a simple American girl named Theodora Goodman, born in Cincinnati, should create the image of fatal love on the screen. Her name was changed and the moment "A Fool There Was" became a success, a systematic but amazingly successful publicity began. Mr. Terry Ramsage notes that Theda Bara was announced as "the daughter of a French artist and an Arabian mistress, born on the sands of the Sahara". "Bara" was indeed a mere cypher, being "Arab" spelled backwards. That proved the rest of the story. "Theda" was just a rearrangement of the letters of "death". This deadly Arab girl was a crystal-gazing seeress of profoundly occult powers, wicked as fresh red paint and poisonous as dried spiders. The stranger the copy grew the more it was printed. Little girls read it and swallowed their gum with excitement.'

¶ It is doubtful, however, if such exotic creatures were the real favourites of the cinema-going public. The vamp could be as wicked as the censor would allow but the heroine of a film had, above all things, to be 'pure'. Elmer Rice provides a playful picture of what was expected:

Elmer Rice,
'A Voyage to
Purilia', 1930 'She was . . . indeed a lovely creature. And a first glance seemed to confirm the suggestion that she was native to the countryside: the daughter of a humble farmer perhaps. Barefoot and dressed in well-fitting rags, she leaned daintily upon the handle of a rake (which, upon reflection, struck me as a little odd, for it was scarcely the season for haying).

'A closer scrutiny . . . raised many puzzling doubts . . . her person seemed to belie a life of arduous toil and exposure to the elements. Although she was hatless, her skin was snowy and unblemished. Her lips were small bows of unusual perfection and each eyelash stiffly proclaimed its individual existence. Her hair, which was literally a mass of golden ringlets, might well have been proclaimed a triumph of tonsorial art. The hand which clasped the rake (as well as the other hand, which fingered the hem of her charmingly tattered dress) was soft and white, and the finger-nails were well-shaped and beautifully polished and tinted. And I was not a little surprised to observe that the dainty toes, that nestled modestly in the grass, were handsomely

64

Marlene Dietrich in 'The Blue Angel'.

Greta Garbo, before the days of fame.

manicured too. But I remembered that I was in a strange country and I surmised that the conditions of rural life in Purilia are unlike our own.'

¶ Life, however, even in this arcadia of the film-makers' imagination was not all roses:

'In Purilia, practically all the small rural homesteads are controlled by a class of unscrupulous wealthy men who, either as landlords or mortgagees, rule the economic destinies of the humble homesteaders. The agriculture of the country is upon a most unsound economic basis, and the rural population is engaged in a constant struggle to meet rent and interest payments which, under this most inequitable system, are perpetually due. To aggravate matters, these grasping landowners are always irresistibly attracted to the fair young daughters of their unfortunate tenants and, by ill-chance, this attraction is never reciprocal. So there is scarcely a Purilian maiden of rural origin, who is not, at one time or another in her life, faced with the devastating alternatives of allowing her aged parents to be turned out of doors, or of giving herself in marriage (or in many cases, I regret to say, to a state far less honourable than marriage) to one of these agrarian despots. It is a flagrant and shameful condition and I marvel that nothing is done about it. Fortunately, in every case that came to my attention (and their number is incalculable), the imperilled maiden managed, by some means or other, to escape her dilemma and to bring the affair to a happy conclusion.'

Elmer Rice, 'A Voyage to Purilia', 1930

¶ The conventions of the screen-story were still those of old-fashioned melodrama. The same witty author reflects upon some of them in an amusing passage. His imaginary travellers arrive at 'the Metropolis Hotel, a palatial hostelry, where the idle rich pass their days and nights in wasteful luxury, mindless of the suffering of the toiling millions':

'With the assistance of some seven or eight liveried attendants, we entered the great doors of the hotel and found ourselves in a rotunda which in size compared favourably with the interior of the Church of St. Peter in Rome. Great columns soared to incredible heights, and the eye lost itself in vistas which faded dimly away in the remote distance . . . we were permitted to ascend to the room to which we had been assigned. Like everything else in the hotel, its dimensions

Elmer Rice, 'A Voyage to Purilia', 1930

E

were colossal, and the furniture exceeded, both in size and profusion, any that I had ever seen in a terrestrial hotel. The bathroom (which was by far the largest that I had ever seen) contained a magnificent sunken swimming bath as its sole furniture. I was more than a little surprised to find so luxurious a hotel lacking in those conveniences to which even the humblest humans are accustomed. But this lack of conveniences (as I discovered only too often to my embarrassment and discomfort) is universal in Purilia — a curious fact which I can attribute only to the physiological differences between the Purilians and ourselves . . .

'This view is supported by the fact that babies are really not born, but merely occur. There is no long and difficult period of gestation. No one in Purilia, has ever seen a woman who gave outward evidence of approaching maternity. There are no lying-in hospitals, no obstetricians, no midwives. Purilian mothers are happily spared all the hazards and the pangs that attend human birth. Often, indeed, the arrival of the little one comes as something of a surprise to the parents. A pair is joined in wedlock, and then, after a while, a baby appears, usually well-developed and fully clothed.'

¶ All this might well seem to be beneath the notice of cultivated people. But there were those, even among the intellectual élite, who were beginning to take the cinema very seriously indeed. 'I no longer ask myself', wrote René Schwob, 'if the cinema is an art. I ask myself if it is not the greatest of all arts. The cinema reveals to us the discontinuous, and carries the spirit with it in a dizzy descent.'

René Schwob, 'Une Mélodie Silencieuse', 1929 'The cinema seems to have been reserved for the epoch when man, having reduced distances to the point of repressing them altogether, may hope to hold before him the image of the whole world.

'Everything, especially this art, shows that we are on the threshold of a planetary era when Humanity, reunited in one immense whole, should recover its integrity and create, at the end of Time, a New Adam.'

¶ The man who really won over the intellectuals to an appreciation of the cinema was a little man in a bowler hat and baggy trousers. His origins were humble enough:

Gilbert Seldes, 'Movies for the Million', 1937 'The Keystone Comedies had . . . nothing to do with the comedy of the theatre. There was no text, there was no plot. They were shot "on the cuff", that is to say, a director, a cameraman, and a group of actors went out with a few properties — perhaps a step-ladder, some painter's supplies, and a wheel-barrow; they proceeded to a street or a park or a lake, and with nothing more than a general idea of an action in their minds, created their picture . . .

'The Keystone comedians were the descendants of all the true comics of the theatre. You can trace them back to Harlequin and Pantaloon and, farther than that, you will find them in the comedies of Terence and of Aristophanes. They used the same material — misunderstandings, disguises, violent anger over imaginary offences — and everything led to physical action whether it was a blow or a kiss. They destroyed the whole solemn framework in which the everyday man had his existence. Of them it might be reasonable to say that they satisfied our desire to escape from the habits and rules of our life and from the logic by which we had to live.

'And yet Keystone Comedies were only inventive. One further step had to be taken — to become imaginative and creative — and this step was taken by a man who began with the Keystone Comedies and went far beyond them, but never forgot what they taught him — Charlie Chaplin.'

¶ The French author we have already quoted really lets himself go when he comes to Charlie Chaplin:

'Some scenes recall the purest works of Velasquez, with one or two of the characters immensely enlarged. But what is unique in Charlot, and in his earliest films, is the quality of interior life which he finds it possible to suggest.

René Schwob, 'Une Mélodie Silencieuse', 1929

'Unbelievable as it may seem it is simply to multiple reactions implied by each of Charlot's gestures that his compositions owe their gifts of eternal youth . . .

'Charlot's gestures always lead to misunderstandings, to catastrophes, to bursts of laughter. But that is because he lives in a world to which he can never adapt himself, and his perpetual disorientation in the midst of the elements of ordinary life, his awkwardness in the world, find their perfect synthesis in *Charlot patissier*, for the dough, an essentially plastic material, serves as the symbol of his confusion. Sometimes his hands, sometimes his feet are stuck in it, even his behind. Or else he uses it as a weapon of defence — or attack.'

67

¶ Who would have thought that so much metaphysics was to be extracted from a tub of sticky dough — or a custard pie?

René Schwob,
'Une Mélodie
Silencieuse, 1929
'Charlot reveals the interior chaos and the unity of its complexity, the organic unity of expressions released from the confines of time and space . . . The unity of that which lies below is thus set forth free from any external influence in a kind of Absolute Virginity . . .

'However far from Christ he may seem to some of his admirers, the contradiction between his life and his art underlines one of the teachings of Christ . . . When he has disappeared with the dough, he continues to pay no attention to it and to pursue his dream as if out in the fields.

'Charlot in his films repeats the same lesson of absolute independence — a lesson which is a caricature of that of the great mystics and which, precisely, finds its function in the fact that it *is* only a caricature.

'But does he understand the lesson of his own genius?'

¶ It would seem extremely unlikely.

M. Schwob had an almost equal admiration for Douglas Fairbanks, especially in *The Black Prince*:

René Schwob,
'Une Mélodie
Silencieuse', 1929
'But Douglas? He poses questions, and in full daylight, answers them.

'In him are joined ease, good humour, strength and courage.

'Charm of simplicity!

'No difficulty troubles him. He sees none; his faith removes mountains . . .

'His acrobatic feats provoke public enthusiasm because he never takes his own existence into account. He risks it first, and glory is added to him . . .

'The negation of self is the door open to the Holy Spirit, the means by which mortal creatures can find eternity . . .

'Thanks to the agility of his body, Douglas realizes the impossible. It is truly one of the emotive poles of the cinema that an unexpected liberty of the spirit should transform the captive language of the body. It is as if the realm of reason were surpassed and, in a manner incomparably more honest than that of literature, space and time lost their habitual rigidity and ceased to put obstacles in our way.'

¶ As the 'twenties progressed, however, the film-makers began to realize that the medium had other possibilities, quite remote from the high-falutin' fancies of M. René Schwob. These 'other possibilities' can be summed up in the one word — Sex.

'The age which sloughed its sex inhibitions . . . was the so-called "jazz age". One fourth of radio time in 1928 [in America] was devoted to torrid tunes like "Baby Face", "I Need Lovin' ", "Hot Mama", "I Gotta Have You", and "Hot Lips". Motion picture production in this decade joined the party when two German directors arrived on American soil and immediately capitalized on a satirization of native taboos. Ernst Lubitsch and Erich von Stroheim exploited the casual infidelities of the socially elect in films like "Blind Husbands", "Kiss Me Again", and "Forbidden Paradise". Contemporary movie titles included "Is Matrimony a Failure?", "Why Be Good?", "Flaming Youth", and "Mad Love". The Lynds, checking Middletown's cinema offerings for one week in 1925, listed "The Daring Years", "Sinners in Silk", "Women Who Give", and "The Price She Paid". Movie culture, the authors commented, is what people have always wanted to do but never dared . . . Only romantic love and crime films outdistanced portrayals of biological sex in movie popularity.'

Sidney Ditzion, 'Marriage, Morals and Sex in America', 1953

¶ *'C'est toujours la même chose'*, said Madame de Pompadour, *'et ça donne toujours plaisir'*:

'The movies . . . drawing millions to their doors every day and every night, played incessantly upon the same lucrative theme. The producers of one picture advertised "brilliant men, beautiful jazz babies, champagne battles, midnight revels, petting parties in the purple dawn, all ending in one terrific smashing climax that makes you gasp". The vendors of another promised "neckers, petters, white kisses, red kisses, pleasure-mad daughters, sensation-craving mothers . . . the truth — bold, naked, sensational". Seldom did the films offer as much as these advertisements promised.'

Frederick Lewis Allen, 'Only Yesterday', 1931

¶ It was small wonder that the world's moral guardians (official or self-appointed) became alarmed. The Child Welfare Committee of the League of Nations met at Geneva in May, 1926 to consider the 'Effect of the Cinematograph on the Mental and Moral Well-being

69

of Children', and called upon a number of experts to express their views:

William Marston Seabury, 'Motion Picture Problems', 1929 'Nearly all those consulted pronounced in favour of educational, historical, etc., films and against the cinema theatre. A German neurologist, having analysed 250 cinema films, had found 97 murders, 52 cases of adultery, 19 seductions, 22 abductions and 43 suicides. Among the principal protagonists were 176 thieves, 25 prostitutes, 35 drunkards, etc. Even if the end of the film was happy, the effect on children of this representation of persons in conflict with society and good morals remained the same.'

¶ The cinema was blamed for the increase (it is always an increase) in juvenile delinquency:

William Marston Seabury, 'Motion Picture Problems', 1929 'M. Rollet said that the magistrates who sat on the children's courts in Paris had always realized the pernicious influence of certain films on a larger number of crimes . . . It was, of course, true that a censorship, even if strictly exercised, did not prevent a certain number of crimes being represented on the screen. He himself had assisted some time ago in prohibiting a film which showed the holding-up of a train. In spite of the exotic character of the costumes and the acrobatic feats of horsemanship, he thought it preferable not to show children that it was possible to hold up a train . . . This prohibition had not prevented a mysterious affair of the holding up and robbery of a train which had occurred two months ago . . .'

¶ The logic of the Frenchman would seem to have been at fault, since the film had not been shown and yet the train robbery took place. The reference to the exotic costumes and the feats of horsemanship shows that it was a Western — perhaps *The Great Train Robbery* itself. How solemn — and how silly — can you get?

The Committee hoped that:

William Marston Seabury, 'Motion Picture Problems', 1929 'Collaboration with the International Institute for Intellectual Co-operation and the voluntary associations . . . would make it possible to influence public opinion in order that good films [i.e. educational films] might be well attended and melodrama neglected.'

¶ Unfortunately 'public opinion' refused to play, and the Canadian representative sadly admitted that there was truth in a newspaper illustration 'showing on one side of the street a cinema giving an educational film the entrance to which was absolutely deserted, whereas on the other side of the street, two policemen could scarcely control the crowd at the entrance to a cinema where there was a bill of "The Admirable Crichton" under the title of "Male and Female", with a note to the effect that it had been condemned by the censorship.' *William Marston Seabury, 'Motion Picture Problems', 1929*

¶ The cinema barons began to think they had better put their own house in order, and so

'Ten of the leading producers of Hollywood joined to ask a member of President Harding's Cabinet to serve them. Mr. Will Hays, an elder of the Methodist Church, became President of the Motion Picture Producers and Distributors of America. The invitation to him said nothing about censorship . . . To this day the official position of the Hays Organization is that it exercises no censorship. Once in a while a slight error may be made; the Hays Office is reported as saying that a certain book or play is not suitable material for a motion picture; but in general the approved method is for a producer to submit a story to the Hays Office and the Hays Office then informs the producer that in all likelihood if he makes the picture he will have trouble with the State boards of censorship. That is all, but the formula, or something similar to it, is sufficient. The producers know that the Hays Office has turned thumbs down.' *Gilbert Seldes, 'Movies for the Million', 1937*

¶ The results were not quite those anticipated:

'Mr. Hays promised that all would be well. "This industry must have", he said before the Los Angeles Chamber of Commerce, "toward that sacred thing, the mind of a child, toward that clean virgin thing, that unmarked slate, the same responsibility, the same care about the impressions made upon it, that the best clergyman or the most inspired teacher of youth would have." The result of Mr. Hays' labours on behalf of the unmarked slate was to make the moral ending as obligatory as in the confession magazines, to smear over sexy pictures with pious platitudes, and to black-list for motion-picture production many a fine novel and play which, because of its very honesty, might be construed as seriously or intelligently questioning the traditional sex ethics of the small town. Mr. Hays, being something of a genius, managed to keep the churchmen at bay. Whenever the *Frederick Lewis Allen, 'Only Yesterday', 1931* threats of censorship began to become ominous, he would promulgate a new series of moral commandments for the producers to follow. Yet of the practical effects of his supervision it is perhaps enough to say that the quotations given above all date from the period of his dictatorship.'

¶ The exercise of film censorship in Great Britain was equally curious and indirect:

Home Office Memorandum, 1929 'The legal foundation of the censorship of films in Great Britain is to be found in the Cinematograph Act, 1909. Although the primary object of this Act was to secure the safety of the audience from special risks, in particular that of fire, attaching to the cinema, means have been found for the exercise, under the Act, of a sufficiently effective control over the character of the films exhibited . . . Responsibility for the granting of licences — which may be refused, and are subject to annual renewal — lies in the hands of local licensing authorities . . . By a series of decisions of the High Court, it has become clearly established that the conditions which a licensing authority may attach to the grant of a licence can properly relate to matter other than the safety of the audience . . . Accordingly it is possible for each licensing authority to assume the functions of a censor.'

¶ This might have been thought likely to lead to chaos, with every local authority imposing its own arbitrary conditions. But fortunately:

Home Office Memorandum, 1929 'There has been in existence for many years an unofficial body, established and maintained by the cinematograph trade, known as the British Board of Film Censors. The submission of films to this body is voluntary and its decisions have in themselves no legal sanction though . . . they have been given such sanction by the action of the licensing authorities . . . It is common for them to conform in practice to the standard set by the Board. In this way, it has been possible to attain throughout the country an approximate uniformity based on the standard set by the Board.'

¶ The authorities concerned have, in nearly every country in the world, drawn up lists of scenes and subjects which it is not permitted to show on the screen. These lists all bear a strong family resemblance so that one will suffice — that issued by the British Board of Film Censors:

72

'Indecorous, outrageous and irreverent titles and sub-titles
Cruelty to animals
Drunken scenes carried to excess
The modus operandi of criminals
Cruelty to young infants, and excessive cruelty to and torture of
    adults, especially women
Profuse bleeding
Unnecessary exhibition of women's underclothing
Nude figures
Offensive vulgarity and impropriety in conduct and dress
Indecorous dancing
Excessively passionate love scenes
Improper bathing scenes
Scenes tending to disparage public characters and institutions
Realistic horrors of warfare
Scenes and incidents in war calculated to afford information to the
    enemy
Scenes in which the king and officers in uniform are seen in an
    odious light
Executions
Gruesome murders and strangulation scenes
Vitriol throwing
The use of drugs, e.g. opium, morphine, cocaine, etc.
Subjects dealing with the deliberate seduction of girls
"First night" scenes
Indelicate sexual situations
Situations accentuating delicate marital relations
Views of men and women in bed together
Illicit sexual relationships
Prostitution and procuration
Disparagement of the institution of marriage
Misrepresentation of police methods
Surgical operations
Commitment of crime by children
Criminal poisoning by the dissemination of germs
Practice of the third degree by the police
Branding men and animals
Women fighting with knives
Exaltation of doubtful characters as heroes
Making the sacrifice of a woman's virtue laudable

Infidelity on part of a husband justifying adultery of a wife
Confinement and puerperal pains
Views of dead bodies
Subjects in which sympathy is enlisted for criminals
Animals gnawing men, women and children
Realistic scenes of epilepsy
Insistence upon the inferiority of coloured races
Advocacy of the doctrine of free love
Salacious wit
The perpetration of criminal assaults on women
Scenes depicting the effect of venereal diseases, inherited or acquired
Incidents suggestive of incestuous relationships
Themes and references to "race suicide"
Scenes laid in disorderly houses
Materialization of the conventional figure of Christ.'

¶ It is a curious list and if its prohibitions had been rigidly adhered to many films, including some of the best which have appeared in the last thirty years, would never have reached the screen. It must have provided many a headache for the film censors. When, for instance, is the exhibition of women's underwear 'unnecessary'? When is cruelty to women 'excessive' (cruelty to babies being ruled out altogether)? When can a drunken scene be said to be carried to excess? What makes a character 'doubtful'? Why is 'profuse' bleeding so frowned upon? And so on. Some of the other national prohibitions contain some strange items. In French films, for instance, there must be no 'displeasing Mexicans'. The Pennsylvania State Board of Censors prohibits '*abnormal* brutality', but allows profanity when it is 'essential to scene or characterization'. The Ohio State Board will have nothing to do with 'Productions that teach fatalism', and Maryland forbids the '*excessive* use of firearms', and the 'shooting of persons' (shades of the 'Wild West'!). The strange thing is that the system, however absurd and illogical, works, in practice, well enough.

Many good films were made in what is now known as 'the old silent days'; and then —

Vivian Ogilvie,
'Our Times', 1953
'In 1927 the cinema was revolutionized by the arrival of sound. Short talking films had been made before that date — in England

74

as well as in America. But it was "The Jazz Singer" that established sound for good and all. It was not intended to be a "talkie"; Al Jolson was to be heard singing "Mammy" and other songs. Unintentionally he spoke a sentence, "Come on, Ma, listen to this!" and these words pronounced the doom of the silent picture. There was no going back. "The Singing Fool" followed and hard-headed business men left the cinemas red-eyed from weeping over Sonny Boy. Overnight silent films with the exception of Chaplin's had become as old-fashioned as long skirts. It was the end too of many a star. Some had no voice or an unsuitable one or could not memorize more than three or four words. But there were many who marched on to fresh success — Greta Garbo, the Barrymores, Wallace Beery, Harry Carey, Donald Crisp, Adolphe Menjou, Laurel and Hardy, Lewis Stone, to name but a few.'

¶ Another commentator notes that

'Garbo kept people guessing until 1930 when huge posters appeared with two words: *Leslie Baily, 'Scrapbook for the Twenties', 1959*

GARBO TALKS

'With the coming in 1930 of such pictures as King Vidor's lyrical "Hallelujah!" and Josef von Sternberg's "The Blue Angel" (with a new discovery, Marlene Dietrich, as the cheap cabaret singer who infatuates the schoolmaster, Emil Jannings), it was clear that the silent film had been buried because something better had taken its place: better, because more satisfying.'

¶ But there were many who regretted the passing of the old silent picture:

'Since talking films have occupied the attention of studios the pictorial value of the screen has greatly deteriorated. The films of the last year of the silent period were far more pleasing from a pictorial point of view. The public has tired of its craze for simply hearing speech and seeing moving pictures of the speakers. Audiences in 1930 failed to maintain the big business created by the talking boom of 1929. Attendances dropped to pre-dialogue level. The season of 1930–31 showed that box-office receipts had fallen 30 per cent in comparison with a year ago.' *Paul Rotha, 'The Film of Today', 1931*

75

¶ The fortunes of the cinema have waxed and waned from that day to this, but the silent picture is now no more than a historical curiosity.

How strange the history is of the two 'mechanical contrivances' we have been considering! For a generation people watched moving pictures without speech, and for almost as long people listened to radio without sight. In the late 'twenties the screen began to speak and in the late 'thirties came television. These are the two *frères ennemis* whose contest we are watching today.

CHAPTER IV

BLAZING THE TRAIL

PROGRESS IN FLYING had been much stimulated by the War of 1914–18. At the time of the Armistice the tiny Royal Flying Corps had become the Royal Air Force and had expanded to the size of 27,906 officers and 263,842 other ranks. In February 1919 the British Air Ministry formed its Civil Department, and in the same month the Air Navigation Act was passed, and civil flying was officially permitted as from May 1st.

In August, 1919, a regular daily air service was started between London and Paris — the first of its kind in the world. The fare was twenty guineas and only two passengers were carried — in conditions of extreme discomfort. In November mails were taken for the first time, the charge for a letter being half a crown. Two years later the operating companies were in difficulties, owing to French (subsidized) competition and the British Government came forward with a temporary aid. In 1924 this was increased to £1,000,000.

This did not please everybody and there were many who thought of the commercial subsidy as well as what was being spent on the Royal Air Force as waste of public money. A writer who called himself Neon made himself the spokesman of these malcontents:

'Since the conclusion of the late War, and increasingly during the past few years, belief in the future of the Air has been ceaselessly fostered in the public mind. As a result of unfortunate propaganda the nation as a whole acquiesces in the strange doctrine that aircraft are of vital importance for transport in peace and will prove the decisive factor in the next war, so the country, therefore, must be supreme in the air, no matter at what cost . . .

'Perhaps the most remarkable feature of the country's enslavement to this false idea is the absence of any clear or systematic opposition.'

Neon, 'The Great Delusion', 1927

¶ Neon's book was an attempt to supply this deficiency. He seems to have had no faith whatever in the future of either airship or aeroplane, and the introducer of his treatise agreed with him:

Arthur Hungerford Pollen, Preface to 'The Great Delusion', 1927

'It is only over short distances — that is, on point-to-point flights — that the speed of the aeroplane is greatly superior to that of a ship or superior to that of a train. One recognizes, of course, that speed may at certain conjunctures be of vital importance. This possibility may justify a national subsidy to keep civil aviation in being. But if the nation chooses to keep it going, it should be for reasons that can be clearly stated. We should not be fooled into thinking that in time it will pay . . . How are we to explain the fact that an impoverished nation, crippled by debt, industrial disputes and unemployment, can afford to spend over twenty millions a year on an activity the proved practical value of which is so very small?'

¶ Money spent on the Air Force was equally wasted since

Neon, 'The Great Delusion', 1927

'Cool and dispassionate consideration of the facts will show . . . that "air power" is illusory and "air supremacy" a will-o'-the-wisp. The development of aircraft for war purposes is a sheer waste of men and money, and moreover constitutes a grave danger, since expenditure and dependence upon unreliable and futile weapons is a sure road to defeat.'

¶ Neon was particularly opposed to money being spent on airship research, and perhaps we should deal with this aspect of the matter first. The history of airships had certainly not been reassuring. The United States Airship *Roma* crashed in flames in 1922 with a death-roll of thirty-four; the French Airship *Dixmude* (taken over from the Germans in 1920) was lost in December 1923 with a crew of fifty-three. The United States Airship *Shenandoah* lasted two years before she crashed in September 1925 with a crew of fourteen. The British 'R' Series was not much more fortunate, in spite of such feats as the Atlantic crossing by the R.34 in 1919.

R.33

Launched March 1919, at a cost of £350,000.
Reconditioned and repaired at a further cost of £77,000.
Total number of hours in the air, 800.

R.34

Launched March 1919, at a cost of £350,000.
Crossed Atlantic in 1919. Totally wrecked 1921. Total number of hours in the air, 500.

R.35

Never completed. Approximate cost £75,000.

R.36

Launched April 1921 at a cost of £350,000.
Reconditioned at a further cost of £13,500. Total number of hours in the air, 97.

R.37

Never completed. Approximate cost £325,000.

R.38

Launched June 1921 at a cost of £500,000.
Completely wrecked on 24th August, 1921 with the loss of 44 lives. Total number of hours in the air, 70.

R.39

Never completed. Approximate cost £90,000.

R.80

Launched July 1920 at a cost of £275,000.
Total number of hours in the air, 73.

¶ However, the optimism of 'persons well qualified to judge' remained unquenched:

'Although much valuable service was rendered by R.27 and R.29 . . . R.33 and R.34 were the first really successful British airships and both achieved distinction. The latter was the first airship to cross the Atlantic, acomplishing this feat in July, 1919 . . .

J. L. Nayler and E. Ower, 'Aviation of Today', 1930

'R.38, larger than any airship previously constructed . . . With a view to lightening the structure and so increasing the disposable lift, certain departures from standard Zeppelin practice were made. Unfortunately, with the knowledge available at the time, these modifications proved to be premature, and during high speed trials on August 24th, 1921, the ship broke in two over the Humber and forty-four of the forty-eight persons on board lost their lives . . .

'Financial stringency after the War . . . together with the severe reaction of public opinion consequent upon the loss of R.38, caused construction to cease for the time being after the Autumn of 1921.

'Persons well qualified to judge, however, regarded with concern the complete cessation of airship construction in this country, and . . . a definite airship policy, including a constructional programme, was formed by the Government in 1924 . . . two ships, to be known as R.100 and R.101, were to be constructed . . .

'These airships were completed in the Autumn of 1929 . . . As soon as the home trials of these vessels are completed, it is expected that demonstration flights to India and Canada will be undertaken.'

¶ In Germany, perhaps naturally enough in view of the 'Zeppelin tradition', there was even more faith in 'lighter-than-air' machines:

J. L. Nayler and E. Ower, 'Aviation of Today', 1930

'Extinction threatened the Zeppelin works, but public subscription came to the rescue. Between the Autumn of 1925 and the end of 1926 a sum of two million marks was raised by collections throughout Germany, and, with the removal of the treaty restrictions the construction of a new Zeppelin, larger than any of its forerunners, was begun. This ship, the LZ.127, better known as the *Graf Zeppelin*, represents the last word in Zeppelin construction . . .

'The *Graf Zeppelin* has accomplished a number of notable flights since her launch in September 1928. With a crew of forty and twenty passengers on board she left Friedrichshaven for Lakehurst, N.J., on October 11th 1928 . . . The weather was far from favourable, and strong head winds encountered over certain stages of the journey caused considerable delay. Moreover, a sudden gust or an unusually large down current damaged one of the horizontal fins, and speed was reduced to 40 miles per hour while temporary repairs were executed in flight. Nevertheless, the journey of about 5,000 miles was completed in 4 days $15\frac{1}{2}$ hours. The criticism has been advanced that this is not as good as the *Mauretania*'s 4 days 10 hours for the sea passage to New York.

'A much more remarkable performance by the *Graf Zeppelin* was her flight round the world in the Summer of 1929 . . . The total distance covered is conservatively estimated at about 21,500 miles and the journey occupied in all 21 days $7\frac{1}{2}$ hours, of which almost exactly 12 days were spent in actual flying, giving an average speed of 78 miles per hour . . .

'Count Zeppelin did not live to see this triumphant vindication of

The R.101 riding at its mooring mast, Cardington, 1930.

The wreck of the R.101, near Beauvais, France. October 7th, 1930.

his confidence in the rigid airship: he died in March 1917. But even the performances of the ships built up to that date must have shown him that his early struggles were justified.'

¶ After a gap of two or three years, the Prime Minister, Ramsay MacDonald announced in the House of Commons on May 4th, 1924, that "after careful consideration H.M. Government share the view of their predecessors that it is essential to carry into effect a constructive programme of airship development. They propose accordingly to authorize a comprehensive programme of "lighter-than-air" research and experiments at Cardington . . . and to undertake the early construction of a new airship with a capacity of 5,000,000 cubic feet [and] the construction of a second ship for commercial purposes."
These two airships were the R.100 and the R.101.

'The R.101 is one of the two airships of the programme sanctioned in 1924. Both ships are of 5,000,000 cubic feet capacity, and will be required to fill certain general conditions; they must be able to fly at 70 m.p.h. at an altitude of 5,000 feet, and must conform with certain airworthiness requirements laid down by the Air Ministry. They must have a range at cruising speed, with an average commercial load, of about 4,000 miles. Subject to such general conditions, the designers have a free hand. *Major C. C. Turner, 'Daily Telegraph', November 20th, 1926*

'Both airships are being designed to carry approximately 100 passengers, luggage, and ten tons of mail. The accommodation will include sleeping cabins with two or four berths, promenade decks, lounges and smoking room, the dining-rooms will be capable of seating fifty people at a time. The kitchens will make it possible to serve normal meals for passengers and crew, and a five or six course dinner should be well within the capacity of the airship steward.

'The whole of the passenger accommodation will be contained within the hull of the airship, while the control car will project slightly underneath the hull. The accommodation will be amidships, divided into upper and lower decks. On the upper deck will be the lounge, fitted to seat all the passengers, and the main part of the sleeping accommodation, while running along each side of the airship will be two promenades.

'Among other features which are contemplated may be mentioned shower-baths, accommodation for dancing and games, and there should be no difficulty in providing headphones or loudspeakers, so

F

that passengers will be able to listen-in to the wireless programmes of the various countries over which the airship will travel.'

¶ Neon, the prophet of doom from whom we have already quoted, was surely justified in pointing out that the pay-load of such aircraft was almost ludicrously small:

Neon, 'The Great Delusion', 1927
'In airship transport the effort is enormous — the whole result in useful load negligible.

'The total lifting power of the . . . R.100, of 5,000,000 cubic feet capacity is (if filled with hydrogen gas) 151.7 tons at sea level, with standard purity of gas and under standard atmospheric conditions; in the tropics there is a reduction of lifting power which may be as much as 7 per cent (or 10 tons in a 5,000,000 cubic feet vessel). The lift for practical purposes of this airship (or R.101) may be taken as 150 tons in this country. From this gross lift of the hydrogen gas must first be taken the weight of the structure and machinery, fittings and fixtures, which "is not to exceed" and most certainly will approximate 90 tons, leaving a balance of 60 tons for disposal. The weight of the necessary ballast (15 tons) and of the fuel and lubricating oil must be subtracted, and an allowance made for the crew, before the useful weight left over for freight, or for passengers and their impedimenta, can be determined . . . For such a giant vessel on the proposed route from England to Ismailia, the weight of fuel and oil could not be less than 30 tons. A crew of fifty with the necessities would add over $6\frac{1}{2}$ tons, leaving for this great passenger airship — a vessel as large as the *Mauretania* — an approximate useful lift, that is, a paying load, of $8\frac{1}{2}$ tons only at sea level in this country.'

¶ A Certificate of Airworthiness for R.101 was issued by the Secretary of State for Air on October 2nd, 1930, and on Saturday, October 4th, as dusk was falling, she left Cardington on her maiden voyage to India. She had on board fifty-four persons of whom six were passengers. Heading the list were Brigadier-General The Rt. Hon. Lord Thomson and Sir W. Sefton Brancker. The crew of forty-two ranged from Flight-Lieutenant H. Carmichael Irwin (Captain) and Squadron Leader E. L. Johnston (Navigator) to J. W. Megginson (Galley Boy). Lord Thomson (who had himself as Secretary of State for Air issued the Certificate of Airworthiness) sent a message from on board: 'She is as safe as a house — except for the millionth chance.'

Other people were not so sure:

*James Leasor,
'The Millionth
Chance', 1957*

'At Chequers, Mr. Ramsay MacDonald, the Prime Minister, admitted to a sudden feeling of inexplicable gloom as he sat down to dinner . . . Thomson had so often dined there with him and only a short time previously at the Prime Minister's table they had joked together about his election to the peerage . . .

'Now there were no jokes at Chequers, for although the Prime Minister had been assured that nothing could go wrong, he did not share the popular confidence in the airship. Indeed, during dinner he spoke his thoughts saying that although Lord Thomson, who was his oldest and dearest friend, assured him that every contingency had been provided for, "Yet", he went on, "I am still uneasy. I confess that my apprehension for unlooked-for danger and disaster, ridiculous, no doubt, and admittedly without the smallest basis in personal knowledge or individual experience, will not be set at rest until I know for a fact that the great airship has arrived safely in India." '

¶ At half-past nine the radio operator sent out a message to the Meteorological Office at Cardington, asking for a weather forecast of conditions between Marseilles and Paris. A few minutes later he sent off a second message.

'Crossing coast in vicinity of Hastings. It is raining hard and there is a strong south-westerly wind. Cloud base is at 1,500 feet. After a good get-away from mooring tower at 18.30 hours ship circled Bedford before setting course. Course was set for London at 18.54. Engines running well at cruising speed giving 54.2 knots. Reached London at 20.00 hours and then set course for Paris. Gradually increasing height so as to avoid high land. Ship behaving well generally and we have already begun to recover water ballast.'

¶ In fact, one of the engines was already giving trouble and one observer near Hastings was so much alarmed by the slow speed and low height of the airship as she passed overhead that he thought of warning the Dungeness lifeboat to keep a look-out, in case she came down in the sea.

Shortly after midnight another radio message was received at Cardington:

'To Cardington from R.101, 24.00 G.M.T. 15 miles S.W. of

Abbeville. Average speed 33 knots. Wind 243 degrees (that is W.S.W.), 35 miles per hour. Altimeter height 1,500 feet. Air temperature, 51 degrees Fahrenheit. Weather — intermittent rain. Cloud nimbus at 500 feet. After an excellent supper our distinguished passengers smoked a final cigar, and having sighted the French coast, have now gone to bed after the excitement of leave-taking. All essential services are functioning satisfactorily. The crew have settled down to watch-keeping routine.'

¶ This was the last message sent out by R.101.

James Leasor, 'The Millionth Chance', 1957

'On most Saturdays Eugène Rabouille would leave his home near Beauvais about midnight and set snares for rabbits in the woods and fields. This Saturday night it was so wet and wretched that he was reluctant to drag himself away from his fireside. But at last he did so [although] . . . the wet unfriendly woods seemed no place for a tired workman of fifty-seven, as he stepped out of his house and the gale almost tore the door from his hand.

'He took a moment's shelter in the lee of a house to regain breath, and looking up at the scudding clouds, he saw the dark shape of an airship over Beauvais about a mile to the north. Even at that distance she looked enormous, a dark and gigantic cigar . . .

'R.101 was over the Bois de Coutumes — not more than 150 feet up moving very slowly. The wind was forcing her towards the east.

' "I clearly saw the passengers' quarters, well lit, and the green and red lights on the right and left of the airship", he said later. "Suddenly there was a violent squall. The airship dipped by the nose several times, and its forepart crashed into the north-west edge of the Bois de Coutumes. There was at once a tremendous explosion, which knocked me down.

' "Soon flames rose into the sky to a great height — perhaps 300 feet. Everything was enveloped by them. I saw human figures running about like madmen in the wreck. Then I lost my head and ran away into the woods."

'He did not stop running until he reached home and barred the door against the memory. Then Eugène Rabouille, the man nearest to the airship as she crashed, crossed himself and went to bed.'

¶ There were six survivors: five engineers and one wireless operator. All the rest of the crew, and all the passengers, perished in the flames.

84

H. G. Hawker at Hendon with his 80 h.p. Sopwith machine.

First England–Australia Flight, 1919. Vickers Vimy bomber with crew.

The Vickers Vimy in which Alcock and Brown flew the Atlantic in 1919.

'Then on the Saturday, exactly a week after the airship had set out, the bodies of the passengers and crew were brought back to Cardington to demonstrations of national grief that had previously only been associated with the death of kings. More than half a million people turned out to watch the funeral procession from Westminster Hall to Euston Station. It was two miles long and took an hour to pass . . .

James Leasor, 'The Millionth Chance', 1957

'Immediately the funeral procession had passed along Whitehall, scores of young men hurried into the Air Ministry to enlist for the Air Force.'

¶ This was the end of airships so far as Great Britain was concerned. The Government scrapped R.100 in 1931 and abandoned all airship activity. The Germans persisted. After all the *Graf Zeppelin*, completed in 1928, flew more than a million miles (including 144 ocean crossings) before being decommissioned in 1937. The *Hindenburg* (LZ.129) was completed in 1936 and crossed the Atlantic safely. But while landing at Lakehurst, New Jersey, on May 6th, 1937, it burst into flames with the loss of thirty-six lives. In spite of this another *Graf Zeppelin* (LZ.130) was built in 1938. It was only the outbreak of the war which put an end to German lighter-than-air projects.

Other nations had abandoned them long ago, but there were many in the early 'thirties who thought that *heavier*-than-air machines had reached the limit of their possible development and so had no future:

'Already it looks as if we are beginning to probe the boundaries of commercial aeroplane performance in certain respects . . .

Christopher Sprigg, 'The Airship', 1931

'It may be thought that an increase in size, so beneficial in the case of the airship, might prove equally so in the case of the aeroplane. The aeroplane, however, suffers the common fate of all heavier-than-air creatures. The grasshopper walks on legs that are but a fraction of his total cross-section, and has a jumping ability (in proportion to his bulk) endowed with which a man could leap St. Paul's Cathedral. The elephant, however, can barely support himself on legs with a total cross-sectional area almost equal to that of his body. As for jumping, imagination boggles at it. And the gigantic monsters of prehistory have long been harried off their weary legs by the vicissitudes of weight.

'The whale alone has appreciated the virtues of being lighter than the medium in which he moves.'

¶ The whale was the airship, the grasshopper the aeroplane:

Christopher Sprigg,
'The Airship', 1931

'The implications of this ... can be explained mechanically in the case of the aeroplane. The aeroplane depends for its support on a pair of wings ... If the size of the aeroplane is increased, its volume will grow faster than its area ... the total structure weight will grow faster than the supporting area ... Moreover, in increasing the aeroplane's size, we have in no way increased its range, as is the case with the airship ...

'Many indications point to the fact that we are approaching the boundaries of rapid advance in performance, speed, and pay load of aeroplanes ... Therefore it may be deduced that heavier-than-air craft will never run a trans-Atlantic service.'

¶ However, those obstinate fellows the aeroplane designers went on trying:

Claude Grahame-
White, 'Flying',
1930

'At one time, when designers tried to build an aeroplane of a fairly large size the results were unsatisfactory ... and this led to a belief that large flying machines ... might always be uneconomic from the point of view of the load they would carry, an unreasonably large proportion of the total weight air-borne being represented by the structure of the machine ...

'A big step forward was taken when designers grasped the fact that the big aeroplane or flying-boat represented a different engineering problem from that of the small machine, and should be tackled in a more advanced way. This led to a new trend in design in which, profiting by the fact that he was working with larger structures, the aircraft designer began to plan big machines on more simplified lines. The most conspicuous feature of this simplification of the flying machine lies in what has been called "the flying wing" design ... The wings ... are so designed as to exercise a double purpose. They not only bear the machine through the air but they also carry, within their hollow surfaces, an appreciable proportion of the load that is to be air-borne ... A huge wing, built throughout on a simplified system of light-weight metal construction, is hollow and can be used not only as a receptacle for mails and merchandise, but passenger cabins can also be constructed within it ... Furthermore, it is possible to house the engines inside their hollow wing ...'

¶ The giant Junkers monoplane built at this period actually had cabins in the wing but this system has not been much used since. On the other hand the engines are fitted in or attached to the wing in nearly all types of modern aircraft. But long before these developments intrepid men had been trying to see what the machines at their disposal could be made to do.

As long ago as 1913 the *Daily Mail* had offered a prize of £10,000 for the first pilot to fly the Atlantic in less than seventy-two hours in a heavier-than-air machine. The War prevented any attempts to win this prize, but almost as soon as it was over competitors appeared.

'The first machines to get away, in May, 1919, on a flight in stages from Newfoundland to Plymouth, were three American flying-boats, the NC.1, the NC.3 and the NC.4. The first stage of their journey was one of 1,380 miles to Horta in the Azores. Two of the flying-boats, NC.1 and NC.3, were obliged to retire from the attempt at an early stage, but the NC.4, which was piloted by Lieut.-Commander Read, duly reached Horta on May 17th. On May 20th a second stage of 190 miles to Ponta Delgada was effected. On the 27th the NC.4 left for Lisbon, and accomplished this stage in a day. On the 30th the flying-boat proceeded 340 miles on to Ferral, and on the next day the last stage of 420 miles to Plymouth was accomplished.' *Claude Grahame- White, 'Flying', 1930*

¶ The prize, however, was for the crossing of the Atlantic in a single hop; and this was attempted by Harry Hawker, an Australian, in a Sopwith biplane powered by one 350 h.p. Rolls-Royce engine. He had with him Commander Greene as navigator and in the late afternoon of May 18th, 1919, they set off from St. John's, Newfoundland.

Day followed day and nothing was heard. The newspapers reported 'Hawker Missing', and then, 'All hope has now been abandoned for the safety of the Atlantic Airmen'. The King sent a telegram of condolence to Mrs. Hawker, and then, on Sunday, May 15th —

'A small steamer, the *Mary*, came in sight of the Butt of Lewis, Scotland. Her siren was blowing, and she signalled to the coastguards that she had important news to communicate. Then came the historic signal: *Capt. J. Laurence Pritchard, 'The Book of the Aeroplane', 1926*

' "Saved hands, Sop-aeroplane."

'The coastguard signalled back:

' "Is it Hawker?"

' "Yes", ran up the signal flags of the *Mary*.'

¶ On the morning of the 19th the airmen had been forced down in the Atlantic, by engine trouble, 750 miles from the Irish coast. They were able, however, to come down near a small steamer, the *Mary*, and had been rescued. But the little vessel had no 'wireless' and so almost a week elapsed before the news was known.

Where Hawker had so gallantly failed, others were to succeed less than a month later:

Claude Grahame-White, 'Flying', 1930 'On June 14th another British crew in a big twin-engined Vickers-Vimy bombing-plane started from St. John's to follow the same air line across the Atlantic as Hawker had taken. The pilot this time was Capt. John Alcock and his navigator was Lieut. A. Whitten-Brown. They encountered extremely trying weather, but had the advantage of a strong following wind, and succeeded in accomplishing their trans-Atlantic flight to Ireland in 16 hours 27 minutes, their speed being just over 117 miles an hour.'

¶ This is Alcock's own account of the landing:

Quoted in Capt. J. Laurence Pritchard, 'The Book of the Aeroplane', 1926 'The mainland (of Ireland) was not visible until we were practically over it, and then only the hills. In another ten minutes the masts of Clifton wireless station suddenly appeared, we circled round these firing Very signals, to which no reply was received. Whilst flying round looking for a suitable landing place, we passed over Clifton town, where more Very signals were fired, again without reply, and observing no suitable ground in that neighbourhood we returned to the wireless station, where I had spotted what appeared to be a suitable field, and decided to descend. On touching the ground, however, this field turned out to be a bog, and the machine was slightly damaged, but we were unhurt. The operators of the Marconi station immediately ran to our assistance, but had no idea who we were until informed; they received us with great enthusiasm and cheers. We were then invited to the Marconi station, where we received every kindness, and messages announcing our safe arrival in Ireland were sent broadcast throughout the world.'

¶ Both Alcock and Whitten-Brown were knighted.

88

The next great flight was that of Ross Smith to Australia, of which he has left a lively account:

'Just after the Armistice was signed, General Borton decided to start out in the Handley-Page for India . . . On November 29th, 1918, we took our departure . . . It took just three weeks to pioneer a route to India, where we arrived, without mishap, on December 10th, 1918 . . .

'This was the longest flight that had ever been made up to this time, and it convinced me that a machine, properly attended and equipped, was capable of flying anywhere, provided suitable landing grounds existed.'

Sir Ross Smith,
'14,000 Miles
Through the Air',
1922

¶ Shortly afterwards the Australian Government offered a prize of £10,000 for the first machine, manned by Australians, to fly from London to Australia in eighty days. Ross Smith's India flight had been made from Cairo; he now hurried back to England, and with the support of Vickers began his preparations.

The machine it was intended to use was an ordinary standard Vickers-Vimy bomber, similar to that used by Sir John Alcock for his trans-Atlantic flight. It was being fitted and tested at Weybridge.

'Eventually the spare parts, personal kit, and miscellaneous gear were assembled and weighed. I decided to limit the total weight of our machine when fully loaded to 13,000 pounds . . .

Sir Ross Smith,
'14,000 Miles
Through the Air',
1922

'We discovered that, after the "weighing in", there was an excess of 300 pounds; so something had to go. Our "spares" were indispensable, and so we drastically attacked our personal kit. It was easy enough to cut down our kit — so soon as we were unanimous in deciding to go without any — and so it eventuated that we left England in the garments we wore and with the proverbial tooth brush apiece . . .

'We discussed the question of carrying a wireless set at some length and finally decided not to take one. It would weigh 100 pounds and take up a great deal of room . . .

'For food we carried an emergency ration consisting of tinned meat and biscuits, together with some chocolate and Bovril . . . A fishing line and a few hooks were also carried in case we should land on some small uninhabited island and have to do the "Robinson Crusoe" act for a time.'

¶ In spite of the fact that the weather was reported as 'totally unfit for flying', Ross Smith, with his brother as navigator and two mechanics, set off from Weybridge early on the morning of November 12th, 1919.

He was obviously a born flyer:

Sir Ross Smith,
'14,000 Miles
Through the Air',
1922
'The aeroplane is the nearest thing to animate life that man has created. In the air a machine ceases to be a mere piece of mechanism; it becomes animate and is capable not only of primary guidance and control, but actually of expressing a pilot's temperament . . . When both engines are going well and synchronized to the same speed the roar of the exhausts develops into one long-sustained rhythmical boom – boom – boom. It is a song of pleasant harmony to the pilot, a duet of contentment that sings of perfect firing in both engines and says that all is well.'

¶ We have no space to do more than summarize this historic flight via Lyons, Rome, Cairo, Damascus, Karachi, Delhi, Calcutta, Singapore, Surabaya, Port Darwin and on to Sydney, Melbourne and Adelaide. Every difficulty was surmounted. Port Darwin was reached on December 10th, and the flyers were received with tremendous enthusiasm. They had flown from London to Australia in 135 hours flying time.

Other remarkable flights followed quickly. In 1924 Wing-Commander Goble and Flying Officer McIntyre made the circuit of Australia between 6th April and 19th May. In the same year Major P. L. Martin and other United States airmen flew round the world in four Douglas 'World Cruisers'. Early in November 1925 the Marquese de Pinedo flew from Italy to Japan, *via* Australia and back again, a distance of 35,000 miles. This was a remarkable feat even if it did take six and a half months. Then Alan Cobham between June 30th and October 1st, 1925, made a 27,000 mile flight to Australia and back. Six months later —

Capt. J. Laurence
Pritchard, 'The Book
of the Aeroplane',
1926
'At 4.20 p.m. on Saturday, 13th March, 1926, Mr. Alan O. Cobham landed at Croydon Aerodrome, after a remarkable flight from London to Cape Town and back, a distance of 17,000 miles. The flight, which was *via* Cairo, Khartoum, Bulawayo and so to Cape Town, was undertaken with the object of finding out the possibilities of air routes between London and Cape Town and intermediate places. During the

90

journey the machine, with an unchanged air-cooled engine, went through every kind of weather, including rain, gales, sandstorms and intense tropical heat, a fine tribute to the construction of the engine and the aeroplane itself.'

¶ In 1926 Commandante Franco flew 6,259 miles from Spain to South America, and Lieut.-Commander Byrd flew 1,300 miles from Spitzbergen to the North Pole and back. But the flight which really captured the imagination of the world took place in the following year. After the triumph of Alcock and Brown —

'No further attempts on the Atlantic crossing were made for a period of eight years until Colonel Charles Lindbergh made his memorable solo flight . . . on May 20th–21st 1927, from New York to Paris, when he flew a distance of 3,726 miles in thirty-seven hours. We read how he arrived at his aerodrome of departure a few hours only before he intended to leave, arranged to be called some two hours after he went to bed, flew off early the next morning with but scanty provisions and a few tablets to help to keep him awake, and carried out his flight almost as though it were a routine. He encountered steady weather conditions throughout . . . He crossed the coast of Ireland and landed safely at Paris, where he was accorded an enthusiastic welcome.' *J. L. Nayler and E. Ower, 'Aviation of Today', 1930*

¶ As well he might be!

'The mere crossing of the Atlantic was not what the mass of the people in this country, France, and Belgium most admired. It was that Lindbergh, with no flourish of trumpets, flew, not from New York to anywhere in Ireland, Scotland, England, or Europe, but that he flew from New York to Paris according to plan, without any fuss or advertising of any kind beforehand. Few people knew on this side of the Atlantic that this flight was contemplated. *Rear-Admiral Murray F. Sueter, 'Airmen or Noahs', 1928*

'The loneliness of Lindbergh's flight fires the imagination; it was a daring feat, and he was twice the time in the air that Alcock was in making the first Atlantic flight . . .

'He had nobody to relieve or help him in any way. He had to do the piloting and navigating himself. It was a wonderful test of endurance. For "four o'clock in the morning" courage, I believe Lindbergh's flight is the best effort a human has ever made.

'The way he managed to remain awake and to keep the machine

on her course for all those hours with no encouragement from a second person, shows he was in the pink of condition, with nerves of steel.'

¶ Shortly afterwards, another American aviator Clarence Chamberlain flew from New York to Germany with a passenger. The passenger, Mr. Levine, carried a few sandwiches and two flasks of soup. He forgot his hat.

Byrd came into the news again with a flight from New York to Normandy; and William Brock flew from Newfoundland to Croydon. The trail had truly been blazed.

Claude Grahame-White, 'Flying', 1930   'In 1928 there were further conclusive demonstrations of the reliability of modern aeroplanes and engines, and of the growing skill of airmen in pilotage and navigation. One of the outstanding events of the year was that of Mr. Bert Hinckler, the famous little Australian airman, who started off alone from England to fly in stages to Australia in a low-powered light aeroplane; and who accomplished this tremendous feat in fifteen and a half days, the flight representing one of the finest personal achievements ever recorded in aviation.

'Another memorable feat of 1928, which represented a fresh milestone in aviation, was that effected by Capt. Kobb, Baron Hunefeld, and Commander Fitzmaurice. Starting from Ireland, they flew non-stop across the Atlantic to Labrador, a distance of 2,300 miles, which they accomplished . . . in thirty-six hours. This flight had the historical significance that it was the first non-stop aeroplane crossing of the North Atlantic from east to west, all the previous non-stop journeys having been effected with favouring winds from west to east.'

¶ Meanwhile women were beginning to fly, at first as passengers.

'Morning Post', 1927   'The Duchess [of Bedford] with her pilot in a Moth aeroplane flew from her place, Woburn Abbey, to Paris, Biarritz, Madrid, Seville, Tangiers, Toulouse, Lyons, Paris and London. She has crossed three ranges of mountains, the Pyrenees, the Guadaramas, and the Sierra Nevada.

' "I went for the scenery alone", the Duchess of Bedford continued, "and that has been wonderful beyond description. As you see, the little Moth has returned without a scratch — and the same may be

92

Charles Lindbergh after crossing the Atlantic solo, 1927.

Amy Johnson after her solo flight to Australia, 1930.

said of its passenger. There is none of the dust, dirt and fatigue of ordinary travel and I return as fresh as when I started . . ."

'The Duchess of Bedford, who is in her sixty-second year, is an enthusiastic air traveller. She enjoys not only straight flying but also acrobatics. Before landing at Stag Lane yesterday her pilot put the machine into a spin and executed some steep Immelman turns.'

¶ But soon women began to qualify as pilots:

'Lady Bailey took her pilot's certificate in 1926. Last July she achieved the world's altitude record for light aeroplanes at Stag Lane aerodrome, reaching a height of 18,000 feet after passing through a layer of thunder-clouds. She had as passenger Mrs. Geoffrey de Havilland, wife of the designer of the Moth light aeroplane. Lady Bailey was the first woman to fly the Irish Sea, alone, a feat which she accomplished in August, 1927.' *'Daily Mail', January 19th, 1928*

¶ In 1929 Lady Bailey flew to South Africa and back in a light Moth. Her only chart was a small-scale map from a travel agent's advertisement. Lady Heath had made the single flight from Cape Town to London in the previous year. There were other brave flights by women. The first solo crossing of the Atlantic by a woman was made by Amelia Earhardt, who later flew the Pacific. But the young woman who captured the popular imagination was Amy Johnson. She was no rich amateur but a working girl with a very non-U accent who made up her mind, after a very short training, to fly to Australia, a distance of 10,000 miles. Her machine was a Gipsy Moth, and she set out on May 5th 1930. She carried a revolver, with which she had practised in her back garden at Hull, in order to defend herself against 'tribesmen'. Her object was to beat the record recently set up by Bert Hinckler.

Many times she was on the verge of disaster. She had trouble with the authorities in Turkey, having omitted to provide herself with a Turkish visa. She crossed the formidable Taurus mountains to Aleppo, having flown 2,000 miles in three days. Between Baghdad and the Persian Gulf she ran into a sandstorm. She was plainly so overtired when she reached Karachi that the authorities urged her to rest for a day. She would have been well advised to listen. As she approached Rangoon she mistook a small football field for the race-course. The aircraft smashed a propeller and damaged a wing. It took two days to repair it. On her way to Surabaya she landed in a sugar plantation and had to beg the shirts of the local Europeans to repair the fabric of the wings.

By this time she was front-page news, and as she started on the last leg of her flight over the Timor Sea —

'*Sunday Express*', March 6th, 1960 'The Australians were already motoring along the dusty roads to Darwin to meet her . . . Amy Johnson flew low through the rain and then climbed into the sunshine at 5,000 feet. From time to time she looked at the clock but it moved so slowly that she swore she wouldn't look again. But after she had waited for what seemed about half an hour, she stole another glance. It had moved only ten minutes.

'Hour after hour the Moth droned on and then there was a tanker. On the deck arms were waving.

'Amy Johnson, delighted, bombed them with a cake she was holding in her hand.

'Then came Melville Island, the surf, the trees and the mainland. Over the side went the air cushion which she had planned to use as a life jacket.

'She rocked in her seat and cheered.

'But as the oil-stained, patched and battered moth glided over the head of the thousands of Australians she was crying.

'It was 3.57 p.m. on May 24th, 1930. She had taken nineteen and a half days for the flight.

'Everyone went mad.'

¶ The King sent her a telegram: 'The Queen and I are thankful and delighted to know of Miss Johnson's safe arrival in Australia and heartily congratulate her upon her wonderful and courageous achievement.'

Six years later, Jean Batten, flying solo from England to New Zealand, reached Australia in five days, twenty-one hours, less than a third of Amy Johnson's time. But in the development of aircraft six years is a long time. The fact that rapid flights to all parts of the world are now a commonplace should not make us forget the courage and endurance of those who blazed the trail.

Knowing what we now know we can smile at the timidity of some of the prophecies of future performance written before the develop-

94

ment of supersonic flight. Even as late as 1948 a learned and informative writer remarked:

'It is unlikely that . . . speed will be very much increased . . . because as the speed of a body approaches the speed of sound in air the effect of compressibility causes a rapid rise in drag, and the problem of cooling becomes acute due to the rise in temperature resulting from such rapid motion. Moreover, aircraft capable of such speeds as three-fifths of the speed of sound have limited practical applications and are of a very costly nature . . . Improvement in engine performance — of the conventional type — will not be great unless some revolutionary discovery in the conversion of the latent energy of fuel into power is made, though marked increase in power output has been obtained by the use of special fuels . . . The recent development of the gas turbine in this country would seem, however, to offer remarkable possibilities in aircraft.'

M. J. B. Davy, 'Interpretative History of Flight', 1948

¶ Perhaps we cannot do better than end with a prophecy by Grahame-White written more than thirty years ago:

'Science, already, has achieved marvellous things. We can talk by wireless telephone across immense distances. Soon, perhaps, we may be able to see, as well as hear, anyone on the other side of the Atlantic to whom we may be speaking. And with the perfection of the long-range high-speed flying machine it will be possible for us not only to annihilate distance with words, and even with scenes transmitted by television, but to travel ourselves at such a pace that oceans will be crossed in hours, and a journey to the most distant part of the world will not occupy more than a few days. That is what the future holds forth; that is what we shall attain as our final conquest of the air. We shall have a "magic carpet" which will span oceans and continents between dawn and dusk, shortening Jules Verne's eighty days circuit of the globe to not more, probably, than about eighty hours.'

Claude Grahame-White, 'Flying', 1930

CHAPTER V

THE GAY TWENTIES

FOREIGN OBSERVERS and serious-minded people at home might be concerned at the serious situation in which Great Britain found itself, but the 'twenties has gone down to history as a 'gay' decade, and, on the surface, it seemed gay enough. The *New Statesman* said it was 'wildly funny', by which it meant, extremely shocking.

'New Statesman',
January, 1919

'VILLAGE TOPICS

'Meanwhile, round about, "shoots" are going on. Hounds are killing or drawing blank. Estimates are being prepared for the refitting of yachts. The merits of rival designs for new motor-cars are being discussed, and dodges for enticing young women into domestic service. Plans are being made for world-wide travel. The wines of the future, the price of season-tickets and of suits and millinery, the decline of the poetry-boom, the fullness of restaurants, the prospects of the theatre — these furnish topics of animated conversation. And the necessity of a bathroom for each guest-room in the after-war house is frankly admitted. It is almost astonishing: it is wildly funny, having regard to the fact that millions of people are starving in Europe.'

¶ In spite of such protests, social life took up again, or tried to take up again, at the point where it had left off when Germany tore up the 'Scrap of Paper' and the field-grey battalions come flooding into France. There were supper-parties again at the Savoy and *thé-dansants* at all the best hotels in London. Some of them even put on cabarets where the 'girls' were supposed to be daringly unclothed, although when one looks at their photographs now there doesn't seem to be

The Charleston: Bee Jackson, World Champion, c. 1925.

Henry Lamb—'Lytton Strachey' (Reproduced by permission of the Executors of Henry Lamb and The Tate Gallery).

anything very daring about it. The young generations, those who were just back from the war and those that had grown up while it was raging, seemed to be determined to enjoy themselves and to make up for lost time. Nothing 'stuffy' was henceforward to be tolerated, and the adjective 'Victorian' — largely owing to the success of Lytton Strachey's *Eminent Victorians* — became one of unqualified abuse.

The people who could afford it (and there were more of them than there are today, for confiscatory taxation was only just beginning) flung themselves into a life of gaiety, hectic perhaps, but enjoyable enough while it lasted. The War had been terrible, but it was over and, since it had been a 'war to end wars', it could obviously never happen again. The League of Nations was ridiculed but people believed in it all the same. The world had plenty of troubles no doubt. Let the politicians look to them. Meanwhile, 'let's have fun'.

One would have to go back to the days of the French *Directoire* to find another period of the same mood and tempo. After the fall of Robespierre, Paris went mad with gaiety. The cry was pleasure at all costs and the dancing mania was universal. A similar dancing mania characterized the 'twenties. People danced all night and almost all day, and the improvement in gramophones made it possible to turn on the music at any hour. Jazz was known before the War, but it now became the only rhythm. And the dances were of course negro dances, even when the performers were white:

'The Dixielanders, a group of White Americans, formed their band in New Orleans in 1916 in order to take up an engagement at Schiller's Café in Chicago. From there they went to play at Reisenweber's Restaurant in Columbus Circle, New York, where they caused a sensation and helped the new style of "Dixieland" or "Dixie" to supplant ragtime. *Jack Glicco, 'Madness after Midnight', 1960*

'Under their new name of "The Original Dixieland Jazz Band" they became the first jazz outfit to tour Europe and in the late summer of 1919 they opened a three months' season at the Hammersmith Palais which, then as now, was London's leading dance hall.

'They were a wow. From their first appearance the Palais was crowded at every session, afternoon and evening, to listen to their hot, sweet music. Some of the numbers they made famous are famous still. Everybody has heard of "Alice Blue Gown", "Tiger Rag" (which they composed), "I'm For Ever Blowing Bubbles", "Livery Stable Blues", "Blueing The Blues" and "Sensation".

'They played entirely by ear — not one of them could read a note of music — and during the intervals they came down to the dance-floor and played dice, gambling for huge stakes. Sometimes their opponents over the dice were "the guv'nors". Perhaps the bosses were trying to get some of their money back, for the Dixielanders pulled down a steady £250 a week — top-rate money in those days.'

¶ It is an extraordinary thing that no sophisticated (one is tempted to say, no civilized) person can invent a dance. All he can do is to take some peasant dance (the dance, that is, of people who have not yet lost all *gaieté de cœur*) and make it just sufficiently decent for the ballroom floor. Gradually through the nineteenth century the upper classes had absorbed the peasant dances of Europe, had taken over the waltzes and mazurkas that had once provided the merrymaking in the villages of Poland and Hungary. In the early twentieth century there were no more left. There was only the negro to go to, and he would have been laid under contribution even if the Kaiser had never launched the First World War. But the War had sharpened people's appetites and at the same time deprived them of their respect for tradition. So, in the 'twenties, the Charleston and the Black Bottom spread like a prairie fire, and the gestures and attitudes of the dancers in the smart restaurants of London and Paris were so many echoes of the jungle.

Frederick Lewis Allen, 'Only Yesterday', 1931 'Not the romantic violin but the barbaric saxophone now dominated the orchestra, and to its passionate crooning and wailing the fox-trotters moved in what the editor of the Hobart College *Herald* disgustedly called a "syncopated embrace". No longer did even an inch of space separate them; they danced as if glued together, body to body, cheek to cheek. Cried the *Catholic Telegraph* of Cincinnati in righteous indignation: "The music is sensuous, the embracing of partners — the female only half dressed — is absolutely indecent; and the motions — they are such as may not be described, with any respect for propriety, in a family newspaper. Suffice it to say that there are certain houses appropriate for such dances; but those houses have been closed by law." '

¶ Dancing had become a public affair. The craze for dancing was similar to that which always takes place after great disasters. There was such a craze after the Black Death, and also, as we have noticed, after the French Revolution. One madness seemed to seize all classes; dance-halls and night clubs sprang up everywhere, the latter not only in England where the licensing restrictions provided some excuse, but in Paris and Berlin. Formal dances were discontinued, largely owing to the new poverty of those who had formerly given them, and with formal dances disappeared the chaperone and all that surveillance of the young which had been considered a duty of parents from time immemorial:

'London's night-life was brighter than ever before or since. Evening dress gave it a glamour it now lacks. After the theatre one could go on to such places as the Hotel Metropole for the *Midnight Follies*, the Piccadilly Hotel for *Piccadilly Revels*, the Savoy, Trocadero, Princes, etc. where first-rate showmen of the calibre of Charles B. Cochran and André Charlot presented supper entertainments with stars of such quality as Beatrice Lillie, Alice Delysia, Sophie Tucker, Jack Buchanan, the Trix Sisters, Grock, and Jack Hylton's Band.

Leslie Baily,
'Scrapbook for the
Twenties', 1959

'Such night resorts, gay but respectable, are not to be confused with dozens of murky night-clubs, the cause of crusades to "purify the night-life of London", nor with gilded night-spots where the law could be cheerfully broken by those prepared to be fleeced by such operators as Mrs. Meyrick.'

¶ That extraordinary woman was already

'THE FABULOUS MRS. MEYRICK

Jack Glicco,
'Madness after
Midnight', 1960

'She sat in a little office just inside the door, smiling her smile of welcome. She was a smallish woman, untidily dressed, with a sharp face and sharp eyes, and to all her visitors she would say: "Will you pay me now?"

'She was completely without glamour. Her clothes were dowdy. Against the wealthy, fabulously dressed visitors, she looked horribly out of place.

'Yet no other night-club owner achieved a tenth of her fame — not even the famous American, Texas Guinan. She was known to the whole world. Her exploits made luscious Sunday reading for millions.

'She was Kate Meyrick, the woman who made the "43" Club the greatest night-club in British history; whose peculiar business sense contrasted sharply with her open-handed generosity.

99

'Kate Meyrick's night-club career lasted only thirteen years. It began in 1919 with Dalton's and ended in 1932 with the Bunch of Keys. A year later she was dead. Yet in those thirteen years she became a legend.

'An Irishwoman, the mother of eight children — six of them girls — she went into the night-club business to help keep her family. In the next few years she owned Brett's, the Manhattan, the "43", the Silver Slipper, the Folies Bergère, the New Follies, the Broadway, the Bunch of Keys.'

¶ But even Mrs. Meyrick's '43' was a model of propriety compared with some of the other night-clubs:

Jack Glicco, 'Madness after Midnight', 1960 'If you walk across Piccadilly, turn into Shaftesbury Avenue, and plunge into the side streets that lead to the Windmill Theatre, and Soho, you will find Ham Yard.

'It is a tiny mews, reached through a narrow entry, and by day it looks sleepy and dilapidated. A few yards away London's scurrying millions fight their way about their business; here all is quiet.

'But in those years between the wars a strange transformation came over Ham Yard as the clocks struck 11 p.m. From ten rooms in ten houses music would blare forth into the night, smiting the ears of the visitor with harsh discord.

'The night-club bands had started up.

'All through the night they played until four in the morning, in the Avenue Club, in the Pavilion, the Oak, the Top Hat, the Hambone, Mother Hubbard's, the Morgue and others.

'And into Ham Yard, and to all the other streets which housed London's clubs, came the motley crew of West End night-lifers. There were smart people in evening dress and jewels; prostitutes with their clients and prostitutes seeking clients; toughs and roughs and (occasionally) a respectable couple from the provinces investigating, at a heavy price, the mysteries of the Wicked City.

'What did they get for their money? A single room, most about twenty-five feet square, crammed with smoke, noise and people. A few tables round the walls; a curtained alcove at one end; a small rostrum on which the band played like men possessed.

'Bottles and glasses on the tables; people laughing and talking; couples dancing so thickly on the floor that no flooring could be seen. And over all, an air of jollity and merriment that had a slightly

Jack Buchanan and Lily Elsie, Daly's Theatre, London, 1922.

Elsa Lanchester in her 'Seven Dials' Club.

Mrs. Kate Meyrick: reception on her release from Holloway Prison, 1930.

hysterical quality, as if at any moment the gaiety would crumble to anger or tears. It often did.

'That was the nightly scene in the average club of the 'twenties and 'thirties. A few of the better-class clubs were decorated in lavish or fantastic styles, but mostly they differed only in the quality of their clients.

'There were the exclusive clubs like the Frivolity, where the clientèle included Royalty. There were bad clubs like the Savoya, where every type of evil customer congregated. In between were clubs in which every shade of difference between the extremes could be found.

'But they all had one thing in common: the clients spent money foolishly, lavishly and illegally. There were no club licences, though extensions could be obtained allowing drinks until 2.30 a.m., but you could drink anything you wanted, at prices double those charged in pubs, until four or five in the morning.

'Unless, of course, there was a police raid.'

¶ The disintegration of 'Society' which had been proceeding ever since Edwardian days, was noticeably speeded up. The *chic* replaced the *comme il faut;* the 'gorgeous fringes' spread over the entire warp and woof. For the first time we hear the gigolo spoken of, perhaps with a shrug, but without any simulated horror. The *divorcée* and the woman with no visible means of support are alike accepted. The catchword is 'amusing', and if that hurdle can be taken — anything goes.

It was the acceptance by 'the world' of customs which had once been confined to the 'half-world' that startled the staid and old-fashioned.

'Supposedly "nice" girls were smoking cigarettes — openly and defiantly, if often rather awkwardly and self-consciously. They were drinking — somewhat less openly but often all too efficaciously. There were stories of daughters of the most exemplary parents getting drunk — "blotto", as their companions cheerfully put it . . . and going out joyriding with men at four in the morning.' *Frederick Lewis Allen, 'Only Yesterday', 1931*

¶ Worse still, they were beginning to paint their faces. Before the War only ladies of doubtful reputation had done that. Nice women sometimes allowed themselves the discreet use of *papier poudré* on their

101

cheeks and they used lipsticks, but they were white lipsticks and
conscience was smoothed by calling them lip-salves. Now every girl
used powder and lipstick, the latter of a red which Nature never knew.
The statistics collected by Frances Fisher Dubosc tell their own story.
In 1917 only two persons in the beauty culture business in America
paid income tax. By 1927 there were 18,000 of them. Great Britain
did not lag far behind, although it is doubtful if any country on this
side of the Atlantic could match Professor Paul H. Nystrom's estimate
of three-quarters of a billion dollars a year spent on cosmetics by the
end of the decade. It is said that if all the lipsticks sold in a year in
the United States were placed end to end they would reach from New
York to Reno — which (it was humorously remarked) to some would
seem an altogether logical destination.

Frederick Lewis
Allen,
'Only Yesterday',
1931
'Perhaps the readiest way of measuring the change in the public
attitude towards cosmetics is to compare the advertisements in a
conservative periodical at the beginning of the decade with those at
its end. Although the June 1919 issue of the *Ladies' Home Journal*
contained four advertisements which listed rouge among other products, only one of them commented on its inclusion, and this referred
to its rouge as one that was "imperceptible if properly applied". In
those days the woman who used rouge — at least in the circles in
which the *Journal* was read — wished to disguise the fact . . . In the
June 1929 issue, exactly ten years later, the *Journal* permitted a
lipstick to be advertised with the comment, "It's comforting to know
that the alluring note of scarlet will stay with you for hours." '

¶ Manufacturers of cosmetics were naturally anxious that even the
neophytes should use their products properly:

W. A. Poucher,
'Eve's Beauty
Secrets', 1926
'Flappers, unfortunately, generally over-do this part of their toilet
and what is still worse, they seem to have the taste for colours which
do not harmonize with their facial make-up.'

¶ It was a difficult problem for school-mistresses:

Neville Williams,
'Powder and Paint',
1957
'A recurrent problem in these years was the position of the girl at
High School, for whom even a powdered nose was regarded with
severity, while girls of her own age, earning their livings, were making
the most of their independence. In the early 'thirties Speech Day

102

addresses began to include an exhortation to school girls to throw away any lipsticks or powder which might be given to them . . . But here again, common sense has eventually prevailed. The Head Mistress of Cheltenham Ladies' College, for instance, allows her more senior pupils to wear make-up, on condition that they apply it properly.'

¶ Some women, not content with face-painting, were beginning to contemplate face-sculpture:

'Women with facial disfigurements — and long enough purses — began in the nineteen-twenties to look to plastic surgery for renovations. Great advances had been made in this specialized branch of surgery through the treatments of the facial wounds of soldiers during and immediately after the first war. A plastic surgeon of great experience, Mr. J. C. Bell of Wigmore Street, considered in 1927 that no woman who had once had her share of good looks need ever despair of entirely losing them. Rhinoplasty, the art of forming or improving the nose, was already a familiar operation but oloplasty which corrected outstanding ears, developed remarkably with the fashion for short hair: the Eton crop, especially, demanded perfect ears. *Neville Williams, 'Powder and Paint', 1957*

'Plastic surgeons were kept busy throughout the 'twenties removing wrinkles, dealing with flabbiness and sagging flesh, and, above all, with face-lifting.'

¶ The Eton crop 'demanded perfect ears' — we can well believe it. But why this mania for short hair?

'Even before the War Bohemian and intellectual women had bobbed their hair, as can be seen quite plainly in some of the early canvases of Augustus John . . . By the middle of 1918 we began to find jokes about young women whose contribution to war work had consisted in cutting off their hair — that is, in having it bobbed . . . In times of war and social upheaval the tendency for women to cut off their hair seems to be almost irresistible, and by 1923 to bob or not to bob had become one of the holiday problems . . . Meanwhile the bob, which did not suit all faces, was being gradually abandoned in favour of the shingle . . . The shingle is quite usual in 1925 and we find a "man-woman" in *Punch* complaining: "In the old days I never paid more than sixpence for a haircut; now they call it a shingle-trim and charge *James Laver, 'Taste and Fashion', 1937*

103

me three and sixpence." A new era of prosperity had opened in the hairdressing profession, for by a curious paradox hairdressers never flourished so mightily as in the days when women wore short hair.

'In the same year, 1925, came the first real signs of the *cloche* hat, a type of headgear which was to become the very tyrant of the mode for the next five years. It consisted of a hat with a very narrow brim and a crown which fitted over the head like a helmet. Such hats became universal, and as it was impossible to wear them with a bun or back hair of any kind, women who wished to be in the mode at all were compelled to cut off their locks. In vain old-fashioned gentlemen exclaimed that hair was a woman's crowning glory; in vain old-fashioned ladies strove to find a hat which they could possibly wear. There seemed to be no alternative; and it is an astonishing thought that in the years between 1925 and 1930 the vast majority of women in Western Europe with the exception of Spain, must have cut off their hair.

'The tyranny of the mode, however, was not yet satisfied and early in 1927 or late '26 the shingle was succeeded by the Eton crop. Those women who adopted it cropped their hair as closely as a schoolboy, and, indeed, there was often nothing to distinguish them from schoolboys but their rouged lips and pencilled eyebrows.'

¶ These goings-on did not pass without protest. The moralists were disturbed not only by women's painted faces but by the shortness of their skirts. It is true that some of the stalwarts of the Suffrage Movement regarded the new modes with undisguised (and, perhaps, somewhat misguided) satisfaction:

Ray Strachey,
'The Cause', 1928

'The dress designers, backed no doubt by the conservative tendency of the world, strove hard to keep fashion and hygiene apart. Trains appeared at the end of skirts already long, and women had to hold them up with their hands whenever they moved; high collars, stiffened with whalebone, were fitted close to the neck, and presently the hobble skirt, so narrow at the ankles that only half a step at a time was possible, were superimposed. It seemed that folly could go no farther; and there were some in the feminist ranks who almost questioned whether women who would endure such clothes deserved their enfranchisement!

'The war, however, brought deliverance. Under the necessities of the time fashion gave way, and short-skirted uniforms, and even breeches, became familiar sights. Women, when they had once really tasted the joys of this deliverance, refused to be put back into the old costumes. The trade tried, indeed, when the war was over, to reinstate the old ideas; but they did not "take". Skirts grew shorter and shorter, clothes grew more and more simple and convenient, and hair, that "crowning glory of a woman", was cut short. With one bound the young women of 1919 burst out from the hampering conventions, and with their cigarettes, their motor-cars, their latch-keys, and their athletics they astonished and scandalized their elders. All through the course of the movement any widening of outlook had been thought dangerous for women, and now it seemed that these fears were justified. Men had said that the knowledge of good and evil, which was necessary to themselves, would only hurt women, and rub off the peach-bloom of their innocence; and in the changed manners of the first years after the war this prophecy seemed to be coming true. Many young women seemed to be mistaking the meaning of their freedom, and to be using it only for excess of excitement. They spent the morning hours upon the make-up of their faces, idled through the afternoons, and danced the night. They discarded the semblance of manners and morals, and replaced them by licence and dissipation. These young women figured largely in the minds of the old-fashioned, who enjoyed the belief that the country had now finally gone to the dogs, and that the emancipation of women was the last manifestation of this fact. In reality, however, all this was ephemeral and unimportant, and was more a sign of the reaction after the war strain than of anything to do with the Women's Movement. It passed and died down, and men and women turned away from night clubs to the more wholesome light of day. And yet, in a sense, the pessimists had been right. The new freedom of women *had* destroyed the old ideal on which their fears were based, and it *had* banished the clinging doll-heroine into the shades of the past. Innocence, in the sense of ignorance, existed no more, but in its place there was that of which the pioneers of the Women's Movement had dreamed, namely, the combination of independence with responsiblity.'

¶ Others were not so sure; and one disgusted old Militant was heard to say, pointing to an example of the New Woman, vintage 1926: 'Did we fight the police and go to prison, to give the Vote to *That*?'

'The fundamental fact about the Great War was this, that it gave liberty not to the old married woman, but to the young girl scarcely out of her teens. In all classes of society she had tasted economic

James Laver, 'Taste and Fashion', 1937

freedom, which is the only freedom that matters. She had money to spend, and this was a more valuable equality than anything that could be obtained by the clamour for women's rights. For probably the first time in history the flapper was free, and it was she who was to dictate the fashion for the next decade. If anyone doubts this let him consider the extremely juvenile form which women's dress suddenly adopted in the nineteen-twenties, culminating in the little girl's dress of 1926.'

¶ To create this schoolgirl effect a new kind of corset came in, without bones and exerting its pressure not on the waist, as all previous corsets had done, but on the breasts, so as to flatten them and make them as little conspicuous as possible. Sometimes no corset at all was worn, and any man who was young in the early nineteen-twenties will remember that it was about this period when, placing his hand round the waist of his dancing partner, he noticed the absence of the rigid bone shell which used to confine the feminine figure.

Frederick Lewis Allen, 'Only Yesterday', 1931 'With the short skirt went an extraordinary change in the weight and material and amount of women's clothing. The boyishly slender figure became the aim of every woman's ambition, and the corset was so far abandoned that even in so short a period as the three years from 1924 to 1927 the combined sales of corsets and brassieres in the department stores of the Cleveland Federal Reserve District fell off 11 per cent. Silk or rayon stockings and underwear supplemented cotton, to the distress of cotton manufacturers and the delight of rayon manufacturers; the production of rayon in American plants, which in 1920 had been only eight million pounds, had by 1925 reached fifty-three million pounds. The flesh coloured stocking became as standard as the short skirt . . . No longer were silk stockings the mark of the rich; as the wife of a working man with a total family income of $1,638 a year told the authors of *Middletown*: "No girl can wear cotton stockings to high school. Even in winter my children wear silk stockings with lisle or imitations underneath." '

¶ It was the triumphs of synthetics which made this revolution possible:

Vivian Ogilvie, 'Our Times', 1953 'The democratization of women's clothes could not have been maintained if it had not been for the invention of new materials and especially of artificial silk . . . This triumph of the laboratory revolutionized the clothing of the average woman and her ideas of what she could and should wear. The old black, tan and white stockings of wool or cotton, the old cambric and linen underclothes became the unenvied prerogative of elderly ladies. Flesh-coloured "art silk" stockings, dainty underclothes, gay blouses and dresses came within the reach of millions of women. The new material was not entirely satisfactory at first, but the researchers were constantly at work removing its defects. It might be fragile, liable to stretch and ladder, but it was cheap. For the first time the ordinary women could follow her natural inclination and prefer attractiveness to durability.'

¶ Efforts were made to dam the flowing tide:

'Birmingham waitresses were forbidden in 1924 by their employers to wear short skirts. Fashions and manners were constantly under fire from moralists. The fact is that the 'twenties were more modest than their reputation allows. Miss 1925's bathing-dress had short sleeves and long legs, and she changed in a tent or discreetly under a wrap. Sun-bathing on public beaches was unheard of. Stockings for tennis and skirts for cycling: the shorts of today would have seemed too little of a good thing. On the stage dresses were sometimes scanty by pre-1914 standards but were ample compared with the near-nudity permitted now.' *Leslie Baily, 'Scrapbook for the Twenties', 1959*

¶ Apart from the sporadic and vain efforts by employers the protests in England against the new fashions were limited to a little grumbling in the clubs and a few letters to *The Times*. The Americans, with their incurable belief that people can be made good by law, tried more drastic methods:

'In Philadelphia a Dress Reform Committee of prominent citizens sent a questionnaire to over a thousand clergymen to ask them what would be their idea of a proper dress, and although the gentlemen of the cloth showed a distressing variety of opinion, the committee proceeded to design a "moral gown" which was endorsed by ministers of fifteen denominations. The distinguishing features of this moral gown were that it was very loose-fitting, that the sleeves reached just below the elbows, and that the hem came within seven and a half inches of the floor. *Frederick Lewis Allen, 'Only Yesterday', 1931*

'Not content with example and reproof, legislators in several States introduced bills to reform feminine dress once and for all. The *New York American* reported in 1921 that a Bill was pending in Utah providing fine and imprisonment for those who wore on the streets "skirts higher than three inches above the ankle". A Bill was laid before the Virginia legislature which would forbid any woman from wearing shirtwaists or evening gowns which displayed "more than three inches of her throat". In Ohio the proposed limit of décolletage was two inches; the Bill introduced in the Ohio legislature aimed also to prevent the sale of any "garment which unduly displays or accentuates the lines of the female figure", and to prohibit any "female over fourteen years of age" from wearing "a skirt which does not reach to that part of the foot known as the instep".'

¶ Legislators never learn. The most cursory study of the history of sumptuary laws throughout the ages might have served to convince them that such laws are never effective. Neither, strangely enough, are the denunciations of the clergy. The Archbishop of Naples committed himself to the statement that the earthquake at Amalfi was due to the anger of God against the shortness of women's skirts:

Jacques Reval

'The Almighty cannot bear to see
The female leg above the knee.
It simply isn't fit to show;
He made it — so He ought to know.'

¶ Women in all civilized communities continued to wear short skirts and to defy the lightning.

The amusing thing is that the Puritans — given their premises — were undoubtedly right. No change in fashion is without its significance, and the abandonment of corsets in particular was full of meaning:

James Laver,
Taste and Fashion',
1937

'It is a curious fact in human history, and one well worthy of more attention than it has received from the social psychologists, that the disappearance of corsets is always accompanied by two related phenomena — promiscuity and an inflated currency. No corsets, bad money, and grave moral laxity; corsets, sound money, and the prestige of the *grande cocotte* — such seems to be the rule.'

¶ At least one modern writer has the courage to stand up for the decade when he was a young man:

108

Revolution in Underwear. Black and coral ribbon-threaded cami-knickers from Paris, 1926.

Fred and Adele Astaire dancing on the roof of the Savoy Hotel, London, 1922.

'To me the fashions of the 'twenties are infinitely alluring. Looking through a fashion magazine of 1926 or 1927, one is above all struck by the simplicity of line with which the fashion illustrators sketched those longer-than-life ladies who, with their short, tubular dresses, cigarettes in long holders, cloche hats, bobbed hair, plucked eyebrows, bands of diamond bracelets from wrist to elbow, and earrings hanging like fuchsias, symbolized the visual aspect of the period.'

Cecil Beaton, 'The Glass of Fashion', 1954

¶ And as the same penetrating social commentator justly remarks:

'There has been no period in my lifetime more abused, more ridiculed, more hailed as damned, ugly, and wild than the 'twenties. Perhaps I am rare among my contemporaries in finding that that period was, on the whole, remarkable and vital. If we try to re-examine it, we find it was in some ways like the one we are now passing through — a post-war period marked by restlessness and diversion-seeking. In literature the first "lost generation" was in command. Many people were building their lives on false, shifting, materialistic, childishly romantic, or epicurean values. Women were cutting their hair short, as they do today; and if skirts were up to their knees, whereas today they are down to the calf, it may be merely due to the fact that the Second World War created a hiatus in fashion such as did not occur in the years from 1914 to 1918.'

Cecil Beaton, 'The Glass of Fashion', 1954

¶ To the moralists it was all very disquieting:

'The new woman did not represent as much of a menace to her male contemporaries as she did to the framework of morals prized by the entire older generation. In the eyes of young men of the time, girls were veering towards masculinity but in a pleasing way. By acting like "one of the boys", the "flapper" of the 'twenties made real boys feel more comfortable in her presence. Slender, saucy and smartly insolent, the boyish girl of this era considered it proper to pursue the young man of her choice. Candid, confident, trim and gay, this New Woman really knew what she wanted and set about unabashedly to get it.

'The feminists of yesteryear had cut their hair, dressed in mannish clothes, and avoided men except in intellectual contacts. The new feminist bobbed her hair and shortened her skirt to make herself not less but more noticeable to men. The shortened hair of feminist

Sidney Ditzion, 'Marriage, Morals and Sex in America', 1953

"Pantsy" Walker was a challenge to the enemy sex; the mannish bob, made stylish by actresses in the last thirty years, has been designed to attract an opposite but friendly sex.

'Minorities which gain a measure of equality with their erstwhile oppressors are wont to take on the habits of the majority in an exaggerated way. A liberated sectarian group imposes its own sectarianism where it can. The economically oppressed engage in ostentatious consumption when money comes their way. Women adopted men's drinking and smoking habits to show that they were able; and then they attempted to imitate his sexual standard.'

¶ Women were certainly smoking, and drinking too:

Frederick Lewis Allen, 'Only Yesterday', 1931

'When the Eighteenth Amendment was ratified, prohibition seemed ... to have an almost united country behind it. Evasion of the law began immediately, however, and strenuous and sincere opposition to it — especially in the large cities of the North and East — quickly gathered force. The results were the bootlegger, the speakeasy, and a spirit of deliberate revolt which in many communities made drinking "the thing to do". From these facts in turn flowed further results: the increased popularity of distilled as against fermented liquors, the use of the hip-flask, the cocktail party, and the general transformation of drinking from a masculine prerogative to one shared by both sexes together. The old-time saloon had been overwhelmingly masculine; the speakeasy usually catered for both men and women ... Under the new regime not only the drinks were mixed but the company as well.'

¶ Even in England the cocktail had 'arrived':

Catalogue of W. & A. Gilbey's Centenary Exhibition, 1952

'In England ... the cocktail — both the word and the thing [had] made slow headway. It was known to the "fast set" of the Edwardian era, and, in that strange world of immaculate diplomats and beautiful spies reflected in the novels of Phillips Oppenheim, cocktails play quite a large part. But ordinary people and the daily Press hardly awoke to the existence of the cocktail until after the First World War. Then, suddenly, they were very much aware of it. The young people of the 'twenties, in particular the most publicized of them, known as "The Bright Young Things", spent, so it seemed, a considerable part of their time and income sitting in bars and imbibing potent mixtures, equally bad for their health and their morals.'

Noël Coward,
'Words and Music',
1932

'The Gin is lasting out
No matter whose
We're merely casting out
The Blues
For Gin, in cruel
Sober truth
Supplies the fuel
For Flaming Youth
A drink is known
To help a dream along
A Saxophone
Provides our Theme Song
Though we dishevel
Our girlish bloom
To the Devil
With Gloom!
The Gin is lasting out
No matter whose
We're merely casting out
The Blues . . . '

Catalogue of
W. & A. Gilbey's
Centenary
Exhibition, 1952

'The cocktail shaker became almost the symbol of the age, and the Poor Little Rich Girls danced along the Primrose Path with their cropped hair, silk-clad legs and short skirts to the wail of the saxophone and the tinkling of "shaved ice". No doubt there was a certain amount of truth in this picture; some of "The Bright Young Things" did come to bad ends . . .

'The original cocktails, if one may call them so . . . [were] three in number: the Martini (a mixture of gin and dry vermouth), the Manhattan (a mixture of Bourbon whisky and sweet vermouth) and the Bronx (a mixture of gin, vermouth and fresh orange juice). But bartenders, who became quite important personages, made it a point of honour to invent new varieties . . . Some of them had strangely provocative names like "Bosom Caresser", "Maiden's Blush", "Widows' Kiss" or "Between the Sheets". Some of them, like the "Bunny Hug", reflected the dance mania of the day. Others, like "Some Moth", enshrined forgotten jokes, others, like "Strike's Off", reflected the social upheavals of the 'twenties. There was a "Corpse Reviver", a "Nose-dive" and a "Depth-Bomb". There was a "Glad

Eye" and a "Gloom Chaser", a "Knockout" and a "Monkey Gland". There were cocktails called "Health", "Hell" and "Honeymoon". There was a "Soul's Kiss" and a "Satan's Whiskers". There was a cocktail called after Lindbergh, after Gene Tunney, and after Mary Pickford, and two after Douglas Fairbanks. There were cocktails containing, in addition to spirits, coffee, ice-cream or marmalade. There was even a cocktail, like the "Prairie Oyster", containing no alcohol whatever.'

¶ It was not of course that the 'twenties were really more 'immoral' than the epochs that had gone before. It was only that things had got a little bit more mixed up. The Edwardian man of the world kept his life in watertight compartments and was even pedantically careful that his wife and his mistress should never meet. In the 'twenties all the barriers were down. There were no more *grandes cocottes*: a general promiscuity had deprived them of their status and even of their livelihood. In the words of a Cole Porter 'lyric' in *Nymph Errant*:

> 'In the days of more strict propriety
> Women like me were covered with glory;
> But now, since these damned Society women
> Invaded *my* territory . . .
> 'A busted, disgusted cocotte am I,
> On the page of this age just a blot am I,
> For since the girls called chic
> Have invented new technique,
> I'm afraid, at my trade, not so hot am I . . .'

¶ Another 'lyric' of the period expresses the regret which many men, in their heart of hearts, must have felt for this state of affairs:

Tom Pickering   'LOVE'S TOO EASY

> 'Love's too easy nowadays,
> And no one seems to care a rap,
> I sometimes wonder if it pays
> To have our pleasures all on tap.
> There's nothing in the world we want
> Enough to go on wanting it.
> We would be faithful, but we can't,
> For no one seems to care a bit.

112

Noël Coward and Lilian Braithwaite in 'The Vortex'.

Iris and Daphne Grenfell at the 'Baby' Party, 1929.

Mrs. Armstrong Jones (later Countess of Rosse) at Austrian Legation Period Ball, 1934.

A Débutante's Swimming Party, 1932.

'Don't be too easy, Baby,
    I want to yearn for you.
I want to flutter round like the moth to the flame,
I want to work out all the rules of the game,
    I want to go slow,
I want to imagine all the things I don't know.

    Don't be in a hurry
    To give me your lips.
    Love's just a worry,
    When it once comes to grips.
    Don't swim with the stream,
    Just be my dream,
    For to my dream I'm true.
    Don't be too easy, Baby,
    I want to yearn for you.

'Be a little hard to please,
And difficult to understand.
Only on my bended knees
Give me leave to kiss your hand.
Let me falter, make me woo,
Learn to say your lover "No".
Lest the proverb prove too true —
Easy come and easy go.

'Refrain

'Don't be too easy, Baby, etc.'

¶ Few young women of the period had any such inhibitions. Indeed, since everybody had now read Freud, and interpreted, more or less correctly, his gospel, inhibitions of any kind were definitely ('definitely' was the most overworked word of the epoch) out of fashion:

'While among the immediate post-war generation of *débutantes* there was a taboo upon the display of interest or excitement of any kind, the next crop were so mortally afraid of being considered *blasé* that they lived, moved and had their hyperbolic being in a world

*Archibald Lyall,
'The Future of
Taboo in These
Islands', 1936*

where everything was "quite too thrilling" or "too, too marvellous" and where, instead of being mildly annoyed or amusing, one was "purple with rage", "mad with passion", "speechless with laughter", or "quite hysterical", such descriptions being generally reinforced by the most inapposite adverb in the language, "literally".

'The curious and somewhat gangaresque phraseology coined by a certain set in London at the end of the 'twenties spread to the suburbs and the provinces with more than usual rapidity owing to its popularization by Mr. Evelyn Waugh in *Vile Bodies*.'

¶ Many would have accepted the picture of the Girl of the Period painted by a modern humorous poet:

Jacques Reval,
'The Woman of
1926'[1]

'Mother's advice, and Father's fears
Alike are voted just a bore,
There's negro music in our ears,
The World is one huge dancing floor.
We mean to tread the Primrose Path,
In spite of Mr. Joynson-Hicks.
We're People of the Aftermath,
We're girls of 1926.

'In greedy haste, on pleasure bent,
We have no time to think, or feel,
What need is there for sentiment
Now we've invented Sex-Appeal?
We've silken legs and scarlet lips,
We're young and hungry, wild and free.
Our waists are round about the hips,
Our skirts are well above the knee.

'We've boyish busts and Eton crops,
We quiver to the saxophone,
Come, dance before the music stops,
And who can bear to be alone?
Come, drink your gin, or sniff your "snow",
Since Youth is brief, and Love has wings.
And Time will tarnish, e'er we know
The brightness of the Bright Young Things.'

[1] As these verses have been several times reprinted — without acknowledgement — perhaps I had better admit that the name 'Reval' should be read in reverse.

¶ Who, then, were these Bright Young Things? Above all, they were young. In the cant phrase of the day 'the accent was on Youth'. It started in America. Count Keyserling had referred in his book *America Set Free* to the youth-cult as a particular characteristic of the period when he was writing. In America it had been pushed to the stage of idealizing the child. 'America', he said, 'is fundamentally the land of the over-rated child.' An English prophet took up this theme:

'The "High appreciation of the qualities of Youth", referred to by Count Keyserling, dates from before the War. The Futurists, led by Marinetti, were fanatical Youth-politicians, and their successors of Fascism "Youthed" away for all they were worth. But the world at large only settled down to intensive Youth-politics upon the conclusion of the War. And the phenomenon of "Slimming" is one of the most obvious illustrations of this. It was the diagnostic of that central, pathologic impulse that still dominates our Society. *Wyndham Lewis, 'Doom of Youth', 1932*

'Where it was impossible to *be* "a Youth", it was at least possible to acquire "the profile of Youth" . . . the silhouette if not the solid or unsolid fact . . . The main reason for the "slimming" dementia was the huge premium put on "youth", the War ended. Every one wished to be, as it were, *new born*. To blot out the Past, especially the "pre-war" — that was the idea.'

¶ Youth! Youth! The newspapers, it seemed, could write of almost nothing else. The *Evening News* ran a kind of symposium in which every point of view was canvassed. The old men accused the young — the young men replied:

'Sir Max Pemberton wrote an article in the *Evening News* entitled "Youth Without Ambition" in which he remarked that the young man of the 'twenties "does not want leadership at any price." This, as the Editor no doubt expected and hoped, produced an avalanche of replies. *C. B. Jones, 'Evening News', June 10th, 1929*

'Let Sir Max consider our position. Our education came at a time when the world was in an uproar. Our fathers and elder brothers were in the trenches. Only the old men remained in their clubs, boasting of the number of grandsons they had "given" to the War. We passed our most impressionable years in an atmosphere of confusion and doubt.

'Now the growth of large combines has made it more difficult for

115

a young man to get clear of the mob. Other things being equal, it is obviously ten times as difficult for the youth of today to reach the top of a business employing 1,000 men as it was for the youth of Sir Max's generation in a business with only 100 employees . . .

'We have a difficult task. A world smashed by the weakness and foolishness of Old Age has to be repaired; but in our own way, we are settling down to work. We shall not do it in a night.'

¶ The Editor, however, had a cheering word:

'Evening News',
September 30th, 1930
'Mrs. Elinor Glyn (who has been studying Youth, as such, for a number of years now, since she rather startled the elders with her book "Three Weeks") especially praises them. She is delighted with the very newest generation, and says so.'

¶ However, in an interview with Beverley Nichols she expressed rather different views:

Beverley Nichols,
'25', 1931
'I gave her a cue — something on the lines of the eternal modern girl, and as she heard that phrase her nostrils quivered, her eyes glared like lamps, her backbone seemed to stiffen like that of a cat on the offensive. And she looked extraordinarily beautiful.

' "Women to-day", she said, "are revolting men's senses. Look at me. Do *I* slouch into the room, with a guilty look, as though I had not been to bed all night? Do *I* take out a lipstick and slash it over my mouth without caring where it goes? Do *I* daub powder all over my nose until it looks a totally different colour from the rest of my face?"

'I answered her that, in our brief but entrancing acquaintance, she had done none of these things.

' "Look at my hands." With a gesture of scorn she held out five very white and exquisite fingers. "Are my hands yellow and horrible through incessantly smoking bad cigarettes?" She leant forward and showed her teeth, looking like some furious goddess. "Are *my* teeth stained, for the same reason? I ask you? No, they are not."

'She relaxed, but she still looked very grim. "I can't bear it", she said, "this abominable slackness. If I saw my daughters slouching through life like that, I should shoot either myself or them. It is worse in England than anywhere else." '

116

The Hon. David Herbert, Lady Plunket and Walter Crisham: 'Gods, Goddesses and Muses mobilised for Charity' 1935.

Mrs. Poppet Jackson (formerly Miss Poppet John) in the costume worn at Mr. Cecil Beaton's 'Fête Champêtre', 193?

Wyndham Lewis (of all people) launched an attack upon some of the new young writers:

'Messrs. Winn and Waugh and some others thought that this citadel of Tradition, *La Vieille Angleterre*, in spite of all its history . . . might be laid siege to and shaken up on the "Youth" ticket, and they started a "Youth" racket. Even if Merry England might never return, a Brighter Britain could be brought about. "Youth-politics" being anyhow in full blast, this was done — it was a cinch. And the Ancient Britons awoke one morning, like Baron Byron, and found themselves Bright (Bright Britain is not only better but more appropriate than Great Britain): the "Youth" racket had come to London.' *Wyndham Lewis, 'Doom of Youth', 1932*

¶ Some of the younger writers certainly trailed their coats. Even the idols of yesterday were assailed:

'Aldous Huxley is not bad; but diluted, over-intellectualised, not really creative or original — a younger kind of Galsworthy. *William Gerhardi, 'Sunday Express', January 18th, 1931*
'I have been driven — not unwillingly — to the conclusion that Hugh Kingsmill and myself, through sheer abundance and concentration of talent, must eventually, when Wells and Bennett are dead, have the field of serious literature pretty well to ourselves.'

¶ After this, perhaps it is not surprising to find a young woman writer who declared that —

'A lot of us are getting very tired of these conceited young men of today. There are such a lot of them . . . *Ethel Mannin, 'Sunday Express', January 25th, 1931*
'And all the distinguished men of letters who have not acclaimed their genius they "put in their place". Thus we get young Mr. Evelyn Waugh pitching into his elders, having no end of quiet fun, and getting paid for it into the bargain, and young Gerhardi declaring that Aldous Huxley is "not bad" . . . Unhesitatingly I place Aldous Huxley as the most important, the greatest intellect and the most serious artist of my male contemporaries.'

¶ Cecil Beaton tells us about the origin of the Bright Young Things:

'In London during the 'twenties, Miss Ponsonby (now Loelia, Duchess of Westminster) was one of the instigators of a new type of gala. She lived with her parents in St. James's Palace (where her *Cecil Beaton, 'The Glass of Fashion', 1954* father held a position close to the King), and preferred less conventional parties to those attended by other courtiers and their folk. Miss Ponsonby would, on an impulse, arrange a last minute party and ask her friends to contribute an essential ingredient: some benevolent godfather would supply a band, other guests provided supper, all brought champagne. Nancy Mitford, and a bevy of new personalities just down from Oxford, Lord Kinross, Evelyn Waugh, Harold Acton and Oliver Messel, were the nucleus of a group who were either of the aristocracy or entertained the aristocracy by their talents. They had a splendid zest for life and an ability for expressing that zest. Friends provided impromptu cabarets with their imitations and impersonations; elaborate and ingenious treasure hunts were organized, and hoax picture-exhibitions were arranged. The spirit of masquerade reached new heights, and almost every night there was some excuse for putting on fancy dress. When others began, in a less imaginative, though wilder fashion, to emulate them, the "bright young things" began to receive unfavourable publicity, and their "bottle parties" fell into disrepute.'

¶ They did indeed. In their day they were the delight of Fleet Street, where their antics provided an almost daily ration of copy, and the despair of all right-thinking people, of all those, that is, who still had the capacity for being shocked at anything. The titles chosen for their parties ranged from ingenuity to sheer silliness. 'Come as your dearest enemy', 'Come as your opposite', 'Come as your secret self'; such were the themes of these junketings of self-expression and self-advertisement. But the height, or depth, was reached by the famous Baby Party, at which grown men and women appeared in the garb appropriate to various stages of infancy, and pushed one another in perambulators round a well-known London square. An enterprising advertiser cashed in at once:

F. R. Holmes   'Bring your toys and Teddies,
Come prepared to crawl,
Shake a wicked rattle at the pop-eyed Babies' Ball.
Choose your socks and rompers,
Sport a sailor suit,
Bonnets trimmed with pompoms look most
    infantile and "cute".

118

'Armed with bibs and bottles,
Prattle and say "Ga!"
Suck a naughty cocktail at the Bad Boys'
    Nursery Bar,
Bright Young Things of thirty
Seeking Life and Colour,
Won't 'oo 'tum and toddle, long time past
    bedtime wiz Abdulla?'

¶ A considerable amount of indignation was caused by this escapade.
It was described as an outrage on the public and as an insult to the
innocence of childhood — as indeed it was. For innocence was hardly
the outstanding quality of the Bright Young Things. On the contrary,
they paraded their vices, they

'Drank, and drugged, and stole each other's men —
It was the fashion, then.'

They became involved in car crashes between one roadhouse and
another, they were picked up drunk in the gutters of Jermyn Street.
A few of them — the toughest — have survived into our own day.
They have settled down, and one or two have even set up as guardians
of modern morality, denouncing the sins and follies of a new generation. Many of them are dead.

The writer who most completely expressed the mood of the age
was Noël Coward. He was never, himself, a Bright Young Thing,
being far too clever, and far too ambitious to waste his time on folly,
except as an object of satire.

'DANCE LITTLE LADY

'*Verse*

Noël Coward,
'*This Year of Grace*',
1928

'Tho' you're only seventeen
Far too much of life you've seen
Syncopated child.
Maybe if you only knew
Where your path was leading to
You'd become less wild.
But I know it's vain
Trying to explain,
While there's this insane
Music in your brain.

119

'Dance, dance, dance little lady,
Youth is fleeting — to the rhythm beating
In your mind.
Dance, dance, dance little lady,
So obsessed with second best
No rest you'll ever find,
Time and tide and trouble
Never, never wait.
Let the cauldron bubble
Justify your fate.
Dance, dance, dance little lady,
Leave tomorrow behind.

'Verse

'When the saxophone gives a wicked moan
Charleston hey hey,
Rhythms fall and rise
Start dancing to the tune
The band's crooning — for soon
The night will be gone.
Start swaying like a reed
Without heeding the speed
That hurries you on.
Nigger melodies
Syncopate your nerves
Till your body curves
Drooping — stooping,
Laughter some day dies
And when the lights are starting to gutter
Dawn through the shutter
Shows you're living in a world of lies.

'Refrain

'Dance, dance, dance little lady, etc.'

¶ Apart from viciousness, however, Coward was typical enough. He shared the scepticism of the age, its determination to debunk everything, in particular those qualities which had ensured the stability of the Victorian period, and 'built the Empire'. His recantation in *Cavalcade* was therefore all the more effective; although rumour has it that he began to write the piece tongue-in-cheek and suddenly realized that the mood of the country, and his own attitude, had changed.

What we think of as the 'twenties was in fact a very brief period — less than a decade. Already in 1926 the General Strike had given a rude shock to public complacency, and before the 'thirties dawned the shadows had begun to close in. What really put an end to the picnic was the American Slump.

CHAPTER VI

THE GENERAL STRIKE — AND AFTER

THERE WAS NOTHING NEW in the idea of a General Strike:

G. D. H. Cole, 'William Morris made it the method of the social revolution in
'The World of *News from Nowhere,* and it has long been a leading feature of Com-
Labour', 1913 munist propaganda. M. M. Pataud and Pouget, in their Syndicalist
Utopia *Comment nous ferons la Révolution* by no means hit on a
new idea in ushering in their "great change" by means of a half-
conscious strike gradually extending over the whole working-class.
The idea is old, and has always exercised a powerful fascination over
young rebels of every school. M. Briand, the most notorious strike-
breaker of all French Premiers, was in earlier days a notable advocate
of it, and it has always been over the idealist and the middle-class
Socialist that it has cast the strongest spell.'

¶ As long ago as 1906, Jaurès, at the Socialist Conference at Limoges,
carried a motion declaring its conviction 'that the working-class will
not be able to enfranchise themselves fully except by the combined
force of political and syndical action, by syndicalism going as far as
the general strike, and by the conquest of the whole political power,
with a view to the general expropriation of capitalism . . .' In one of
his earliest books, published before the outbreak of the First World
War, G. D. H. Cole, gives this account of the attitude of the C.G.T.
(Conféderation Générale du Travail):

G. D. H. Cole, 'Direct Action is for them at once a great educative influence and
'The World of the actual method of capitalist expropriation. It has therefore taken
Labour', 1913 on an almost religious aspect, and has felt the need of providing itself
with a theology. The dogma of the General Strike is a formulation of
the philosophy of Direct Action in a popular and compelling manner.

122

The General Strike is presented as historically in the future; but the workers are meant to recognise in it the type of the strikes of the present . . . Every strike is more or less general, and the same conception embraces all; from the petty strike in a single workshop to the local, regional, national and international general strikes, all are touched with something of the glamour which attaches to the one great "social general strike" in which is envisaged the complete overthrow of capitalist society. It is not necessary to go into the complicated theory of social myths and the analogy of the Second Coming which M. Sorel has woven round the conception of the General Strike: we are concerned only to notice how extraordinarily compelling the idea is.'

¶ In Italy, although 'M. Sorel's influence has been there also very great, and, as Italian Socialism has always been much devoted to the criticism and interpretation of Marxian doctrine, his neo-Marxism has probably had even more effect on theory there than in France', in practice the Italian workers were far too unorganized to make Direct Action possible.

The German Trade Unions were, on the other hand, extremely well organized but 'in Germany . . . the General Strike has found practically no supporters. The theoretical General Strike has been received there even more coldly than in England . . . The policy of the German Unions is, on the whole, peaceful; they prefer getting their advantages by means of conciliation to fighting for them.' A General Strike was actually staged in Sweden in 1909, but was a complete failure.

Some Left-wing idealists had high hopes of the *anti-militaristic* General Strike:

'Of this there is no actual case, though France has several times come near to furnishing one. Its most popular form is that generally preached by Mr. Keir Hardie, the "strike against war". When two powers declare war on each other, it is urged, let the workers of both countries go on strike, and refuse to play the capitalists' game. This looks very well on paper, and it is possible, in times of peace, to get up, among a limited class, quite a lot of enthusiasm for such a proposal. But there is nothing so certain as that at the first breath of a war-scare, all the peaceable professions of the workers will be forgotten, and jingoism will sweep like a scourge over the country. However true it may be that the interests of the working-class are in all countries

G. D. H. Cole, *'The World of Labour'*, 1913

identical, there is assuredly no working-class educated enough or sober enough to recognise the identity in the midst of a war-scare. A strike against war on a large scale is, in this country at any rate, absolutely inconceivable; in Germany the attempt is more possible, but its failure is equally sure. The strike against war may be ruled out at once as a sheer impossibility.'

¶ Considering that these words were written in 1913, we are compelled to admire the acuteness of G. D. H. Cole's diagnosis. But the undertone of regret is obvious. Cole made no secret of his own sympathies:

G. D. H. Cole, 'The World of Labour', 1913

'Industrial peace . . . must not be permanent. There is a real class-antagonism, a quarrel that can only be adjusted by the overthrow of capitalist society. The fact that strikes inconvenience the public and are "brutal" in their effects is an argument, not for prohibiting strikes, but for altering the social system. A public that acquiesces in exploitation, has no rights against workers who are up in arms against it: the State has no right to interfere *as an impartial person* . . . At present, it interferes, as a rule, merely to stop the strike at any cost: its motto is "anything for peace and quietness". But it has no right to peace till it has secured all men their rights — and from the State of today, it is more than a little fantastic to expect that.'

¶ To 'secure all men their rights' might seem an ambitious programme for any State, however constituted, and Cole admits sadly that even

G. D. H. Cole, 'The World of Labour', 1913

'The Trade Unions have to take men as they find them, and revolutionary methods only succeed, for long, with revolutionary people. In England, the rebel is a very rare phenomenon. Trade Unionists, as a whole, have very little revolutionary spirit. They will bear the slaughter-house meekly, provided the market does not demand the slaughter of too many at once; they will lie down gladly in their thousands in the green pastures of Liberalism and Reform. Meanwhile, profits will go up, and real wages will fall. Capitalism has not yet to die in its last ditch.'

¶ Once again we must admit that Cole was right. When the General Strike came at last to England it was not due to any 'formulation of the philosophy of Direct Action', nor did it envisage 'the complete overthrow of capitalist society'. The T.U.C. simply blundered into it.

124

Super 'Oxford Bags', 1926.

L. S. Lowry—'Street Scene' (Reproduced by permission of Howard Spring, Esq.).

'May (1926) saw the General Strike in England. Never was a great gesture so confused. Sympathy for the miners and discipline to the T.U.C. leaders brought out the rank and file of the Unions . . . The Government hit back. The Emergency Powers worked well. As a collar of steel prevents a tourniquet from strangling an artery, so the Civil Commissioners' plans and powers prevented the strike of transport from strangling the cities. The middle classes could think of the struggle only in these terms and gave a highly emotional and enthusiastic support to "elected authority". It was clear in England, as it had been in Italy and was to be in Germany, that the only class which is fully class-conscious is the despised middle class: rouse it, and from it spring the storm troops, though the dictators may be blacksmiths' sons or builders' apprentices. England, however, always uses even violence with inconsistent moderation.'

Gerald Heard, 'These Hurrying Years', 1934

¶ At first the Left-wing was jubilant:

'Tuesday, May 4th, started with the workers answering the call. What a wonderful response! What loyalty!! What solidarity!!! From John o' Groat's to Land's End the workers answered the call to arms to defend us, to defend the brave miner in his fight for a living wage . . .

A. J. Cook, 'The Nine Days', 1926

'It was a wonderful achievement, a wonderful accomplishment that proved conclusively that the Labour Movement has the men and women that are capable in any emergency of providing the means of carrying on the country. Who can forget the effect of motor conveyances with posters saying "By permission of the T.U.C."? The Government with its O.M.S. (*sic*) were absolutely demoralised. Confidence, calm and order prevailed everywhere, despite the irritation caused by the volunteers, blacklegs, and special constables. The workers acted as one. Splendid discipline! Splendid loyalty!'

¶ Was this the rosy dawn of Revolution at last?

'On Friday (May 7th) in a desperate effort to increase the pressure, the leaders of the railway and transport trade unions issued orders that everything was to be done to break down the supply of food, and attempted intimidation by pickets was increased. Large stocks of flour were lying at the London Docks and could not be moved owing to the obstruction of the strikers. On Saturday (May 8th) a great train of lorries, escorted by a battalion of Grenadier Guards, with armoured

'British Gazette', May 10th, 1926

cars, marched from Hyde Park to the docks, where the flour was loaded and taken away, the watching crowds offering no opposition.'

¶ Of course the General Strike was an *inconvenience* to everybody:

Mrs. C. S. Peel, O.B.E., 'Life's Enchanted Cup', 1933 'Discontent boiled up in the Great Strike of 1926, when we saw in the streets convoys of food supplies under the protection of armed soldiers and armoured cars; when Hyde Park became a food depot from which the public was excluded; when newspapers shrank to one-page leaflets and those of us who had wireless sets invited others who had not to gather and listen to the news. Then we, like most other people, used our car to take workers to and from their work, and the few omnibuses which ran had boarded-up windows and engines protected by an entanglement of barbed wire.

'Young men from the universities drove these omnibuses or took the place of drivers and stokers on the trains, and women turned to as they had done in the War and made themselves useful wherever they could.

'It says much for the common sense and good feeling of the nation that the strike which began on May 4th and ended on Wednesday, May 12th, was, for the most part, a good-humoured and disciplined strike. On one of the strike days I went in the late afternoon to play bridge at a certain club. I happened to know that an elderly woman who was then on duty in the cloak-room lived at Camberwell. "How did you get here?" I asked. "I had to walk ma'am. Perhaps I'll be lucky in getting a lift home." I asked her if she would care to come and stay with us while the trouble lasted. One of the club members overheard this conversation.

' "Oh, I suppose you are one of those Reds yourself", she said in scathing tones. "The working classes want a lesson. Those damned strikers ought to be shot."

'The cloak-room attendant watched her as she walked indignantly away and then she looked at me. "Those are the people who make revolutions", she said.'

¶ For many people it was all a 'tremendous middle-class lark':

Christopher Isherwood, 'Lions and Shadows', 1933 'The General Strike which everybody . . . said was impossible and sure to be called off at the last moment, began without any visible fuss at midnight . . . As I took my ticket home on a bus, the conductor

126

said: " 'Fraid you'll have to drive this thing yourself, tomorrow, sir."

'And sure enough, next morning, the tremendous upper-middle-class lark began: by lunch time, the Poshocrats were down from Oxford and Cambridge in their hundreds — out for all the fun that was going. And the Medical students — "spoiling for a fight", as elderly Kensington ladies admiringly said of them — paraded the streets in their special constables' armlets, licensed to punch at sight. Every bus and underground train was a ragtime family party; goodness knew where you were going or how long it would take. If you fussed because they took you to Mornington Crescent instead of Hyde Park Corner you were a spoil-sport, an obstructionist, even a trifle unpatriotic. Not that anybody talked about patriotism — this wasn't 1914. Everything was perfectly all right, really. The strikers were all right — except for a few paid agitators controlled by Moscow, and some groups of professional roughs. The great mass of the working class entered "into the spirit of the thing" . . .

'I couldn't laugh at the strike. From the first moment, I loathed it and longed for it to end. It wasn't that I seriously expected street fighting or civil war. But "war" was in the air: one heard it in the boisterous defiant laughter of the amateur bus drivers, one glimpsed it in the alert sexual glances of the women. This was a dress rehearsal of "The Test": and it found me utterly unprepared. I wanted to lock myself away in a corner and pretend that nothing was happening. For the first time, I knew that I detested my own class: so sure of themselves, so confident that they were in the right, so grandly indifferent to the strikers' case. Most of us didn't even know why the men had struck. I didn't know, myself, I couldn't think about such things: I could only shudder with fear and hatred; hating both parties . . . I hated myself, too, for being neutral . . .

'After a miserable week of doubts and self-reproaches, I sneaked round shamefacedly to the Chelsea Town Hall and volunteered for duty . . . However, before I could be called up, the strike had ended. The Poshocracy had won, as it always did win, in thoroughly gentlemanly manner . . . it was quite prepared magnanimously to pretend that nothing more serious had taken place than, so to speak, a jolly sham fight with pats of butter.'

¶ Christopher Isherwood's soul-searchings implied a certain amount of Left-wing sentiment. The vast majority of undergraduates had no such doubts:

H. W. Austin, 'Lawn Tennis Bits and Pieces', 1930 'During my first summer term at Cambridge the normal lawn-tennis programme was upset by the General Strike. However, the greater part of the University rejoiced at the prospect of being able to help defeat the strikers. I went with a batch of undergraduates to help conduct buses from their depot at Chiswick Park. Unfortunately there were six hundred of us all equally keen to conduct the same bus. After one or two idle days and uncomfortable nights endeavouring to sleep on the top of a bus, and having contracted colds of considerable violence, a friend and myself took seats as passengers in one of the many buses we had endeavoured to conduct. We went to look for work elsewhere and obtained an excellent job on the railway; but this was too much for the strikers, and before we were able to undertake our duties the strike was at an end. After one or two pleasant days of golf, we returned to Cambridge to continue the term.'

¶ Such sublime *insouciance* was incomprehensible to foreigners:

'Illustrated London News', May 15th, 1926 'There was little to indicate, in London, that any very extraordinary state of affairs existed. Some foreign visitors, who went forth armed with cameras in search of dramatic incidents were reported to have asked where the strike was to be found and to have returned in disappointment, having failed to locate it . . .

'The strike did not interfere much with the amusements of the people, such as cricket and lawn-tennis. The Australians, after it began, played Essex at Leyton and Surrey at the Oval, and Mr. Woodfull and Mr. McCartney made their centuries as though nothing untoward were afoot. It would be a great error to suppose, however, that the crisis was not taken seriously, in spite of the general cheeriness prevailing . . .

'We feel that the heart of England must be sound when . . . we read that "Mr. C. E. Pitman, the Oxford stroke, is driving a train on the G.W.R. from Bristol to Gloucester" . . . "The Headmaster of Eton (Dr. Alington) and about fifty of his assistant masters have enrolled as special constables" . . . Lord Chesham is driving a train. The Hon. Lionel Tennyson is a "special". Mr. Roger Wethered, the golfer, was yesterday working on a food convoy from the docks . . . But perhaps the most encouraging fact of all was that at Plymouth, on May 8th, the police played a football match with the strikers, and the wife of the Chief Constable kicked off.'

128

The General Strike, 1926: An armoured car escorting food convoys.

George Lansbury speaking at a Means Test Rally in Trafalgar Square, London.

¶ This seemed an extraordinary way of conducting the Class War. Was Great Britain in the midst of a revolutionary upheaval, or wasn't it?

'Throughout the General Strike the eyes of all observers throughout the world were turned to Britain. One of the most acute and experienced observers, J. V. Stalin, was following it with close attention.'

R. Page Arnot, 'A History of the Scottish Miners', 1955

¶ We can well believe it! Some eight years later, in his talks with H. G. Wells, 'J. V. Stalin' expressed his astonishment:

'The first thing any other bourgeoisie would have done in the face of such an event, when the General Council of Trade Unions called for a strike, would have been to arrest the Trade Union leaders. The British bourgeoisie did not do that, and it acted cleverly from the point of view of its own interest. I cannot conceive of such a flexible strategy being employed by the bourgeoisie of the United States, Germany or France. In order to maintain their rule, the ruling classes of Great Britain have never foresworn small concessions, reforms. But it would be a mistake to think that these reforms were revolutionary.'

Stalin-Wells Talk, Verbatim Record, 'New Statesman', December, 1934

¶ One of the early successes of the T.U.C. had been, by calling out the printers, to make it impossible to publish newspapers in the usual form. However, the *British Gazette* took their place to some extent and the principal papers were often able to struggle on although in a much reduced format. Little more than a week after the beginning of the General Strike, one of them was able to announce:

'MEN DEFY UNIONS

PRINTERS, IRONWORKERS, AND BREWERY EMPLOYEES
GO BACK TO WORK

'Daily Mirror', May 12th, 1926

'There was a continuance yesterday of the "back-to-work" movement with which the second week of the strike opened.

'Stanton Ironworks, Derbyshire, employing over 4,000 men, resumed operations, which will absorb 2,000 hands.

'Printers have returned at Rochdale, Hinckley, Galashiels and Hawick. At Bristol, 1,100 are at work in one house.

'Many *Daily Express* strikers have applied for reinstatement, and strikers have resumed work on several provincial newspapers.

'Railwaymen on strike presented themselves in a steady stream to the G.W.R. at Slough for re-engagement.

'Union men at three Northampton breweries were called out, but at a meeting of employees only four men voted for the strike.'

¶ In the same issue the *Daily Mirror* announced Preparations for its Normal Re-issue.

'Daily Mirror',
May 12th, 1926
'The Directors of the *Daily Mirror* will consider applications from any members of its staff now on strike who desire to resume work in preparation for the re-issue of this journal in its usual form. Such applications will, however, not be considered unless they are clearly unconditional. They must be sent by post and not delivered by hand.

'The Government have pledged themselves to protect any strikers who return to work, and the *Daily Mirror* Newspapers Company Ltd., associates itself with that undertaking.'

¶ Meanwhile what was happening behind the scenes? Alan Bullock's recent book, *The Life and Times of Ernest Bevin,* throws a new light on this complicated story:

Alan Bullock,
'Life and Times of
Ernest Bevin', 1960
'Much criticism was later directed at the General Council for calling a national strike without adequate preparations. But this does not go to the heart of the matter. At a pinch, as Bevin and the local strike committees showed, organisation could be improvised.

'The real criticism to be made of the trade union leaders, including Bevin, is that they had not sufficiently thought out the consequences of the course on which they had embarked. The lack of preparation was only a part of a wider failure to grasp clearly where their policy was leading them . . . Jimmy Thomas was quicker than any other member of the General Council to see the quandary in which they were now placed and he was determined to find a way out.'

¶ Sir Herbert Samuel, as he then was, had presided over a Royal Commission on the Coal Industry, and its findings had led the Labour leaders to look upon its chairman as at least favourably inclined to the miners' claims. After the publication of the Report Sir Herbert had left for Italy, intending to settle there, but, on the outbreak of the

130

General Strike, he returned to England and, entirely on his own initiative, offered to help. He was told by the Government that any negotiations he might undertake could not have 'even a vestige of official character'. Samuel himself made this quite plain. Nonetheless the Labour leaders, especially Thomas, welcomed his intervention, and—

'A series of secret meetings took place in the house of Thomas's friend, Sir Abe Bailey, the South African mining magnate. With the advice of Thomas, Pugh (chairman of the General Council) and the other members of the Negotiating Committee, Samuel drew up proposals for implementing the Commission's recommendations. *Alan Bullock, 'Life and Times of Ernest Bevin', 1960*

'Samuel and the Negotiating Committee tried to meet the miners' objection that the promised re-organisation of the industry was only another trick to get them to agree to wage reductions.

'Both the miners' representatives on the General Council were absent throughout the dispute. It was doubly unfortunate that the first discussions between the Negotiating Committee of the General Council and Sir Herbert Samuel — for which Thomas was again responsible—took place without the knowledge of the miners' leaders.

'In a joint meeting with the Miners' Executive that evening (Monday, May 10th), the General Council told the miners that they regarded the Samuel memorandum as a satisfactory basis for re-opening negotiations. The miners did not . . .

'In the course of a heated argument, the strongest pressure to accept the proposals came from the railwaymen's leaders, Thomas and Bromley, who threatened to take their men back if the strike were not called off.

' "Take them back", was the only reply this threat elicited from Herbert Smith, who retorted by asking pointedly what guarantees the T.U.C. had received that the Government or the mine owners would accept Sir Herbert Samuel's proposals.

'Bevin, preoccupied with the work of the Strike Organisation Committee, had so far taken no direct part in the negotiations. There was, in fact, no one on the Negotiating Committee who could stand up to Thomas, a master of negotiating tactics who was bent upon getting a settlement, whether the miners liked it or not.'

¶ What followed may be gathered from Ernest Bevin's own account:

131

Alan Bullock,
'Life and Times of
Ernest Bevin', 1960 'I did not happen to be at the General Council, but I must not try
to escape responsibility . . . When I got there, I met the Negotiating
Committee coming out. I said to George Hicks "What has happened?"
He said, "They have adopted the Samuel proposals." I asked what that
meant and his reply was that, if they were accepted, it meant the finish.

'I urged him to be very careful and pointed out that they had not
yet seen the Miners. I also urged care with regard to demobilising our
forces. I told him to hesitate a bit.

'That was all in the street . . . now this is the crucial point. The
Miners were sent for.

'Pugh, tired, worn and a little bit sick of things, did tell the Miners
they had to take it or leave it. Well, with a temperament like Smith's[1]
that was asking for a stubborn opposition, but it was due to an
unfortunate tiredness.

'Smith immediately wanted to know why he had not been at the
negotiations that afternoon when the final document was arrived at.
He was there the previous day discussing it with Samuel and the
Negotiating Committee. He wanted to know the reason for being
left out.

'Then a hullabaloo took place on that point. I appealed to the
Miners that, with all the strain and stress of running a strike on their
behalf, they should not exaggerate every little incident that occurred
but that they should take the document on its merits, examine and
see whether it offered a solution to their trouble.

'After a good deal of persuasion, the Miners retired, returned about
11 p.m. and rejected the document.

'After the Miners went, everyone on the General Council felt that
there would be no solution in conjunction with the Miners' Executive,
but that it had become necessary to reach a decision without them.
We were responsible for four times as many people as they had in the
field and therefore the question of whether the Miners accepted it or
not was discarded altogether . . .'

¶ Next day the Labour leaders (without the Miners' representative)
went to see Mr. Baldwin: Bevin tells us what happened:

Alan Bullock,
'Life and Times of
Ernest Bevin', 1960 'Before we got there, the decision of the Miners had been given to
the Press. When we got to Downing Street it was on the tapes . . .
Baldwin knew that the movement was split.

[1] Herbert Smith, the miners' leader.

132

'When we went in, Sir Horace Wilson (Permanent Secretary, Ministry of Labour) came to the door of the Cabinet Room. He said, "You want to see the Prime Minister?" Thomas said, "Yes!" Wilson then said, "Well, Mr. Pugh and Mr. Thomas, what do you want to see the Prime Minister for?" They replied, "We want to see him on the position." The reply to this was, "You know the Prime Minister will not see you before the strike is called off."

'I said at the back, "For Christ's sake let's call it on again if this is the position." Thomas then said,"We have come to call the strike off." '

¶ The strike was off. The miniature *Daily Mirror* for Wednesday, May 12th, was crudely overstamped 'Strike Over' and for the general public that was that. All but the miners went back to work. The miners themselves held out for another six months in growing bitterness and then accepted lower wages and longer hours. The country had been saved — but had it?

The General Strike had been the writing on the wall; but what really brought the fools' paradise of the 'twenties to an end was the Great American Slump. Throughout the decade America had been fabulously prosperous. The German mark might have slid into the abyss, the French franc was visibly shaky. The pound and the dollar, both still based on gold; these were the shining beacons of international finance. But was the financial situation as sound as all that, even in America?

For the moment everything looked rosy:

'Through 1927 speculation had been increasing. The amount of money loaned to brokers to carry margin accounts for traders had risen during the year from $2,818,561,000 to $3,558,355,000 — a huge increase. During the week of December 3rd, 1927, more shares of stock had changed hands than in any previous week in the whole history of the New York Stock Exchange. One did not have to listen long to an after-dinner conversation, whether in New York or San Francisco or the lowliest village of the plain, to realize that all sorts of people to whom the stock ticker had been a hitherto alien mystery were carrying a hundred shares of Studebaker or Houston Oil, learning the significance of such recondite symbols as GL and X and ITT, and whipping the early editions of afternoon papers to catch the 1.30 quotations from Wall Street . . .

'How many Americans actually held stock on margin during the

Frederick Lewis Allen, 'Only Yesterday', 1931

133

fabulous summer of 1929 there seems to be no way of computing, but it is probably safe to put the figure at more than a million ... The rich man's chauffeur drove with his ears laid back to catch the news of an impending move in Bethlehem Steel; he held fifty shares himself on a twenty-point margin. The window-cleaner at the broker's office paused to watch the ticker, for he was thinking of putting his laboriously accumulated savings into a few shares of Simmons. Edwin Lefevre told of a broker's valet who had made nearly a quarter of a million in the market, of a trained nurse who cleaned up thirty thousand following the tips given her by grateful patients; and of a Wyoming cattleman, thirty miles from the nearest railroad, who bought or sold a thousand shares a day — getting his market returns by radio and telephoning his orders to the nearest town to be transmitted to New York by telegram. An ex-actress in New York fitted up her Park Avenue apartment as an office and surrounded herself with charts, graphs, and financial reports, playing the market by telephone on an increasing scale and with increasing abandon. Across the dinner table one heard fantastic stories of sudden fortunes: a young banker had put every dollar of his small capital into Niles-Bement-Pond and was now fixed for life; a widow had been able to buy a large country house with her winnings in Kennecott. Thousands speculated — and won too — without the slightest knowledge of the nature of the company upon whose fortunes they were relying, like the people who bought Seaboard Air Line under the impression that it was an aviation stock. Grocers, motor-men, plumbers, seamstresses, and speakeasy waiters were in the market ... The Big Bull Market had become a national mania ...

'Thursday, October 24th ... On that momentous day stocks opened moderately steady in price, but in enormous volume. Kennecott appeared on the tape in a block of 20,000 shares, General Motors in another of the same amount. Almost at once the ticker tape began to lag behind the trading on the floor. The pressure of selling orders was disconcertingly heavy. Prices were going down ... Presently they were going down with some rapidity ... Before the first hour of trading was over, it was already apparent that they were going down with an altogether unprecedented and amazing violence. In brokers' offices all over the country, tape-watchers looked at one another in astonishment and perplexity. Where on earth was this torrent of selling orders coming from? ...

'As the price structure crumbled there was a sudden stampede to get out from under. By eleven o'clock traders on the floor of the Stock Exchange were in a wild scramble to "sell at the market". Long before the lagging ticker could tell what was happening, word had gone out by telephone and telegraph that the bottom was dropping out of things, and the selling orders redoubled in volume. The leading stocks were going down two, three, and even five points between sales. Down, down, down . . . Where were the bargain-hunters who were supposed to come to the rescue at times like this? Where were the investment trusts, which were expected to provide a cushion for the market by making new purchases at low prices? Where were the big operators who had declared that they were still bullish? Where were the powerful bankers who were supposed to be able at any moment to support prices? There seemed to be no support whatever. Down, down, down. The roar of voices which rose from the floor of the Exchange had become a roar of panic . . .

'The Big Bull Market was dead. Billions of dollars' worth of profits — and paper profits — had disappeared. The grocer, the window-cleaner, and the seamstress had lost their capital. In every town there were families which had suddenly dropped from showy affluence into debt. Investors who had dreamed of retiring to live on their fortunes now found themselves back once more at the very beginning of the long road to riches. Day by day the newspapers printed the grim reports of suicides.

'Coolidge–Hoover prosperity was not yet dead, but it was dying . . . Americans were soon to find themselves living in an altered world which called for new adjustments, new ideas, new habits of thought, and a new order of values. The psychological climate was changing; the ever-shifting currents of American life were turning into new channels.

'The post-war decade had come to its close. An era had ended.'

❡ In America itself the effects were terrifying. There seemed no way out of the abyss:

'The depression seemed endless. Each month the number of un-employed mounted till it reached 14,000,000. Each month more and more farm mortgages were foreclosed, and the farmers rose in something like armed rebellion, threatening to hang judges who issued decrees. Each year millions of children left school to hunt for a diminishing number of jobs. Hundreds of thousands of boys and

D. W. Brogan, 'Picture Post', December 11th, 1954

135

tens of thousands of girls took to the road, entered what were called the "Hobo jungles" by the railroad tracks where they lived in semi-savage and semi-criminal conditions. Unemployed veterans of the First World War marched on Washington and had to be dispersed by the Army. Banks, big and small, failed all over the Union. Insurance companies were badly threatened. Building stopped, housing rapidly deteriorated, and an enterprising reporter found people literally living in caves in Central Park, in the heart of the richest city in the world.

'Many cities went bankrupt. Chicago could not pay its teachers for over a year. Schools were shut down or remained open without heat and without proper repairs. The strain on family life was very great, for the rigours of the poor law forced any working member of a family to keep his kinfolk. Hundreds of thousands drifted back to the land, usually from desperate poverty in the cities to hardly less desperate poverty in the countryside. Evicted unemployed took refuge in shanties bitterly called "Hoovervilles". The most representative song was no longer a cheery ballad in the manner of the gay 'twenties, but "Brother, can you spare a dime?" '

¶ The effects of the American financial collapse were felt all over the world:

Gerald Heard, 'These Hurrying Years', 1934 'The crash of 1929 continued even more crashingly into 1930. From the beginning of the collapse, late in September, 1929, to the end of that October the United States citizens lost 50 billion dollars, a sum five times more than all those debts the erstwhile Allies still owed America. On one day, 23rd October, sixteen million shares were sold — a record which broke by 100 per cent the former "biggest ever" crash. Three million unemployed resulted . . . 1930 . . . witnessed a second crash and one that buckled the very props of the economic life. Not only did millions of private people's bank accounts vanish. The bankers themselves began to go. Only 400 broke in 1929; 13,000 collapsed in 1930 . . . Material wealth had not been destroyed. All the misery and ruin was due not to an economic fact but to a psychological state of mind. Credit had been shaken, and credit, it was proved, though not a material fact, can nevertheless give such seismic shocks to the material property of millions that they may be reduced to begging their bread and finding none to give it them.'

¶ In Great Britain unemployment was intensified; and many men had been unemployed for years:

136

'There are men of forty-five and even less who have to face a future *Cicely Hamilton, 'Modern England', 1938* without hope of regular employment. A few months ago I was in a northern district where such "elderly" unemployed abound and where, accordingly, a centre had been started to give them occupation and interest; when I enquired what was the age qualification for admission to membership, I was told that the rule was, no member under thirty-five! Thirty-five — and no liklihood of permanent employment . . . The plain fact being that, in England of today, many men and women are only past work because the work is not there for them to take.'

¶ The situation was particularly bad in South Wales:

'I gazed out of my hotel bedroom at P —— in South Wales. The *'The Sphere', February 28th, 1931* sight . . . was one of the most doleful I have ever seen in my life. It consisted chiefly of this: Men — obviously dressed in their Sunday best — standing with their hands in their pockets along the street kerb. Just standing . . . I knew that if I asked some of them, they would tell me they were "waiting for something to pass by" — a chance to run an errand, or do something to earn a few pence. Others, especially the men over thirty-five (and they are becoming bitter realists now) would answer they were waiting for the Old Age Pension to come along.

'These were some of the 15,000 hale, hearty, and capable miners of X (a population of about 104,000 people) who will probably never go down a mine shaft again in their lives. A problematical chance of improved markets will be met by nationalisation; and it was the conclusion of practically every one I talked with in that "valley of despair" that, unless there is found some way to drain them off, there will always remain about that number of unemployed . . . One man when I asked him what he looked forward to said: "I am just lingering. That's it — lingering."

'There is one question, especially after you have been among them for a time, that you will never ask these miners in South Wales; and that is whether they would rather work or live on the Dole. That peculiar dead-alive look in their faces as they stand in the streets is enough to save you from that.'

¶ It was equally deplorable in the North, in places like Jarrow:

Cicely Hamilton,
'Modern England',
1938
'When I visited Jarrow in the depth of its worklessness it was not for the first time; I knew the Tyneside well in my younger days, when all along the river you were never out of hearing of the clang, clang, clang, of hammers from the shipyard. At the best of times — the busiest and the most prosperous — Jarrow was not an attractive place for the stranger; its streets had been built in response to the industrial needs of the nineteenth century and were as dreary and grubby-looking as most of the streets that were built at that period, for that purpose. But when I first knew it there was bustle of activity in those dreary, grubby streets; men going about their work, women going about their shopping, the baker and the grocer busy with their customers; a squalid town like so many in the north, but alive!

'On my last visit I was taken to see an exhibit in urban lifelessness; a street which had once been a shopping centre of the town, tenanted by bakers and grocers and drapers, and where now almost every trader had despaired and put up his shutters. It reminded me of some deserted town in the war zone; there were back streets in it that looked much like that when I saw them shortly after the Armistice. Between thirty and forty, I think, was the number of shops that had closed in that little street; their shutters the outward and visible sign of broken homes and hopes.'

¶ Some of the individual stories make very sad reading:

H. L. Beales and
R. S. Lambert,
'Memoirs of the
Unemployed', 1934
'A SKILLED ENGINEER'S TRAGEDY

'I am an engineer by trade, forty-seven years of age, married and the father of one child. Until four years ago I worked for a large engineering firm in the North Midlands. I had worked for this firm for many years, but owing to loss of contracts the firm was compelled to close down and I found myself unemployed for the first time in my life. Up to this time I had lived the life of an ordinary respectable artisan. I earned the standard rate of wage, round about £3 a week, and maintained a decent house at a rent of 15s. 3d. I have been happily married some twenty years and was devoted to my wife and child. My activities were divided between home, garden and public affairs. I had held every office possible in my trade union branch. I took a keen interest in politics both locally and nationally.

'During the first months of unemployment I felt confident in being able to find another job. I received unemployment pay and a few shillings weekly from my trade union. But the trade union's funds were low and this latter source of income ceased after a few months. Nevertheless, by the aid of our little savings we were able to get along . . .

'After a year of vain efforts I decided to accept any job I could get . . . but I soon found that outside my trade I could get nothing . . . In the meantime my wife . . . obtained a job as house to house saleswoman, and was able to earn a few shillings to supplement our dole income. It was from this time that the feeling of strain which was beginning to appear in our home life became more marked . . . Life became more and more strained. There were constant bickerings over money matters . . . The final blow came when the Means Test was put into operation . . . Quarrels broke out anew and bitter things were said. Eventually, after the most heartbreaking period of my life, both my wife and son, who had just commenced to earn a few shillings, told me to get out, as I was living on them and taking the food they needed.

'I left and took with me a little furniture. I rented an unfurnished bedroom for 4s. 6d. a week in the house of an unemployed man who had a wife and three children. This happened some fifteen months ago. Since then I have drawn 15s. 3d. weekly from the dole and have had to sell every bit of furniture I had . . . and try to exist on 8s. 0d. a week for food. I have never been able to afford coal for a fire . . . The outlook as far as I am concerned is hopeless. I've given up dreaming of any return to my former life and work, and just hang on hoping something big will happen before I die.'

¶ That was the tragedy. The unemployed gradually became unemployable:

'The moral fibre of the unemployed cannot resist either the life they are now leading, or the complacency with which it is accepted. A feeling of slackness pervades the atmosphere; inspectors report that they often find the inveterate unemployed stretched out in bed during the day. For these left-overs, hour follows hour with nothing to do except an occasional visit to the Labour Exchange to see if by chance there is a job to be had. Finally, all effort, aptitude, and energy are benumbed.'

André Siegfried, 'England's Crisis', 1931

¶ A young poet gave poignant expression to the prevailing despair:

Stephen Spender, 'Collected Poems', 1955

'Moving through the silent crowd
Who stand behind dull cigarettes,
These men who idle in the road,
I have the sense of falling light.

'They lounge at corners of the street
And greet friends with a shrug of shoulder
And turn their empty pockets out,
The cynical gestures of the poor.

'Now they've no work, like better men
Who sit at desks and take much pay,
They sleep long nights and rise at ten
To watch the hours that drain away.

'I'm jealous of the weeping hours
They stare through with such hungry eyes.
I'm haunted by these images,
I'm haunted by their emptiness.'

¶ This, however sincere, was the outsider's view. Here is another account from one of those actually affected:

H. L. Beales and R. S. Lambert, 'Memoirs of the Unemployed', 1934

'A SOUTH WALES MINER

'It was in June 1927, that I first began to draw unemployment benefit at the rate of £1 9s. 0d. a week. At that time my eldest boy, who was then fifteen, had not started work as he could not find a job . . . until at last the manager of one colliery told him he would give him a start because he was ashamed to keep turning him away. He is still working at the same colliery . . . his wages being 15s. a week, which made our income up to £2 4s. 0d. and enabled us to buy him some clothes. After paying our rent we still had £1 15s. 0d. a week to live on. Then my second son came out of school and found he could not get work, but he went to the training centre and there eventually got work. His wage was 15s. too, so that we had £2 10s. 0d. after allowing for rent . . .

'My unemployment benefit came to an end in March, 1932, when

140

I was disallowed because I had not qualified for the necessary contributory period of thirty weeks. After this I was given a food ticket for 23s. a week, which continued until January, 1933, when it was stopped because of the Means Test. Before the stoppage our income was over the minimum limit of £2 17s. 6d. So now we have to depend on the boys and they have to keep all six of us, including my wife and the two children who are still going to school . . .

'What effect has unemployment had on me? It has definitely lessened my interest in politics, because it has led me to believe that politics is a game of bluff, and that these people do not care a brass farthing for the bottom dog . . . the same applies to the trade unions; when it comes to the real test they are hopeless.'

¶ Despair of the politicians! It is a dangerous mood. For what were the bemused and wretched men to do?

'Any leader could have been excused for confusion and puzzlement concerning the economic situation of 1929–31. But MacDonald was more avuncular, more eloquent, more uplifting in his confusions than any man of his generation . . . George Lansbury (*le bon vieux papa* of the Party), who became for a short time leader of the Parliamentary party after the Great Schism, when the crash came simply chanted the Party hymns. All would be solved when we had "complete socialism and power as well as office. Let's sing the Red Flag." Tom Mosley had already shaken off the dust of the Party and began his Fascist experiment. What one saw of his character made one shudder; its arrogant angers and intolerances, and hint of utter ruthlessness . . . John Strachey flirted with the nascent Fascist organization and seemed to oscillate between it and the Communists . . . Dalton, when it came to the Schism, could talk of it all with the best of the demagogues as just another bankers' ramp.'

Sir Norman Angell, 'After All', 1951

¶ Well! England got the Baldwin–MacDonald Coalition; America got Roosevelt and the New Deal; and Germany got — Hitler. But that is a subject for another chapter.

141

CHAPTER VII

ICH HATT' EINEN KAMERADEN

THE BRITISH PEOPLE had been aware of Mussolini since 1922, the year of the March on Rome. On the whole they — at least those of them who were sufficiently prosperous to go for holidays to Italy — approved of him. 'He made the trains run on time' — that was the accepted phrase. No one foresaw that a movement similar to his might arise in Germany.

Visitors to that country were impressed by its *pacifism*. The typical German phenomenon was thought to be the Wandervögel:

Cicely Hamilton
'Modern Germanies',
1931
'Interest in things German is general nowadays and we are most of us aware of the existence of a *Jugendbewegung*. We are not, however, as a rule aware of its scope; outside Germany it is often assumed that the Youth Movement means the peregrinations of the Wandervögel only; of its many other aims and activities the foreigner, at any rate the British foreigner, seems to have little understanding. And even as regards the Wandervögel his ideas are frequently more picturesque than accurate; he imagines them wandering over forest and fen as irresponsibly as the birds their namesakes; strolling hither and thither as the spirit moves them, sharing pot-luck and finding shelter in barns; creatures of impulse and taking no thought for the morrow! Whereas, in reality, the goings and comings of these migratory young people, like the generality of Teutonic activities, are systematized, very neatly and carefully systematized. As indeed they have to be — considering the dimensions of the movement and the number of young people who take their pleasure afoot . . .

'The *Jugendvereine* . . . are producing — there cannot be a doubt of it — a marked effect upon the energy and health of the race. It is thanks, in part at least, to the training of these Youth Associations

142

that the direct effects of the War are being overcome and a generation that might have been sickly is winning back its sturdiness . . .

'It would be idle, however, to shut one's eyes to the reverse of the medal; more than once of late I have heard the opinion expressed that there is a danger in the Youth Movement which may be summed up in the one word, Politics.'

¶ Mr. John Mander sums it up even more neatly:

'The "Wandervögel" movement, founded in Berlin in the years before the First World War . . . was a more romantic edition of the Boy Scouts . . . Its attitudes were un-Prussian in the extreme and were part of a much wider revolt against the "world of the Father" reflected in such Expressionist plays as Hasenclever's *The Son* or Arnoldt Bronnen's *Patricide*. Wandervögel was libertarian and individualistic, and more concerned with free love than with free speech. But while the Youth Movement was romantically unpolitical in its beginnings its post-war successors were to become more and more the protégés and later the instruments of the political parties.'

John Mander, 'Berlin: The Eagle and the Bear', 1959

¶ Troops of quite young children were to be seen marching about on Sundays preceded by the Red Flag. There was also a junior branch of the Stahlhelm, originally an association of ex-soldiers. And there was something else of which the British people had hardly yet heard:

'The other formation which, like Communism and Stahlhelm has no difficulty in attracting the enthusiasm of youth is National Social-ism, the party which made a sudden leap into strength at the General Election of 1930. Its full name and title is National-Socialist-German-Workers'-Party which being impossible for everyday use, is mercifully shortened to Nazi. The Nazis are also dubbed Fascists, especially by the foreign Press; but they do not seem to apply the name to them-selves though they would hardly deny their kinship with Mussolini's followers — the Brown Shirt has certainly derived from the Black and they use the Fascist salutation. Their badge is the Hakenkreuz (the hooked cross, which we call the Swastika) and the younger section, the counterpart of Mussolini's Avanguardisti, is usually known as the Hitlerjugend, from the leader of the party, Adolf Hitler. When the Nazis walked abroad in their uniform, they were Brown Shirts to themselves and others; but if the Brown Shirt uniform continues to

Cicely Hamilton, 'Modern Germanies', 1931

be forbidden in Prussia and Bavaria — the larger part of Germany —
it is possible the name will lapse . . .

'With the possible exception of their enemies the Communists,
these Brown Shirts, or ex-Brown Shirts, are the most striking example
of youth trained to partisan thinking. I hasten to add that, so far as I
have seen them, they are not an unfavourable example. Their doctrine
may be dangerous and their methods provocative but the lads
themselves — so far as I have seen them — are of clean, upstanding
type.'

¶ It is odd in retrospect to reflect that what had attracted the English
intellectuals to Germany in the late 'twenties was its *left*-wing
atmosphere.

Goronwy Rees,   'It is hard now, nearly thirty years later, to explain even to myself
'A Bundle of   the kind of attraction which Germany exerted on young men of my
Sensations', 1960   generation at Oxford . . . To try to recover the original image of
Weimar Germany by which I, and so many others, were attracted is
like trying to restore some lost masterpiece which has been painted
over by a succession of brutal and clumsy artists; and in this case the
task is all the harder because the masterpiece never really existed
and the Germany of Weimar in which we believed was really only a
country of the imagination.

'First of all, one would have to reconstruct the illusions under
which we suffered at the time; the illusion, for instance, that in the
war of 1914–18 there was no distinction of guilt between the Allies
and the Central Powers . . . to which we added the emotional and
irrational corollary that somehow or other the defeated were less
responsible than the victors. In this illusion we were happily con-
firmed by reading Brandenburg, Lowes Dickinson and Sidney Fay . . .

'We were all agreed, therefore, that the terms of the Treaty were
unjust; it was equally obvious that they were futile. This illusion was
firmly founded on Maynard Keynes's *Economic Consequences of the
Peace* . . .

'To those who said that, whether the Treaty was just or unjust,
Germany might one day try to redress her defeat by force or arms,
we replied scornfully . . . For did not the League of Nations, supported by all the power of the Allies, exist to prevent the recurrence
of war . . . Even if the League, as an instrument of Anglo–French
capitalism, could not be trusted, was it not clear that there was an

144

Eldorado Night Club, Berlin: Four of the 'ladies' are men

Hitler taking the salute at a parade of Brown Shirts, early 'thirties.

Hitler taking the salute at a military parade, mid 'thirties.

even stronger foundation for our belief in the maintenance of perpetual peace between nations? For the real bulwark of the peace was not the League but the international working-class movement, and was not Germany, with its massive trade union and social democratic organization, the strongest representative of that movement?

'In saying this, of course, we were expressing our feelings just as much about our own country as about her defeated enemy. To sympathize with Germany was a mark of revulsion against the Great War and its consequences, and against the generation which had helped to make it and to conduct it to victory. Germany was for us at the opposite extreme from everything we disliked in the land of our fathers . . . and to adhere to her cause and her culture was for many of us the most effective and the easiest protest we could make against the England of Mr. Stanley Baldwin, Lord Birkenhead, and Sir William Joynson-Hicks.

'For politics were only a part of our infatuation with Germany. Weimar also represented to us all those experiments, in literature, in the theatre, in music, in education, and not least in sexual morals, which we would have liked to attempt in our own country but were so patently impossible in face of the massive and infuriating stupidity of the British middle classes . . .

'We received reports of these experiments not only through the Press, through German films, through books, but by word of mouth. Ever since the inflation young Englishmen had visited Germany in greater and greater numbers, and they returned to us in Oxford with wonderful travellers' tales of this land of freedom and, even better, of licence; where one could be on the right side, the proletarian side, in politics, and at the same time take advantage of the fact that social disapproval had ceased to exist; where morals had been discarded as a bourgeois prejudice; where sex was permitted, even encouraged to take any form it chose, however eccentric; where night-club tables were decorated with phalli made of marzipan . . .

'I was very much a creature of fashion; I found the attraction of Germany irresistible; and so, in my first year at Oxford, I determined that in the summer vacation I too must make the pilgrimage to Weimar and Wedding to see the whores and the queers and the Lesbians on the Kurfürstendamm, observe the violence and confusion of German politics at first hand, so that I might have at least some idea of what politics were like if they were properly conducted; I too must tramp in the Black Forest with the Wandervögel, and breathe

the inexpressibly sweet air of a society in decay . . . I used to wonder bitterly why I could not win scholarships to maintain myself in some *Nachtlokal* in Berlin instead of in the Wykehamist respectability of New College.'

¶ Mr. Rees, in his fascinating book, describes his disappointment at finding himself, not in left-wing Berlin but in a family of Prussian Junkers. And what were the Junkers doing?

John Mander,
'Berlin: The Eagle
and the Bear', 1959 'The *Junkers* had followed their *Kaiser* into voluntary political exile. They retired to their country estates in Pomerania and East Prussia where they occupied themselves with hunting, shooting and fishing until better days should return. And their absence from the political scene was Hitler's chance. He had only to mobilize the little men from the provinces and to impose their will on the vacillating centre. The German people who had been accustomed to receiving orders from Berlin in the past, longed to receive orders again from an authoritarian centre. Hitler did not succeed in marching on Berlin in 1923 as Mussolini had marched on Rome; but organization was to succeed where force had failed. Red Berlin was not taken by storm, it was swallowed whole by the provinces.'

¶ While the Junkers were biding their time, Hitler was getting on with the job. But who was Hitler? What kind of a man was he? He was born at Braunau in Austria, the son of an 'Inspector of Customs' (in fact a humble *douanier*) and his father wished him to be a Government official too. But Adolf had what is called the artistic temperament. He wanted to be a painter and, after his father's death, he went to Vienna and sought admission to the Academy of Art. He was refused 'for want of talent' so, miserably poor, he became a painter in another sense, i.e. a house painter. It was in Vienna that his character and ideas began to take shape.

Philip Guedalla,
'The Hundredth
Year', 1940 'The War was fifteen years away when Adolf Hitler rose to power. But his reflections on his country's fate were largely a war-time production. Before the war this son of an Austrian *douanier* passed through an undistinguished youth with an increasing sense that he was not as other men. Two bound volumes of an old illustrated paper filled his mind with the events of 1870, with images of war and military power. A random course of reading gradually imparted to the

growing youth the deadly certainties of the uneducated. As an Austrian, he felt an envious inferiority to Bismarck's Germany. Why should he be denied a share in the glories of St. Privat and Sedan? Why could not all Germans be members of one glorious community? It was quite natural for a provincial lad in Upper Austria to have such feelings. They lived so near the frontier of Bavaria and had so much more in common with their German neighbours than with many of their fellow-subjects in the Dual Monarchy. For as Austrians they were compelled to share their politics with unintelligible Czechs and questionable Magyars and even more exotic elements. But just across the German border there were people who spoke German like themselves. It was almost inevitable that a provincial upbringing in Linz should make him a Pan–German; and when he tried his fortunes in Vienna the same lesson was enforced by much that he encountered in the capital. For on the pavements of Vienna he discovered those Jewish fellow-subjects who were so painfully unlike himself. He noted how they dressed and how they cut their hair, and asked himself how anyone who looked so odd could really be a German. Their dissimilarities offended his provincial taste for German uniformity . . . Already a Pan–German, he now found himself an anti-Semite!'

¶ When the War came he welcomed it. He was then living in Munich and he joined a Bavarian regiment. He served throughout the conflict and claimed afterwards that he had been awarded the Iron Cross. At least he always wore it on ceremonial occasions, but he does not mention it in *Mein Kampf* and, as hostile critics have pointed out, 'it was only a very stupid ranker in the four years of decimation on the Western Front, who did not receive, if he survived, promotion above the rank of orderly-corporal, and that for one who had been awarded the Iron Cross to fail to do so was quite incredible.'

However that may be, at the end of the War, Hitler found himself back in Munich. The Bavarian Socialists had set up a Government of their own, the so-called 'Bavarian Free State' with an East Prussian Jew, Eisner, as President. Eisner was assassinated, and the Communists tried to set up a 'Soviet Republic'. This was brought to an end by an Army *putsch* and the right-wing separatist Kahr was appointed as Governor.

Hitler was already involved in these events. While the Workers' and Soldiers' Councils were still in control he 'resolved to become a politician'. In plain language he became a police spy.

Anon., 'Heil', 1932 'It was a day of splinters and petty sects, of eccentrics among parties, and among these tiny groups was one tinier than others, the little German Workers' Party of Anton Breder, the locksmith, with his friend Feder, the engineer, who had discovered the solution of the world's ills in the "breaking of interest-servitude". To a meeting of this party Hitler allowed himself to be sent by his superior officers in the Reichswehr to make a report. Feder interested him, and he joined it. His fees of membership were paid by the Reichswehr and the materials for his first lecture to it — on Brest–Litovsk — were supplied him by his officers.'

¶ Hitler admired Gottfried Feder and even copied his toothbrush moustache. He saw that Feder's ideas could be used as the platform of a re-constituted party which would not be content to discuss politics in beer halls, but would act. The name was changed, under Hitler's influence — he had now got himself elected to the committee — to the National Socialist German Workers' Party, or Nazi for short. The military men saw that Hitler could be useful to them:

Anon., 'Heil', 1932 'Under the patronage of three prominent members of the Bavarian Government apparatus, Epp, of the Reichswehr, Pöhner the Police President and Frick, head of the political section of the police, the little party grew and flourished. With Epp's help, Roehm, also from the Reichswehr, gathered in an army of mercenaries and terrorists. Pöhner and Frick saw to it that the activities of these in popularising Hitler's oratory and smashing opponents' meetings were undisturbed. In 1923 discussions took place with Kahr, with a view to a putsch to establish a separate Bavarian Kingdom. "Yes, excellency, it is due most decidedly to the monarchy, sacrificed so shamefully by the November criminals of 1918, that a serious injustice should be atoned. If your excellency will agree, I myself will proceed directly from this meeting to His Majesty (Prince Rupprecht) and inform him that, by means of the German resurrection, the injustice upon his late father will be made good." '

Wickham Steed, 'That Bad Man', 1942 'Hitler . . . always meant to be number one . . . and to use the Bavarian Government as his tool instead of being used as a tool by von Kahr and the army officers. At that time General Ludendorff had come to Munich and had linked up with Hitler. A famous, and rascally, German airman, named Captain Hermann Goering, had also joined the Nazi party . . .

'*I am a Jew but I* will *not grumble about the Nazis.*'

Hitler addressing 20,000 Nazis at the Sportspalast, Berlin, 1938.

'Hitler thought he could do in Germany what Mussolini had done in Italy. But von Kahr and von Lossow (the military member of the Government) forbade him to start a revolution on May 1st, 1923; and Hitler had given them his "word of honour" that he would do nothing except under their orders . . .

'Von Kahr [and] von Lossow . . . made up their minds not to work with Hitler . . . Hitler seems to have felt that things were not going well. He heard that von Kahr had turned against him [and] . . . thought he had better run away. Ludendorff wouldn't hear of it, saying that no German soldier would fire a shot against him, the great commander of the war, and that Hitler with his Storm Troops must seize the Government buildings. Then the people, who looked on Hitler as a national hero, would rise and all would be well.

'So, at midday, Ludendorff, Hitler, Goering, Roehm and 2,000 Nazis marched through the city to the big square while the people cheered them. On the big square they found armed police drawn up. Somebody fired a shot. A Nazi rushed forward to order the police not to shoot at Ludendorff. The police fired all the same. Fourteen Nazis fell. Ludendorff, who was not hit, passed through the police ranks and was arrested. Goering was wounded but managed to escape. Hitler threw himself on the ground so furiously that he hurt his shoulder. Then he picked himself up, ran away and took refuge in a friend's house where the police caught him and put him in prison. There he was kept until he, Ludendorff and seven others were tried for high treason by a Munich court. The trial lasted a month, from February 26th to March 27th, 1924. Hitler was sentenced to the lowest possible punishment for high treason — five years' imprisonment in a fortress. Ludendorff was declared innocent; and even Hitler was set free after six months.'

¶ Hitler had to wait for eleven years to have his revenge on Kahr. On July 1st, 1934, Kahr's body was found near Munich chopped to pieces with hatchets.

Meanwhile, Hitler's confinement was far from rigorous:

'I spent my period of detention in the fortress of Landsberg, where *Adolf Hitler,* I was treated by everyone, from the governor down to the warders, *'Mein Kampf'* with the greatest politeness and together with my friend Hess wrote my memoirs and drew up the programme of the National Socialist German Workers' Party. Later I presented this programme to some of the Fatherlands' industrialists and bankers, and after precise elucidation received their enthusiastic applause.'

¶ These are the closing words of *Mein Kampf*.

Wickham Steed, 'That Bad Man', 1942 'Little by little a good many business men [gave] him money when he told them that he wasn't really a Socialist at all, that he wanted to save Germany from having to pay any more reparations, and to smash the Jews, Socialists and Communists. He also got money from abroad. The head of a big Anglo–Dutch Oil Company, some of whose oil wells had been taken by the Russian Bolsheviks, paid him to go on cursing the Bolsheviks. A rich American who hated the Jews paid him to go on cursing the Jews. With this money Hitler began to live like a prince, to drive about in big motor cars and to make people believe that his pockets were full. Yet they weren't really full until an old German business man named Kirdoff made up his mind that Hitler could help the big German iron and steel makers to get rich by selling secretly guns and other weapons for a new German army. Through Kirdoff, and Kirdoff's business friends, Hitler got as much as £4 millions in a year.'

¶ It would be outside our purpose to follow all the labyrinthine intrigues which brought Adolf Hitler to power in Germany. It is enough to note that there came a time when Hitler had to choose. The price he had to pay for the support of the generals and the big industrialists was the liquidation of his own left-wing. This is how it was done:

Wickham Steed, 'That Bad Man', 1942 'You remember that it was Captain Roehm who first helped Hitler at Munich. It was Roehm who then began to get together and to drill gangs of Nazis, and who used them to break the heads of people at Hitler's meetings. It was Roehm who formed them into Storm Troops; and it was he who, when Hitler was hard up, tried to get money for them by pawning them to the Army. Then, in 1925, Hitler quarrelled with Roehm because Hitler wanted to keep the Storm Troops for himself and not let the Army use them. So Roehm went off to Bolivia in South America and trained the Bolivian army. In 1930 Hitler called him back, and Roehm obliged. He built up the Storm Troops again; and when Hitler got the iron and steel makers to give enough money, Roehm soon had half a million Storm Troops under his command.

He really was a smart soldier, though he was a brutal fellow with such rude beastly habits that Hitler often got into trouble because of them. A good many other Nazis wanted Hitler to turn Roehm out of the Nazi party, especially Goering, who thought Roehm was getting too strong. But Hitler wouldn't do it. He still found him useful.

'Things began to change after Hitler became Chancellor and had begun to make himself master of Germany. Then the number of Storm Troops grew until there were three millions of them. By 1933 most of them were oldish fellows in shabby uniforms who looked more like rabble than real soldiers. They were jealous of the smart young Black Guards who watched over Hitler and they were disappointed because Hitler had not given them the well-paid jobs they would have liked to have . . .

'On April 8th, 1933, Hitler had told them in a broadcast speech: "I will be true to you to the last drop of my blood". This didn't stop their grumbling. They talked among themselves of a second Nazi revolution, a really bloody one this time, whether Hitler wanted it or not . . . Roehm wanted the Storm Troops to be taken into the Regular Army, with himself as a General in command of them. Hitler's Defence Minister, General von Blomberg, wouldn't hear of this . . . So Hitler had to make up his mind whether to go with Roehm and use the Storm Troops to swamp the Army or whether to go with the Army and smash up the Storm Troops . . .

'Hitler told Roehm that as soon as old President von Hindenburg was dead, there would be a second revolution which the Storm Troops would carry through. He advised Roehm to take a holiday in June, and to call together the Storm Troop leaders on June 30th at a place near Munich where Hitler would join them . . .

'At two o'clock on the morning of June 30th Hitler got into an aeroplane with Goebbels at Godesberg and landed the same morning at four o'clock, on the Munich aerodrome. At Munich he had a few people put in prison. Then he ordered five car-loads of Black Guards and Gestapo, or Secret Police, to drive with him to a place called Wiessee where Roehm was staying. A well-known Nazi murderer, Edward Heines, and several other Storm Troop leaders were staying there too. Roehm had been expecting Hitler to come at midday to join the meeting of Storm Troop leaders which he had told Roehm to get together. Roehm, Heines and the others had got drunk the evening before; Hitler found them in bed. He cursed Roehm and had him handcuffed. Then he told the Black Guards to take Roehm back to their barracks at Munich, to lock him up there in a cell and to leave him a revolver with a single cartridge in it, so that Roehm might shoot himself. Heines and some of the other drunken leaders were shot by the Gestapo or the Black Guards as they slept. The rest were taken to Munich and shot there. Finding that after some hours Roehm had not shot himself, Hitler had him dragged out of the cell and shot.

'On the way back from Wiessee to Munich, Hitler and Goebbels, with their procession of cars, met a number of other cars that were bringing Storm Troop leaders to the expected meeting with Roehm and Hitler. These cars were stopped and ordered to follow Hitler back to Munich. There most of the men in them were taken into the courtyard of the Munich prison and shot. One of them was killed because he knew too much ... and dozens of others who were known as the oldest comrades of Hitler, were shot one after the other ...

'The exact number was never known. So many people vanished in those days, and weren't heard of again, that nobody could tell what had become of them. A list was drawn up some time afterwards. There were 1,183 names on it. Still, it wasn't certain that all the names were there. Hitler said at first that fewer than fifty "comrades" had been killed ...

'On July 13th he said in a long speech to his Nazi Parliament — where a good many seats of the butchered Nazis were empty — that seventy-six had been killed. "Mutineers", he shouted, "are crushed according to eternal, iron laws. I was responsible for the fate of the German nation. Therefore I myself was for twenty four hours the Supreme Judge of the German people . . ." Old President von Hindenburg telegraphed his best greetings and deepest thanks to Hitler for having "smothered the germs of treason". The Minister of Justice declared that what Hitler had done was not only lawful but his duty as a statesman. And a Protestant Bishop held a thanksgiving service at which he preached a sermon telling everybody to thank God for the salvation of the German Church and people by Hitler's manly action. He prayed that God might protect the Leader and give him strength to carry through his great work.'

Anon., 'Heil', 1932

'Why did Hitler slay such a man [as Roehm]? The excuse for the widespread slaughter of June 30th was that the victims were plotting together. This explanation could last just until their names became known and not a moment longer . . . To offer an analogy for the

English reader, it was as though Mosley had slain on pretext of a joint plot, Baldwin, Maxton, Lord Lloyd, the Bishop of London and the trunk murderer. It was just faintly conceivable that the professional soldiers and terrorists, like Roehm, Heines, Schmidt, Hayn might have made some contact with "left-wing" Nazi elements like Strasser, or conservative intriguers like Schleicher, but to allege that these could have the faintest connection with Jung and Bose, Papen's associates, with Dr. Klausener, President of the "Catholic Action", with the aged von Kahr (never forgiven by the Nazis for his prevention of the Munich putsch), with Dr. Beck of the International Students' Exchange, with Dr. Walter Lütgebrune, defending council to Ludendorff in his trial with Hitler, or that this or any could have plotted with the Communist poet Mühsam, safely in prison for eighteen months past, is to snap the limits of the plausible. Yet all these and others died. The very names of the victims proved that, whatever its inception, June 30th was in execution a night of private vengeance.'

¶ Why did the German people put up with such a man?

'Hitler was something new at the time when millions of Germans felt that things could anyway scarcely be worse than they were. Hitler could afford to offer everybody everything: socialism to the workers, nationalism to the bourgeoisie, violence to would-be rebels as well as strict authority to those who had wearied of a generation of revolt . . . *John Mander, 'Berlin: The Eagle and the Bear', 1959*

'New above all . . . was the apocalyptic note. *"Das Dritte Reich"* is a concept that can be traced back to Joachim de Flora in the thirteenth century, a vision of a Third Kingdom of the Holy Ghost which has been cherished by generations of heretics and never quite died out. When the economic crisis broke out in 1929 and the anarchy of the inflationary period returned, the German people became more and more susceptible to this apocalyptic extremism. For a time the extreme Left and extreme Right seemed to be running neck and neck. But Communism had a fatal handicap; its revolution had already taken place and the German people had been able to observe it at fairly close range. The German people were sick of the class struggle, sick of unemployment, sick of capitalism, sick of the Jews, sick of democracy, and above all sick of Berlin, that modern Gomorrah and the source of all their ills. There is no great mystery about Hitler's coming to power. The simplest explanation is the best: the German people chose him.'

¶ Otto Dietrich, one-time Hitler's Press Chief, remarks:

Otto Dietrich,
'The Hitler I Knew',
1957
'In 1933 Hitler had said: "Give me four years." Since then he had provided millions with work and bread, had raised the standard throughout Germany. Why should the people distrust him? The people were, of course, aware that Hitler was vigorously rearming Germany. They saw that the preponderent reason for re-employment was armament contracts. But they also believed that the growing domestic strength of the Reich brought with it external dangers: they took it for granted that this rearmament was for defence.'

¶ But John Mander reminds us:

John Mander,
'Berlin: The Eagle
and the Bear', 1959
'It is as well to be frank about Nazi Germany in the 'thirties. For the average citizen these were happy years. Unemployment vanished, the currency became stable, there was greater social security and a new sense of national pride and prosperity . . . the man in the street got a reassuring impression of directed energy and reconstruction in public life and it would be foolish to deny that he preferred it to the anarchy of the Weimar period. Two products of the Third *Reich* impressed him particularly: the vast new airfield at Tempelhof and the Olympic Stadium . . . And the Berliners were not alone in praising the monster outlay for the Olympic Games in 1936. Anglo–Saxons came home full of enthusiasm for the bold planning of the new dictatorship and its appreciation of the values of sportsmanship. Berlin was a revelation: the shops so clean! The people so honest! The streets so full of purposeful activity! It was the Nazis' greatest triumph; all the world had come to honour the new Germany, and not a drop of foreign blood had yet been shed. For the Berliners, if they are frank, these were among the best years of their lives.'

¶ And so the Second World War became inevitable, and the stage was set for *Götterdämmerung*.

CHAPTER VIII

THE SUN WORSHIPPERS

NOTHING BRINGS HOME TO US more vividly the difference between the Edwardian Age and the period 'between the Wars' than remarks like the following:

' "My life is all a 'season'," was said by a very fashionable English- *'Graphic',* man some thiry years ago, and the statement was fastened on by the *June 8th, 1907* serious-minded of the time, who used it as a text for many meditations and reflections. There are hundreds of women in England today who could repeat the assertion, but the condition is comparatively so common that it would not occur to them to suppose the circumstance worth mentioning.

'There are the London season, from the middle of May to August; German–Bath season, from August to the middle of September; the country-house season from the middle of September to the middle of December; and the South of France season, from the middle of December to the middle of May. That programme regulates — more or less — the movements of several hundreds of men and women.'

¶ The South of France season from the middle of December to the middle of May! The 'several hundreds of men and women' fled to the South of France in order to escape the English winter; it had never occurred to anyone, except to the French *petite bourgeoisie* to visit the Riviera in summer.

It was, in the first place, supposed to be extremely unhealthy; and in the second place, it would have ruined the ladies' complexions. A lady never exposed the delicate bloom of her face — still less any other part of her body — to the direct rays of the sun. Veils and sunshades were *de rigeur*. A lady (it was taken for granted) had a white skin, and this notion is, of course, a very ancient one. It goes back to the days when it was easy to distinguish the peasant girl — the 'nut-brown maid — from the lady of the manor. Perhaps the sentiment was reinforced by the mem-sahibs of India who had no ambition to resemble the natives.

This fair-skin complex vanished after the First World War; and we can regard this as a victory for democracy, a reaction against the colour-bar, or an increased interest in health — as we please.

It had been found that the under-nourished German children, after the War, benefited by being exposed to sunlight, either real or artificial. Why should not healthy and quite well-fed people benefit also? Fresh air and sunlight was the cry and this seems sound enough. But some have thought that more than mere hygiene was involved:

Gerald Heard, 'These Hurrying Years', 1934

'Just below the level of full consciousness were the . . . changes in ideas of hygiene. Fresh air had won and pushed its victory against the curtain, blind, wrap and flounce so far that it began to pass the Plimsoll Line of prudery. A new issue was then joined, and the Hygienists, who till then had been allies of the Puritan, began to swing over towards the libertine. "To the pure all things are pure" was extended to the rather different and not so clear assumption that "to the naked all things are unexciting". It may be true, but up to the present passion prevents sufficient scientific experiment. What is clear is that the fresh-air campaign had ceased to be physiological and had become psychological. That change involved a discussion of issues much wider than costume, though to the psychologist costume had always been a clue to understanding the subconscious sex life. Quite sane and kindly people went on to ask not whether clothes helped chastity but whether chastity itself was helpful.'

¶ This passion for fresh air and sunlight led, in its extreme form, to nudism; in more moderate minds it led to smaller and smaller bathing costumes. But England took a long time to catch up:

James Laver, 'Taste and Fashion', 1937

'It is surprising how recent the extremely exiguous bathing costume is. Even in 1928 *Vogue* shows ladies bathing, or rather posing before a studio scene, in quite ample over-skirts and extremely limited décolletage . . .

'It was not sea-bathing, but sun-bathing which really effected a revolution in the form of bathing costumes. If it was really helpful to expose the skin to the action of sunlight, obviously the more you

156

Sports costume and walking costume, 1926.

Bathing costumes at Deauville, 1926.

could expose of it the better. Bathing costumes accordingly became shorter and shorter. The over-skirt in some instances disappeared altogether, or else was reduced to a dimension of two or three inches. The armholes grew larger and larger, and the décolletage more pronounced.

'In 1930 we get the first backless bathing costume, no more backless however, than the evening dresses of the period . . . In German bathing places before the Nazi reaction young girls often appeared in public wearing only shorts, leaving the breasts exposed; but this has never been allowed in England except in the privacy of sun-bathing societies. In Scandinavian countries men and women frequently bathe without any costumes at all, which is perhaps the only logical kind of bathing costume.'

¶ Nowadays we take near-nudity so much for granted on our bathing beaches that we have to remind ourselves that, as recently as the early 'thirties, it was unknown in England and created surprise and shock when seen abroad. Even so enlightened a person as Cicely Hamilton records her surprise during a visit to Germany:

'The tourist . . . will not have to look very far for examples of a scarcity of garment which, in England, would flutter the Puritan. One such example, I remember, I came on in the course of a walk; on the edge of a lake, in a district known as the Switzerland of the Mark, which is one of the favourite week-end resorts of the Berliner. Tramping through the woods that fringe the water, I rounded a miniature cape and found myself in a lakeside clearing and in the presence of a party of holiday campers. One member of the party, a middle-aged gentleman of protuberant figure, lay close beside my path and sunned himself contentedly, in a state of all but nakedness. He was clad in nothing but the very attenuated species of trunks which an acrobat wears above his tights. In this case, however, there were no tights. A few yards further on four young people, two male and two female, were playing what looked like a variety of tennis, with round wooden bats in the place of rackets and, as substitute for net, a string drawn from post to post. The two young men of the party, like their elder companion, were clothed in nothing but attenuated trunks. Of the girls one wore shorts, or loose bathing drawers, and the garment known as a brassiere — a considerable expanse of diaphragm being visible between the two. While the other, an agile slip of a lass,

Cicely Hamilton, 'Modern Germanies', 1931

157

contented herself with bathing-drawers only and was naked from the hips upward. As, girls and men alike, they were entirely unembarrassed by the passing spectator, the passing spectator was entirely unembarrassed by them.'

¶ Miss Hamilton herself did not investigate further, but she notes:

Cicely Hamilton, 'Modern Germanies', 1931

'There are devotees of the cult of nudity who refuse to be satisfied with the half-measures of shorts or bathing-garb and insist on the Nude and nothing but the Nude; for them, accordingly, are provided bathing establishments where bathers of both sexes splash about and sun themselves, uncovered by so much as a wisp; and these, I believe, are fairly numerous and well patronized. It is hardly needful to state that these *Naktkultur* establishments are not for the use or the sight of the casual visitor; admission, in the interest of morals and manners, is strictly an affair of membership.'

¶ The real devotees of Nudism, or Naturism, were animated, or thought they were animated, by the highest Moral Principles.

Robert Graves and Alan Hodge, 'The Long Week-End', 1940

'Pacifism had been introduced from Germany at the time of the Weimar Republic. So had three other libertarian fashions — sun-bathing, nudism and hiking. Sun-bathing had originally been found useful in Germany to cure children of "deficiency diseases" caused by the British blockade and by the severities of the post-war years. It now became a general cure-all . . .

'Nudism was of psychological rather than medical origin. Though some of its more zealous supporters wished to abolish the consumption of meat, tobacco, and alcohol, as well as clothing, nudism proper had no such simple-life background. It was supposed to eradicate repressions by teaching people to take their bodies for granted, and to promote health by open-air life and exercises. A nudist society had to be extremely strict, in order to avoid all charges of immorality: prospective members must convince the secretary of their sincerity and, if they happened to be married or engaged, obtain the written consent of their husbands or wives or fiancées. The societies tried to keep the numbers of the two sexes equal but men tended to predominate because a woman took greater social risks by becoming a member.'

158

¶ It was not only that. Women who had 'lost their figure' preferred not to abandon the assistance of corset and brassière; so that most of the women members of nudist societies were young. This was, perhaps, an advantage, from the *male* point of view, but it made a balance of the sexes almost impossible to achieve. The same penetrating authors offer an amusing social comment on nudism in England:

'Nudism was not so popular in Britain as in Germany or the United States: it was not suited to the climate. At first nudists gathered in muddy and midge-ridden corners of solitary woods, but later built luxurious nature camps and in the winter held indoor meetings with sun-ray lamps. They adopted the Hellenistic Greek name "Gymnosophists", and brought their children along with them. After a time most members found the routine of these camps monotonous, despite the earnest psychological and valetudinarian talk that went on in them. Women especially grew bored sitting about with no clothes, while attracting no erotic interest in the opposite sex, and being made wonderfully healthy by compulsory drill and by lettuce and tinned-salmon teas. Far better to wear a bathing-dress on a beach and be conscious of its daringness, than to sit about with no clothes on and with everyone politely unconscious of it. At the superior nudist camps, a nice class distinction was made: the butlers and maids who brought along the refreshments were forced to admit their lower social status by wearing loin-cloths and aprons respectively.'

Robert Graves and Alan Hodge, 'The Long Week-End', 1940

¶ Perhaps it is only fair to give the other side of the picture, even if it is only an imaginary picture of life at the German nudist colony at Himmelheim:

'The days passed so quickly that Evangeline lost count of them, aware only of a growing physical well-being, the placid contentment of a healthy open-air life. Her first sensation emerging naked from the shelter of the hut into the undergrown woods of Himmelheim had been a consciousness of the prickliness of the world. She picked her way delicately over pine-needles, she avoided stones, she sought for the mossy edges of paths, and, unable to keep her foothold on them, bruised her ankles and cut the delicate soles of her feet. When her companions flung themselves down carelessly on the ground, she lowered herself gently, in fear of spikey grasses and sharp pebbles. But the inconveniences of the natural life soon passed.

James Laver, 'Nymph Errant', 1932

'In a week she could run easily through the glades of the forest; in a fortnight she stretched her lithe body at full length among the bracken, heedless of the brittle stalks. Her skin grew tougher and more elastic, and gradually changed its colour; the white phantom became a brown gazelle. The flesh grew firmer, the joints more supple, the separate parts of her body took on a life of their own. She was conscious of her own legs running, like the movement of a horse beneath her; her hair sang as she bounded forward. When she stopped for a moment to listen she had the strange sensation that her two breasts were listening too; they seemed to hold their breath, while beneath them the heart pounded, and the blood coursed intoxicatingly through her veins. The sensation of touch which in ordinary life is narrowed to the tips of the fingers, spread over her whole body. Her thighs stirred, the belly rose from its long sleep in darkness, the hidden flanks awoke.

'Evangeline discovered with wonder and delight that her feet, while they had grown hardened to the roughness of the ground, had not lost their sensitiveness. Rather had they acquired a more delicate perception. The sole of the foot, weary of the monotony of treading always on the inside of a shoe, found a whole world of sensation before, or rather beneath, it. The rough silkiness of turf, the soft sponginess of moss, the hard brittle feel of dried sticks, the pleasant tickling of pine-needles, the sudden cool exhilaration of a rain-puddle — Evangeline's emancipated feet found and rejoiced in them all. They poked delighted toes through masses of dead leaves, savouring the crispness above and the soft earth-mould below. They not only rested upon the ground, they grabbed it with the instinctive reaction of hands; they rose and fell with a regular springy rhythm, delighting as they did so in the sharp contact of earth and air.

'Sometimes Evangeline was overcome with the desire to experience with her whole body this new-found earth ecstasy, and she flung herself face downwards on the ground, and felt against her legs and her abdomen and her breasts the close imprinted pattern of the flattened turf. Or else she ran shouting through fields of tall grass, the feathered tops whipping against her thighs, the parted stems hissing against her knees, until she fell exhausted and out of sight, gazing up at the sky, a narrow lane of blue between two green walls, like those of parted Jordan, one on the right hand and one on the left.'

¶ Nudism was never *fashionable* in England. The present author

Highlights of summer at Haslemere (Reproduced by permission of Léon).

once asked an acquaintance who confessed to 'practising nudism'.[1] 'What kind of people do you find in nudist clubs?' and he answered: 'Exactly the same kind of people who, fifty years ago, would have attended the Sunday School Outing, or the Band of Hope.' The fashionable — the playboys and their friends — took advantage of the new liberty but 'sought the sun' merely for pleasure. For them it merely meant the discovery of new playgrounds. Yet it is surprising that it was not until almost the end of the 'twenties that they found them:

'The most notable change in the last ten years of Continental luxury life is the popularity of the summer season on the Riviera. In the winter the younger generation make for the ski resorts, while their parents sit gracefully in the sunshine of the Côte d'Azur. In the heat of the summer the parents wisely seek cooler climes, while youth answers the call of what has been described as "The International Drinking Season", the headquarters of which carry the postal address "Alpes Maritimes".' *E. H. Tattersall, 'Europe at Play', 1938*

¶ The next quotation is even more explicit:

'Monte Carlo in 1926 was a winter resort only. It wasn't until a year or so later that Elsa Maxwell, after her tremendous success in attracting summer tourists to Venice, was asked to do the same for Monte Carlo, and I think it was mainly her ideas that made it the world's most fashionable summer playground.' *Gloria Vanderbilt and Thelma Lady Furness, 'Double Exposure', 1959*

¶ The Lido had been quite unknown to the fashionable world of a few years before. Now, it suddenly became 'the thing' to go there:

'To reach the Lido one must first go to Venice. And so to the pearl of the Adriatic do I tender humble apologies for presuming to write about its island-suburb before uttering a word of praise for the city, in describing which romantic novelists and poets have excelled themselves ... Description of the beauties of the Lido can be very short — for there are none. It is just a bank of land which breaks the flow of the Adriatic towards Venice; it is the sea-bathing resort not only of Venetians but of every mid-European country too; it is about a quarter of an hour in a motor-boat[2] from Venice, and it is dominated by a huge hotel, The Excelsior. *E. H. Tattersall, 'Europe at Play', 1938*

[1] The accepted phrase — but a curious one. It suggests that you have to go on "practising" for some time before you succeed in being absolutely nude.
[2] The journey can now be made in four and a half minutes.

Eden Roc, Cap d'Antibes, 1932.

'The hotel, in its turn, is dominated during the season by Princess Jane di San Faustino, who, although over seventy years old, organises all the big galas for charity, directs the social politics of the neighbourhood, and has a passion for backgammon. Every morning at eleven thirty she holds a court, sitting outside her *capanna* (bathing hut), a very imposing figure with her white hair and long, flowing white dress. Friends regale her with all the news of the previous evening, and upon their information does she deliver judgment upon new visitors. If "socially O.K." they are invited to her parties, must attend at the court each morning, and are given a good reference to the Countess Morosini, who rules correspondingly in Venice.

'And at two-thirty punctually in the afternoon, the Princess Jane sits down outside her *capanna* and issues summonses to play backgammon, and woe betide delinquents to the call. For she voices her opinion in no uncertain manner, and she is American. So are many wives of the Italian nobility — for instance, Princess Chito di Bitteto, Princess Torlonia, Countess Zoppola, and Countess Frasso.'

¶ Noël Coward added his own apt and acid comment.

Noël Coward,
'This Year of Grace',
1928

'A narrow strip of sand
Where Byron used to ride about,
While stately ships would glide about
The sea on either hand.
But now the times have changed,
For civilized society
With infinite variety
Has had it rearranged.
No more the moon
On the still Lagoon
Can please the young enchanted,
They must have this
And they must have that
And they take it all for granted.
They hitch their star
To a cocktail bar
Which is all they really wanted,
That narrow strip of sand
Now reeks with asininity
Within the near vicinity

162

A syncopated band
That plays the blues — all the day long —
And all the old Venetians say
They'd like a nice torpedo
To blow the Lido away.

¶ Magazines like *The Sketch* began to carry pages of pictures of High Society — and others — enjoying themselves at the Venetian paradise. Here are some of the captions:

'WHERE THE SUN SHINES WARMLY

'Basking on the Lido sands: the Hon. Mrs. Evelyn Fitzgerald, Prince Jean de Faucigny-Lucinge, Count Giovanni Sangro di Buccino, Princess Jean de Faucigny-Lucinge, Señor Bestigui, M. Lucien Lelong, Mme. Lelong, and M. Serge Lifar.'

'Mrs. Evan Morgan, in bathing dress [obviously], and Mrs. Sacheverell Sitwell, in pyjamas [equally obvious], on their way to lunch at the beach restaurant on the Lido.'

'T.R.H. Princess Marie Adelaide of Savoy and Princess Bona of Bavaria on their *patina* [a kind of catamaran] off the Excelsior Beach.'

'Princess Jane de San Faustino is one of the leading figures in Lido society. She constantly dresses in white, to match her wonderful white hair.'

'This is a lovely snapshot of a lovely lady. Viscountess Castlerosse.'

'Lady Mendl, the wife of Sir Charles Mendl, was formerly Miss de Wolfe. She is here posed in delightfully picturesque summer attire.'

'Miss Elsa Maxwell, one of the most popular of Parisian party-givers, is here posed with Mr. Cecil Beaton, in his fez.'

¶ E. H. Tattersall, 'some time an officer of the Fifth Princess Charlotte of Wales' Dragoon Guards', gives an admirable account of Lido Life:

'The day's programme on the Lido is not strenuous: there are tennis courts, though except . . . when the tournament is in progress, I have rarely seen them used . . . *E. H. Tattersall, 'Europe at Play', 1938*

'Bathing in the sea and in the sun occupies the morning assisted by eating the lovely green fresh figs which are one of the best local products. After a light luncheon there are bridge, backgammon, gossip, and more sun-bathing on the beach; towards five o'clock people retire to dress preparatory to going into Venice for the evening. For there is nothing to do here after sunset . . .

'As regards dress, women have their beach-dresses of every hue, and men are content with ordinary bathing suits when on the beach; otherwise flannels and short sleeved jerseys, blue for preference, and hardly ever a hat . . .

'Mr. Cecil Beaton races up and down the foreshore each morning to see if his friend Mr. Peter Watson is about, stopping to buy a fig for Miss Olga Lynn, or to bid "good morning" to a posse of princesses . . .

'In the fading light at about seven o'clock, just about the time you will be crossing from the Lido, Venice . . . looks her most romantic . . . A drink at Harry's Bar on the Grand Canal will transport you at once to the atmosphere of any other bar at any luxury resort. Dispensing with this I wander slowly from the Danieli Hotel, where our motor-boat leaves us, to the Piazza San Marco, and sit in meditation upon the question of dinner. This usually develops into telling a *rampino* (local waterman) to call out "Puppe!" when a gondola will appear; even though the Taverna restaurant is reasonably close, it is more pleasant to arrive there feeling cool for dinner . . .

'Let us look round to see whom we can recognize. There are M. and Mme. Sert dining with Mr. and Mrs. Denis Conan-Doyle (she was Princess Nina Mdivani) and Mr. Peter Watson; Signor de Facci Negrati, that very popular attaché in the Italian Embassy in London; Mr. Ralph Hall Caine, M.P. for East Dorset; the Duke of Alba with his famous black pearls in his evening shirt, and the Duke de Laurino, who was married to one of the Joel family, and whose white plus-fours with hearts on the knees are such a familiar sight in all Italian summer resorts.'

¶ In spite of the presence of so many Italian princesses, Mussolini, it is recorded, did not altogether approve of the goings-on on the Lido. The redoubtable Elsa Maxwell, as we have been informed by Lady Furness, then turned her attention to Monte Carlo, and made it a summer playground also, to the astonishment of the older habitués. E. H. Tattersall, in his fascinating account of the life of pleasure, makes the following revealing remark:

E. H. Tattersall,
'Europe at Play',
1938

'Captain D'Arcy Rutherford helps the Directorate at Monte Carlo in the entertainment of visitors. Being a first-class golfer, dancer, ski-boarder, with "Guardee" good looks and perfect manners, he has all the qualifications for his post. Age about forty-three, he is almost the youngest man here in the winter, whereas in the summer he is about the oldest inhabitant: there is a complete reversal of ages with the change of seasons.'

¶ Monte Carlo retained her fascination:

'There is something splendidly artificial about Monte Carlo, like a skilfully made-up woman, who never allows herself to be seen at dawn; you feel you could not be surprised to see Fred Astaire or either of the Jacks (Buchanan or Hulbert) come dancing down the steps of the Casino and up those of the Hotel de Paris opposite, evening coat-tails flying and top-hats neatly askew.' *E. H. Tattersall, 'Europe at Play', 1938*

¶ The playboys of the period were not entirely unaware of the existence of Culture:

'On the coast road from Monte Carlo, just before reaching Nice, if you turn off to the left you will find yourself on the promontory Saint Jean–Cap Ferrat. Here you can meander along several by-roads before you find the villa for which you are searching, and, should it be the Villa Mauresque, all that you will see will be a Moorish sign in red on a white gate-post. *E. H. Tattersall, 'Europe at Play', 1938*

'It is the home of that great playwright and novelist, Somerset Maugham . . . Mr. Maugham is a very keen golfer, and plays frequently on the pleasant little course at Cagnes, near Nice. Here he fights dour battles with Mr. Michael Arlen, who still preserves in his conversation that cleverness which we had from his pen; everyone is hoping for a renewal of his literary articles.'

¶ These literary interests, however, were hardly shared by the majority:

'A few minutes after arriving at the Carlton Hotel at Cannes, one is in touch with the wins and losses at the Casino. The Greek Syndicate had been having a grand run in its favour, with all the punters cheerfully contributing to the yachts, villas and fortunes of the combine. *E. H. Tattersall, 'Europe at Play', 1938*

'But the Syndicate had a bad night recently, and what a change! The young Greek nephew of M. Zagraphos had been playing the cards, and his face got very long and anxious; they all held a conference at 3 a.m. because somebody had won £12,000 back from it. And, worse still, a young Viennese girl had thirteen successive winning coups against the bank, netted about £7,000, and got up to leave, remarking: "Oh, I see it's half past one; my mother wouldn't like me to be out so late." '

¶ The authorities of Riviera resorts were beginning to find their feet again. The 'Battle of Flowers', perhaps with a certain self-consciousness, was still an event not only at Nice but at Monte Carlo. There is a certain faded charm in the social gossip of the period:

E. H. Tattersall,
'Europe at Play',
1938

'A maroon and some startled pigeons announced the "off". It was nice to see a friendly face or two peering out of the flower-bedecked carriages . . . There was one really exquisite Norwegian blonde who travelled alone in her glory, Mlle. Kari Aarbus.

'In the royal box were Princess Juliana and Prince Bernhard Lippe-Biesterfeld; they thoroughly enjoyed the contest and had a noble battle, especially with Mlle. Aarbus . . . Prince Bernhard has a great sense of humour, speaks perfect English, eternally chews gum, and appears to take a cheerful view of life. In their party were Mrs. Robert Wilson, Count Hans Czernin, and Baron Hubert Pantz (our friends "Hans and Pants" of Mittersill Club fame in Austria) and Miss Penelope Maffey (now Mrs. William Aitken), who was responsible for Princess Juliana having her hair cut short.'

¶ For those who wanted a quieter, but still fashionable life, there was Eden Roc, on the tip of the Cap d'Antibes. It consisted of a hotel and an ingenious construction of concrete platforms over the rather jagged rocks, and here it was possible to be all day in the sun and — unless you scorched and peeled — to acquire the hue of a mulatto *almost* all over. The *Sketch* carried a full-page picture in 1932, remarking:

'Sketch',
August 17th, 1932

'We publish so many portraits of the patrons of Eden Roc, the Riviera bathing and basking paradise, that it's only fair to give the place itself a look-in for once. This photograph gives a good idea of what it's really like, and shows the swimming pool, the diving-boards, the famous orange mattresses, and how the population is distributed among them. Backgammon is in progress in the foreground.'

166

¶ You could push further south to Capri — Who, a generation before, would have thought of visiting Capri in the summer? Or Majorca either, which became very popular in the early 'thirties. How pleasant if all these playgrounds could have been preserved for ever, with picturesque and attentive "natives" to minister to the visitors' wants! But, although the physical sun might continue to shine over the Mediterranean, the political climate grew more and more menacing as the decade moved on. 'Those nice Italians' began to shout 'Sanzionisti!' and other rude words at the visitors, and the streets of Majorcan villages were stained with blood.

CHAPTER IX

ILLUSION AND REALITY

AFTER THE FRIVOLOUS 'TWENTIES, the guilt-haunted 'thirties! After the party, the hangover, and what a headache it was! The play-boys, of course (at least, those who had not lost all their money in the American Slump), continued to have fun. But for anybody with a conscience it was a disquieting time. A universal *malaise* was in the air and, on the Left, a sense of betrayal. Three of the leaders of the Labour Party, MacDonald, Snowden and Thomas had (so it seemed to their erstwhile followers) gone over to the other side. 'Treason' said cynical old Talleyrand, 'is a matter of timing': and the action which History praises in a Monck it condemns in a Dumouriez. It all depends on whether or not your followers will follow you; MacDonald's did not, and the three Labour statesmen found them-selves alone among Tories. On the other hand, the Labour Party had been decapitated, and the fury of the rank and file is easy to understand. Some of them were not above imputing disreputable motives, especially to MacDonald.

Claud Cockburn,   'Ramsay MacDonald [was] at the moment of his "betrayal" the
'Crossing the Line',   visible darling of Lady Londonderry — so that the late James Maxton
1958   asked in the House of Commons whether the anthem of the Labour
Party was now the "Red Flag" or the "Londonderry Air".'

❡ If in terms of power, there was a swing to the Right, in terms of ideas, however, especially among the younger intellectuals, there was a pronounced swing to the Left. In his profound analysis of the state of affairs at this time, a recent commentator remarks:

Neal Wood,   'A British Radical intelligentsia, comparable to the long-established
'Communism and   continental intelligentsias, did not appear until the nineteen-thirties.
British   In the main British intellectuals have always been Liberal or Con-
Intellectuals',   servative. Then between 1928 and 1933 a change occurred in their
1959

outlook. Just before the opening of the new decade G. D. H. Cole sensed a "disquieting insecurity" among young intellectuals. Their pursuit of pleasure ceased to be satisfying. A new seriousness came to the fore in place of the former *"joie de vivre"*. Increasing attention was given to politics. Whereas sex and aesthetics had been the major topics of conversation, now everybody began to talk politics. As time passed the politics of the intellectual moved leftward to socialism and communism. What began as a political awakening became a great radicalization.'

¶ It was inevitable in the circumstances of the time that such a 'radicalization' should take extreme forms. Wyndham Lewis was one of the first to realize this: he notes:

'I know of no militant, professional "Youth" today in England (whether of fifteen or fifty) who is not militantly "radical". And the solitary and unique way of being "radical" that the Anglo–Saxon has . . . is to be communist: Communist, more or less, he must therefore be for there is no other organisation in sight. In France or Germany and, of course, Italy, and in all the smaller countries of the north and centre of Europe, there *is* an alternative that, today, the greater number of the active young men have taken. But in England or America there are only these two things: (1) the *status quo* (namely, just not ever to think politically at all), or else (2) Russian Communism (i.e. Marxism).'   *Wyndham Lewis, 'Doom of Youth', 1932*

¶ Russian Communism was in fashion, especially among those (that is to say, nearly all the intellectuals) who had very little notion of what was really happening in Russia. Even when they visited that country they saw only the façade:

'No longer was social disgrace the penalty for visiting Russia as it had been in certain circles during the nineteen-twenties. Now, one was much more likely to be ostracized if he criticized the country of the Bolsheviks . . . Every allowance was made for the obvious lack of political democracy in the Soviet Union . . . political democracy in capitalist countries was really only a sham . . . the dictatorship of one party and even one man was compatible with democracy because Soviet dictatorship was in the interest of the majority. All this was confidently being stated in Great Britain at the very time, as we are   *Neal Wood, 'Communism and British Intellectuals', 1959* informed by the present Soviet leaders, that Stalin was securing his dictatorship by means of an inquisition of terror and violence.'

¶ What was not realized in England was that, in Russia, the winter of Stalinist dictatorship had already set in:

Neal Wood,
'Communism and
British
Intellectuals',
1959
'Playing one intellectual leader against another Stalin succeeded in removing all from positions of power. His attack upon the intelligentsia was manifest in the decline of Soviet culture beginning about 1928. The brilliant experimentation of the early years disappeared. Creative activity was affected. The day of the party line in culture had arrived!'

¶ Such things being hidden from their eyes, the intellectual young were content to chant in chorus the praises of

'Glorious Russia, mighty and strong;
Glorious Russia can do no wrong.'

Even among their grave elders there were those who looked upon them with a certain approval:

J. M. Keynes, in
'New Statesman
and Nation',
January 28th, 1939
'There is no one in politics today worth sixpence outside the ranks of liberals except the post-war generation of intellectual communists under thirty-five. Them, too, I like and respect. Perhaps in their feelings as intellectuals they are the nearest thing we now have to the typical nervous nonconformist English gentlemen who went to the Crusades, made the Reformation, fought the Great Rebellion, won us our civil and religious liberties and humanised the working classes last century.'

¶ The 'nervous nonconformist English gentleman' was certainly well to the fore in these days. He had found a new Crusade:

Claud Cockburn,
'Crossing the Line',
1958
'For years people have been going around and about saying that in Britain Communism is an alien thing, that it is repugnant to all but the physically starved or the mentally distorted or those who may imagine that they are going to float on a high tide of troubles . . . Paradoxical as it may seem Communism has — or at any rate very often has — a particular appeal to people brought up in British public schools and universities, especially people with a classical and

Christian education . . . And if you ask me what first — long before I experienced central Europe in the inflation time, or attended the American crash of 1929 — "conditioned" me to be susceptible to the appeal of Communism I should have to say that it was, for example, the Magnificat I listened to every Sunday at evensong in the village church, and Antigone's defiance of Creon in Sophocles' play!'

¶ C. Day Lewis in his recently published autobiography makes the same point:

'Nearly all my friends who during this period became active in Left Wing movements, or at least sympathetic to Left Wing ideas, had had the same kind of upbringing. Rex Warner, MacNeice and myself were sons of clergymen; Auden had a devout Anglo–Catholic mother; Spender came from an "old-fashioned Liberal" family. We had all been to public schools, with their traditions both of authoritarianism and of service to the community. We had all, I think, lapsed from the Christian faith, and tended to despair of liberalism as an ineffective instrument for dealing with the problems of our day, if not to despise it as an outworn creed. Inoculated against Roman Catholicism by the religion of my youth, I daily felt the need of a faith which had the authority, the logic, the cut-and-driedness of the Roman church — a faith which would fill the void left by the taking away of traditional religion, would make sense of our troubled times and make real demands on me. Marxism appeared to fill the bill . . .

'My leanings towards Communism came less from any intellectual conviction they afforded me than from my heritage of romantic humanism, a bent of mind quite incompatible, as I would discover, with the materialism and rapacity of Communist doctrines . . . If my faith was shakey — I was and remained sceptical about a good deal in Communist theory and practice — at least I had hope: no one who did not go through this political experience during the 'thirties can quite realize how much hope there was in the air then, how radiant for some of us was the illusion that men could, under Communism, put the world to rights.'

C. Day Lewis, 'The Buried Day', 1960

¶ Day Lewis himself edited a little book which included contributions from most of the young Left Wing intellectuals of the day: Rex Warner, Edward Upward, Arthur Calder-Marshall, Charles Madge, Edgell Rickwood, and the redoubtable, if not so young, Professor

J. D. Bernal. Their essays show their complete acceptance of the communist idea in every department of life. In literary criticism, for example:

Edward Upward, in 'The Mind in Chains', 1937
'Literary criticism which aims at being Marxist must begin by recognizing that literature does reflect social and economic conditions, and must proclaim that no book written *at the present time* can be "good" unless it is written from a Marxist or near-Marxist viewpoint... No modern book can be true to life unless it recognizes, more or less clearly, both the decadence of present-day society and the inevitability of revolution...

'A writer of today who wishes to produce the best work he is capable of producing, must first of all become a socialist... Unless he has in his everyday life taken the side of the workers, he cannot, however talented he may be, write a good book... He must be told frankly that joining the workers' movement does mean giving less time to imaginative writing, but that unless he joins it his writing will become increasingly false, worthless as literature. Going over to socialism may prevent him, but failing to go over *must* prevent him from writing a good book.'

¶ Rex Warner was equally convinced that Culture had now passed out of the hands of the 'cultivated classes'. 'Capitalism', he wrote, 'has no further use for culture.' It could only be preserved by bringing a new class into power:

Rex Warner, in 'The Mind in Chains', 1937
'Those who will support the change will be those who think that they will gain by it; that is to say, firstly, the working class, and secondly those people who, guided by the accepted principles of morality and reason, have come to the conclusion that only socialism can satisfy the demands which mind and body can reasonably make of life. The force which alone can bring about the change must be, in the last resort, the organized working class, and that is what we mean when we say that the working class has now become the guardians of culture...

'Those who fight desperately to maintain the old order are forced into "immoral" and "uncivilized" methods in their defence; the revolutionaries, on the other hand, are found to be "moral" and "civilized" in their methods.'

172

¶ In the light of what we now know of communist methods such remarks seem almost incredibly naïve. But another contributor to the same volume assures his readers that —

'There is no foundation for the misgivings of those intellectuals who, whilst deploring the degeneration of quality inseparable from capitalist mass-production, see no difference in the socialist application of the same method. Nor need the art worker fear that grim standardization with which the apologists of individualism (as they term the *bourgeois* anarchy) seek to terrify his innocence.'

Edgell Rickwood, in 'The Mind in Chains', 1937

¶ Since Lenin himself had said that 'in this matter it is absolutely necessary to secure great scope for personal initiative and individual tendencies, scope for thought and fantasy', everything was going to be all right. Charlotte Haldane, looking back on this search for a father-figure, makes the acid comment:

'I would define the middle-class Communist convert as an "Aginner" — the type of person who, as a result of psychological strains and stresses, endured in childhood or adolescence, rebuts the discipline in which he has been brought up but is compelled to seek another, still more rigorous, who has an emotional need for direction, who, however eminent intellectually, can find no inner peace, save on the basis of surrendering his intellectual, moral and political judgment to "democratic centralism".'

Charlotte Haldane in 'Tribune', 1947

¶ The acknowledged intellectual who pushed this 'surrender' to extreme lengths was Middleton Murry, even if he never actually became a member of the Communist Party:

'To believe in, to pursue, to give oneself to Communism in this country does not mean to become a "Communist", it means to devote oneself to the task of making the Labour Party Marxist and revolutionary once more. The English Communist is the man who works with those and for those who aim at a real social *revolution*, at the complete eradication of the capitalist system. It is the revolution that matters, the name of Communist does not. It seems to me fantastic to suppose that in this country the social revolution should ape the manners of the Russian revolution; it seems to me natural to suppose that the experience of the next few years will be such as to make

John Middleton Murry, 'The Necessity of Communism', 1932

173

Communism appear to a decisive minority of Englishmen completely reasonable. In England, too, we can expect to be allowed to put the Communist case in season and out of season without hindrance. How long that freedom will continue I have no idea. It depends upon how quickly the fundamental Marxist version permeates the Labour Party, which is the natural instrument. If the Labour Party becomes radically Marxian, instead of parasitic and sentimental, why, then the cause is as good as won. And the condition of the permeation of the Labour Party is the increase of those intellectuals to whom Communism is veritably the one religious faith. If this book has served to increase their number by a dozen, or even by one, it has not failed.'

¶ Some of the hard-headed members of the inner councils of the C.P. must have been more than a little puzzled by Murry's high-falutin' approach to the whole question.

'Marxian Communism', he told them, 'is a combination into a perfect dynamic unity of ethical passion and intellectual objectivity.'

And again:

John Middleton Murry, 'The Necessity of Communism', 1932 'Intellectually, spiritually, ethically, the choice before the conscious Englishman is to be a Communist *or nothing*. His nothingness may take the most diverse forms; aesthetic dilettantism, snobbish economic sapience, superficial "action", pessimistic neo-Catholicism. But each and all are forms of nothingness: manifestations of non-belief. Ultimately a man has to believe. At a crucial moment of the world's history he must believe or perish. There is now, and always has been, only one way of achieving a belief — through the final sacrifice of the ego. To-day it is Communism. Therefore Communism is the enemy of all "religions", because it is itself the one religion.'

¶ In his footnotes he urges the reader to:

John Middleton Murry, 'The Necessity of Communism', 1932 'See my *Life of Jesus,* and, for a statement of his story in the terms of a *complete* materialism, *God: An Introduction to the Science of Metabiology.* The title of this book has, I fear, been an impediment to many.'

¶ Such fears were no doubt amply justified. But Murry went on booming from his own particular cloud-capped Sinai:

174

'It is quite conceivable . . . that the type which we ourselves may be said to represent — the "intellectuals" who have carried their disinterestedness through their fragmentary opportunities of economic freedom — will not survive. It cannot be helped. But it is not wholly accidental to the purpose of this book that it may teach some of these how to endow themselves with a survival value. For there is only one way — to be ready to sacrifice their all. By that readiness they will have earned the right to survive; in virtue of that readiness, if they see no prospect of surviving, they will not care.'

John Middleton Murry, 'The Necessity of Communism', 1932

¶ Whether this hysterical appeal for an intellectual suicide-pact had much effect may be doubted, but Middleton Murry's writing helped to reinforce the general impression that all intellectuals were moving in the same direction. Certainly there was ample cause for alarm:

'If January 1933 marked the economic nadir in Britain, for world diplomacy it opened an event-crammed year which would propel mankind into the greatest war of history. British journals struck a particularly pessimistic note from the beginning of the year. The democratic nations seemed to be floundering on with no purpose or direction to their actions. Hitler on January 30th became Chancellor of Germany, and shortly afterwards the Reichstag was burned. Japan withdrew from the League of Nations, launching an attack on China. Threatened with the collapse of its banking system, the United States in the Spring abandoned the Gold Standard, and depreciated the dollar. The collapse of the deliberations held in the Summer ended the hope of world economic co-operation. Arabs and Jews clashed in Palestine in October. Withdrawing from the World Disarmament Conference, Hitler announced his decision to leave the League of Nations. Corruption at its worst was revealed in the sordid Stavinsky scandal in Paris, followed by the fall of the Daladier Government in February 1934. The rise to power of Pierre Laval, one-time member of the Communist Party and now an arch Conservative, and an attempted Fascist *coup* in Paris, brought little relief to despairing hearts. Chancellor Dollfuss, after repressing the Social-Democrats in Austria, was assassinated by the Nazis in July 1934.'

Neal Wood, 'Communism and British Intellectuals', 1959

¶ The Communists themselves began to be alarmed by the rising flood of the Fascist tide. A man who was at that time in their inner councils in England, comments:

175

Douglas Hyde,
'I Believed', 1951
'The shock to the world Communist leaders caused by Hitler's virtual destruction of the mighty German Communist Party was terrific. If this could happen, then anything was possible. And so, in approved Marxist fashion, the Comintern did a complete switch . . .

'Communism had been our aim and we had said so . . . It could only be achieved by bloody revolution, civil war and Red Terror — and we made no bones about it . . .

'If we worked to assist the return of a Labour Government we did so only that the social democrats, or "social fascists" as we more often called them, might reveal their bankruptcy and so that the disillusioned workers would then turn to us. And we told the world that this alone was our reason. There was at least a certain grim, contemptuous honesty about our attitude.

'But the new situation created by the Nazis' successes ended all that. It resulted in the tactic of the Popular Front, the decision to enlist the aid of the middle-class, the intellectuals, the "social fascists" . . .

'Books . . . which stated our position with frankness, such as the *A.B.C. of Communism,* were withdrawn and destroyed. (Thoroughness was carried to a point in the Soviet Union where the two authors of that work were, in fact, liquidated) . . .

'It was all very thorough but very phoney, for we went back on none of the fundamentals; we simply put some into cold storage and found new methods of dishing up the rest.'

¶ The 'Popular Front' had a strong appeal for many middle-class intellectuals of Leftish views, and an agitation began for the admission of the Communist Party into the ranks of the Labour Movement:

John Strachey,
'The Theory and
Practice of
Socialism', 1936
'The essential principles of working class policy in this world situation were established at the Seventh Congress of the Communist International in August 1935 . . . Over a large part of the world a situation, in which for the first time the Marxist parties affiliated to the Communist International find themselves able to re-animate, to join in a working alliance, and ultimately to fuse, the other working class parties of their countries, has been brought about by the sheer pressure of circumstances.

'This swirling stream of world events is now beginning to have its effect in Great Britain. In less than a year it has set up a remarkably strong current of opinion in favour of the accomplishment of the

176

Policemen arresting a demonstrator against the march of Mosley's Fascists in the East End of London, 1936.

Sir Oswald Mosley giving the Fascist salute.

unity of the British working class by the acceptance of the British Communist Party's recent application for affiliation to the Labour Party. As the situation develops, this current of opinion will flow more and more strongly.'

¶ The same writer had hopes that the 'capitalists' themselves might be brought in, and he propounded:

'The interesting question of whether the abolition of capitalism (since capitalism entails war) is not in the true interests of the capitalists themselves . . . But we must, I fear, take the violent opposition of the capitalist class as a whole to the abolition of their class privileges as a dictum — although we must not for a moment suppose that this will be true of every individual member of the capitalist class. On the contrary, as Marx clearly recognized in the *Communist Manifesto* and elsewhere, more and more individual members, both of the capitalist class and of the intermediate groups, will break away from their class and join the workers as and when they realize the nature of the issues which are being decided in our epoch.' *John Strachey, 'The Theory and Practice of Socialism', 1936*

¶ If the capitalists failed to see the light they must take what was coming to them:

'The power of the capitalist class now rests predominantly upon their control over what we have called the means of production of opinion: upon their control over men's minds. If their power to keep men in ignorance and unconsciousness of social processes could be removed, then the process of social transformation could be swift, easy and bloodless . . . we must take it as a constant factor in the social equation that the capitalists will succeed in obscuring, both from the workers and from themselves, that vital knowledge [of Marxism] without which the process of social change is bound to be arduous, blind and therefore to some extent violent.' *John Strachey, 'The Theory and Practice of Socialism', 1936*

¶ Not only the capitalists but the Labour leaders themselves seemed curiously reluctant to accept the Gospel. However:

'In Britain today new forces assure us that it will be increasingly impossible to prevent the British workers from realizing the nature of the task which faces them. A totally unprecedented number of *John Strachey, 'The Theory and Practice of Socialism', 1936*

M

177

young workers, of students in the universities, and, for that matter, of men and women of every age, and from every class, are making a serious study of the science of social change . . . What is above all necessary is that this renewed, spontaneous and inevitable movement of resistance to capitalism should be infused with a more scientific, and, for that very reason, far more militant, political consciousness than has ever been the case before . . . So long as the leaders of the Labour Party and Trade Union movement exclude the Communist Party, and all organizations connected with it from full participation in every side of working-class activity no decisive advance can be made. In the first place the Communist Party, although still small in numbers, today contains, or groups round it the majority of those devoted, tireless, impassioned men and women who always form the living heart of every working-class movement . . . The re-union of the working-class with its most active and advanced members is the pre-requisite of everything else.'

¶ Strachey was perhaps the most forceful of those who were putting forward this point of view. Charlotte Haldane notes:

Charlotte Haldane, 'The claim that the evils of Nazism and Fascism, then developing
'Truth Will Out', at an alarming rate, were due solely to the expanding contradictions
1949 of capitalist economy, seeking desperately to bolster up its tottering edifice against advancing Soviet Communism, was at that time constantly made by Left-wing Labour politicians and polemicists, as well as by the Communists. The foremost British exponent of this view was John Strachey, whose book, *The Coming Struggle for Power,* was avidly read and widely applauded by the Left-wing intellectuals. The Left Book Club was started by the publisher, Victor Gollancz.'

¶ The influence of the Left Book Club was enormous:

G. D. H. Cole and 'In . . . 1935, took place two events, little noticed at the time, which
Raymond Postgate, foreshadowed a profound change in public thought. The Left Book
'The Common Club was founded, and the first Penguin Books were published. Both
People', 1946 of these speedily found imitators, none of which were as successful. The Left Book Club, an enterprise of Mr. Victor Gollancz, rose to have 50,000 members, most of whom received one and sometimes more large books of Socialist propaganda a month. Some of these may have been shallow, some no doubt were sold but unread, some were

criticized as following blindly official Communist policy; but the majority were books of value and depth, likely not to cause momentary excitement so much as to make solid converts. The Penguin Books, and their subsidiaries the Pelicans and Penguin Specials, had no direct political bias: indeed Mr. Allen Lane, their producer, sought anxiously for Right-wing books to balance the Left Specials which alone it seemed possible to find, but with very infrequent success. The total number of books issued must have been astronomical . . . A vast shift of public opinion was on the way.'

❡ An amusing example of the far-reaching influence of the Left Book Club is provided by Cicely Hamilton:

'In the course of exploratory wandering through one of the outer suburbs of West London, I perceived in the window of a bookseller's shop a type-written document, pasted to the glass, which the pattern of its lines proclaimed as verse. The shop, a small one, had already attracted my attention by its prominent recommendations of the Left Book Club; and a nearer view of the type-written product revealed it as yet another advertisement of the reddish volumes which disseminate like coloured views. The Poem (I pencilled it down in my note-book) was brief and to the point; it ran as follows:

*Cicely Hamilton,
'Modern England',
1938*

> Forced to make the choice themselves,
> Our rude forefathers loaded shelves
> With Tennyson and Walter Scott
> And Meredith and Lord knows what!
> But we don't have to hum and ha,
> Nous avons changé tout cela —
> Our books are chosen for us — thanks
> To Strachey, Laski and Gollancz!

'As I stood and scribbled, I noticed that the owner of the shop had drawn nearer to his doorway and was watching me — evidently desirous of knowing what I thought of the poem. Nothing loth to make an opening, I asked was it his work? He nodded assent and entered into talk concerning it. Yes, he told me, the lines had attracted a good deal of attention; passers-by often stopped to read them and, as a general rule, they were approved by progressive opinion. Once, it was true, an objection had been lodged, presumably by a fellow Left-winger; at any rate a note had been pushed under the door, suggesting alteration of the last couplet. The statement that our books were chosen for us by Strachey, Laski and Gollancz was not altogether to the writer's liking; it would be better, he thought, to put it that the three gentlemen in question *helped* us choose our books . . . His own version the bookseller maintained, was the more accurate of the two. It wasn't a case of helping to choose; the books were chosen by Strachey, Laski and Gollancz, and, being chosen, were sent out to members of the club.'

¶ The Communists — naturally — were delighted:

Douglas Hyde,
'I Believed', 1951

'When the Left Book Club began early in 1936 it provided me with just the weapon I wanted. To all those who had so often told me that they were of the Left rather than the Right I said, "Join the Left Book Club and prove it." To the liberal-minded who argued that they liked to read both sides I said: "You can't do so without reading the Left as well as the Right."

'Soon I had dozens of people whom I had regarded as political foes reading a Left book each month and discussing it with me.'

¶ The books were well written, well printed — and cheap. The young especially mopped them up eagerly. They had a particularly large sale among undergraduates — and made many converts. It became something almost indecent not to be politically minded, which meant, in general, being of the Left:

Frank Hardie, in
'Growing Opinions',
1935

'The general tendency of the opinions of the politically minded undergraduates is what might perhaps best be called "radical". In the case of each Party the tendency is for the Oxford undergraduate view to be a point or two to the Left of the official London view. Thus, for example, the Conservatives would anywhere else be described, and rightly described, as Liberals.

'The Labour Club has advanced from strength to strength, but the point to note here is that the standpoint of its members seems on the whole to be that of Sir Stafford Cripps and the Socialist League rather than that of the official authorities of the Labour Party . . . On the left of the Labour Club there sprang up the October Club, a definitely Communist organization, subsequently driven underground by what was commonly held as excessive severity on the part of the authorities at the time of the free speech controversy (November 1933). A Fascist Club has been founded, but its membership seems extremely small.'

¶ The young poets all seemed to be on the same side:

'Wystan Auden's poem *The Orators* was published in 1932; and the works of Stephen Spender, Cecil Day Lewis and Louis MacNeice were gradually becoming known . . . The new poets were partisans of the Left; and their sympathies, heightened by a sense of impending conflict, coloured or clouded much of the verse they wrote . . . That long sad courtship of the Russian Communist Party by Western Men of Good Will . . . exposed the wooers to so many rebuffs, provoked such bitter heart-searchings . . . plunged some of them into a state of moral perturbation from which they have not yet recovered. But it is clear that the "Fight against Fascism", notwithstanding the valour that a number of young poets displayed in the Spanish Civil War, and the eloquence displayed by an ever larger number in support of democratic principles, was directly productive of no more genuine poetry than the struggle against Napoleon Bonaparte.'

Peter Quennell,
'The Sign of the
Fish', 1960

¶ W. H. Auden was their acknowledged leader. He was very bitter against those who would not join the ranks of the Left:

'Brothers, who when the sirens roar
From office, shop and factory pour
  'Neath evening sky;
By cops directed to the fug
Of talkie-houses for a drug,
Or down canals to find a hug
  Until you die . . .

W. H. Auden,
'Look Stranger',
1936

'On you our interests are set
Your sorrow we shall not forget
  While we consider
Those who in every county town
For centuries have done you down.
But you shall see them tumble down
  Both horse and rider.

181

'O splendid person, you who stand
In spotless flannels or with hand
      Expert on trigger;
Whose lovely hair and shapely limb
Year after year are kept in trim
Till buffers envy as you swim
      Your Grecian figure . . .

'Dare-devil mystic who bears the scars
Of many spiritual wars
      And smoothly tell
The starving that their one salvation
Is personal regeneration
By fasting, prayer and contemplation;
      Is it? Well . . .

'Coward; for all your goodness game
Your dream of Heaven is the same
      As any bounder's;
Your hope to corner as reward
All that the rich can here afford
Love and music and bed and board
      While the world flounders.

'And you, the wise man, full of humour
To whom our misery's but a rumour
      And slightly funny;
Proud of your nicely balanced view
You say as if it were something new
The fuss we make is mostly due
      To lack of money.

'Ah, what a little squirt is there
When of your aren't I charming air
      You stand denuded.
Behind your subtle sense of humour
You hide the boss's simple stuma,
Among the foes which we enumer
      You are included.

182

'Because you saw but were not indignant
The invasion of the great malignant
    Cambridge ulcer
That army intellectual
Of every kind of liberal
Smarmy with friendship but of all
    There are non falser.

'A host of columbines and pathics
Who show the poor by mathematics
    In their defence
That wealth and poverty are merely
Mental pictures, so that clearly
Every tramp's a landlord really
    In mind events.

'Let fever sweat them till they tremble
Cramp rack their limbs till they resemble
    Cartoons by Goya:
Their daughters sterile be in rut
May cancer rot their herring gut,
The circular madness on them shut,
    Or paranoia . . .'

¶ In later years the poet was not quite so sure of his anger — or his aim:

'The original of this appeared in the avant-garde anthology *New Country*, edited by Michael Roberts and published in 1933 at the Hogarth Press by Leonard and Virginia Woolf. In this form it bears the title "A Communist to Others", and in the first line, instead of "brothers" we have the more unmistakable Marxism form of address, "comrades". In revising this for *On This Island* the poet cut it down by half a dozen stanzas, but kept it pretty much the same radical partisan propaganda as he found it in its earlier form . . .

'Like the earlier piece from the 1930 *Poems*, this one, even in its revised form, is unredeemed (for later reading) by being a counter-blast to fascist statism. It is straight Marxist propaganda, based on the concept of class struggle, and not excluding an anti-religious bias.'

Joseph Warren Beach, 'The Making of the Auden Canon', 1957

183

¶ When it was first issued the poem was a clarion call for political action. In Oxford and other universities the tide was flowing strongly:

Neal Wood, *'Communism and* *British* *Intellectuals',* *1959* 'Changes in the intellectual life of a nation can often be perceived at an early date among university students. Prior to the nineteen-thirties British students had never exhibited the political fervour so characteristic on the Continent. Consequently, it must have been with some satisfaction that Karl Radek was able to announce to the Congress of Soviet Writers in 1934 that "In the heart of bourgeois England, in Oxford, where the sons of the bourgeoisie receive their final polish, we observe the crystallization of a group which sees salvation only together with the proletariat . . ."

'Student radicalism took firm root during 1932. Several radical publications appeared . . . Contingents of Hunger Marchers passing through Oxford and Cambridge on their way to London were met by militant students and dons, who placed themselves at the heads of the columns. Meeting these straggling processions of unemployed men was the first real contact that many of the undergraduates, coming from affluent middle-class families, had made with the proletariat. It proved to be a profoundly moving experience for the more sensitive ones. About this time the Oxford Union voted by a majority of 67 that "in Socialism lies the only solution to the problems facing this country." Shortly afterwards on Thursday, February 9th, 1933, the Union resolved by 275 to 153 that it would "in no circumstances fight for its King and Country." '

¶ A vivid account of this famous debate was published shortly afterwards by an eye-witness:

Alan Campbell *Johnson, in* *'Growing Opinions',* *1935* 'To many who were members of Oxford University at the time of the now famous "King and Country" Union resolution, when the furore was at its height, it must have seemed that yet another Oxford movement was being launched. Undoubtedly a large portion of the public has a subconscious feeling that "Oxford" and "Pacifism" are correlated terms. This is but a further heresy, a further false emphasis. The importance of that motion was largely accidental. It acted as a match setting alight a highly inflammable tinder of repressed speculation. In fact, the motion itself created little or no impression at Oxford for three or four days, until enterprising journalism discovered its news value. I count myself fortunate to have been present at that debate and to have assumed some small symbolic significance with 272 others who voted for the motion. If C. E. M. Joad had not spoken, it is more than likely that it would not have been carried. A clever defence of the existing status of nations, and of the orthodox attitude in general, had been made by Quintin Hogg, who got a good reception. Then came Joad's superb emotional appeal . . . He proved beyond a doubt the absurdity of war. He proved that expense on armaments and vast military preparations were worthy only of derision. It was high comedy to see the futile gestures and ambitions of nations, men all calling on presumably the same God to help them, and God doing his best not to show favouritism. We laughed at the manifold anomalies . . . It was all very wittily put together, and a pointed beard, a squeaking lisping voice, a twinkling eye, added piquancy. We were greatly diverted — and then he changed the tone; a perfect piece of emotional timing . . . We were laughing at ourselves. In fact, hysteria — a symptom of insanity . . . No comedy after all, but a very dark, bloodstained tragedy — and the end uncertain.'

¶ This, of course, was a victory not for Communism as such, but for Pacifism, and, by an absurd over-valuation of the importance of an undergraduate debating society, it contributed in no small measure to persuading Hitler that the British would not fight for King, or Country — or anything. Thus it did a grave disservice to the cause of peace. Beverley Nichols, putting aside the frivolity of his earlier writing, now entered the fray:

'The generic name for all these poisonous germs which cause war is . . . Patriotism . . .

Beverley Nichols, 'Cry Havoc', 1933

'I believe, with every fibre of my being, that the hour has struck in the world's history when every man who wishes to serve his country must realize that Patriotism is the worst service he can offer to it. The time has come when it must be definitely admitted that Patriotism is an Evil, in every country — that the German patriot is as great a sinner as the English patriot or the American patriot or the Italian patriot. The time has come when this word — a hallowed word, I admit, a word that calls up memories of sublime sacrifice and deathless heroism — must be recognized as having changed its meaning, and as having lost its sense and its virtue.'

¶ Beverley Nichols, after urging parents not to give little boys toy soldiers to play with, tried to answer what he calls "the militarist's standard question":

Beverley Nichols,
'Cry Havoc', 1933 "What would you do if you found a great hulking German attacking your sister?"

'The quickest and most effective reply is, "I should behave exactly in the same way as if I found a great hulking Britisher attacking my sister — i.e. I should give him a sock in the jaw."

'As soon as you introduce this parallel [the militarist's] argument becomes ridiculous. By giving the imaginary assailant of your sister a sock in the jaw you are merely temporarily taking the part of the police. The army and the police have entirely different functions — one exists to break the law, the other to keep it.'

The out-and-out Pacifists must have been a little confused by this, and perhaps still more confused when our author added:

Beverley Nichols,
'Cry Havoc', 1933 'I have at last come to the conclusion that in certain circumstances I would fight in an international army, in an international cause, under some commander appointed by the League of Nations.'

¶ However, the pacifism of the Left was shortly to receive a severe jolt. Was it any good preaching universal brotherhood in a world where Reaction seemed to stalk triumphant? Early in 1935 Hitler repudiated the disarmament provisions of the Versailles Treaty and little more than a year later occupied the Rhineland. Mussolini invaded Ethiopia, and shortly afterwards something else happened:

Philip Guedalla,
'The Hundredth
Year', 1940 'On the Summer day [in 1936] that London saw King Edward ride across Hyde Park to meet the Guards a plane came swooping from the West on Tetuan. The little town lay in the dusty Moorish sunshine between the grey mountains and the sea five miles away. Its pattern of white houses, crooked alleys, the tall minaret of Sidi Es Saïdi, town walls, grey olives, and flat roofs tilted suddenly as the plane circled overhead; and when it landed, the civilian passenger (who had alarmed his pilot by a complete and dazzling change of costume on the long passage from Las Palmas) stood up, and General Francisco Franco stepped out to start a civil war in Spain . . .

'The outbreak . . . was more than usually punctual, although its appointed leader, General Sanjurjo, started two days late from Portugal and owing to an air accident failed to arrive at all. The garrisons were duly raised by their insurgent officers — successfully at Seville, Saragossa, and Pamplona, and without success at Barcelona and Madrid. But though Goded failed in his attempt on Catalonia Franco had come to Tetuan. His duty was to raise the army of

Morocco in revolt . . . The Spanish army had not been very good at conquering Morocco. But there was a fair chance that, with Moorish aid and enough German and Italian support, it might conquer Spain.'

¶ The poets sent forth a clarion call for action:

> 'Leave your gardens, your singing feasts,
> Your dreams of suns circling before our sun,
> Of heavens after our world . . .
> No spirit seek here rest. But this: No one
> Shall hunger: Man shall spend equally,
> Our goal which we compel: Man shall be man.
>   That programme of the antique Satan
> Bristling with guns on the indented page,
> With battleship towering from hilly waves:
> For what? Drive of a ruining purpose
> Destroying all but its age-long exploiters.
> Our programme like this, but opposite:
> Death to the killers, bringing light to life.'

Stephen Spender,
'Collected Poems
1928-53', 1954

¶ But who were the 'killers'? Not those who were murdering nuns in Segovia and Madrid, but Franco and his followers. Surely it was right even for pacifists to combat 'militarism'? Hatred for Franco was universal among the men of the Left:

'In spite of meetings from end to end of England, and the spate of peace literature that pours from the press, there is, if I mistake not, more organized hatred in England today than there was before 1914 . . . One would have thought that pacifist associations would have been anxious to mitigate hate propaganda of the kind, but, so far as I know, none of them have protested against it . . . All the world, I suppose, has grown more callous in the last quarter of a century and England has not escaped the general infection; it is a sober and also unpleasant fact that large sections of our public have little objection to cruelty as a policy, cruelty in itself — only to cruelty inflicted by those they disagree with.'

Cicely Hamilton,
'Modern England',
1938

¶ Spain was the rallying cry:

> 'What's your proposal? To build the Just City?
> I agree. Or is it the suicide pact, the romantic
>   Death? Very well, I accept, for
> I am your choice, your decision: yes, I am Spain.'

W. H. Auden,
'Collected Shorter
Poems', 1950

187

¶ Another poet who had visited Spain just before the outbreak had seen what was coming and painted an evocative picture:

Louis MacNeice,
'Collected Poems',
1949

'I remember Spain
   At Easter ripe as an egg for revolt and ruin
Though for a tripper the rain
   Was worse than the surly or the worried or the
      haunted faces
With writings on the walls —
   Hammer and sickle, Boicot, Viva, Muerra . . .
And the day before we left
   We saw the mob in flower at Algeciras
Outside a toothless door, a church bereft
   Of its images and its aura . . .

And next day took the boat
   For home, forgetting Spain, not realising
That Spain would soon denote
   Our grief, our aspirations;
Not knowing that our blunt
   Ideals would find their whetstone, that our spirit
Would find its frontier on the Spanish front
   Its body in a rag-tag army.'

¶ Only a few of the extreme pacifists were still convinced that moral suasion was enough:

Cicely Hamilton,
'Modern England',
1938

'A body of Oxford undergraduates once openly declared they would refuse to fight at the call of their King and Country. Not many years have gone by since that flamboyant resolution was passed and duly applauded; but events have moved swiftly in the intervening years, and by this time, doubtless, some of those who cast their votes on the side of what they thought was pacifism will have learned that loyalty to king and country is not the only reason for which men turn and rend each other. We have been near to war since those votes were cast but not in the name of the British nation — in the name of collective security and sanctions! and it was not loyalty to their native land but belief in democracy or hatred of Fascism that sent volunteers to the Spanish International Brigade — among them men of the English race who had classed themselves as pacifists. "The pacifists from the

English universities are said to be excellent machine-gunners" — so from Madrid wrote the *Manchester Guardian* correspondent.'

¶ The Communists were naturally delighted. They set out to canalize this surge of Popular Front enthusiasm:

'The organization of the International Brigade was one of the most romantic enterprises of our time. In all countries the call went forth: "Aid for Spain! Arms for Spain! Volunteers for Spain!" In all countries the first underground army began to stream towards the Spanish front. The Communist Parties were charged with the local and national organization . . . The British Communist Party was also given a quota to raise. It was one of the smaller and more insignificant of the European parties . . . Harry Pollitt, William Gallacher and their colleagues of the Politbureau in London had to make terrific efforts to raise their volunteers for Spain . . . Yet the volunteers came trickling in slowly. The vanguard were Communist Party members under discipline to show an example to their fellow-proletarians. It had at first been decided only to send unmarried men over twenty-one. But the smallness of their numbers compelled the British C.P., under orders from the C.I. (Communist International) to furnish its quota of volunteers to extend its recruitment among married comrades and the youth of the Young Communist League.' *Charlotte Haldane, 'Truth Will Out', 1949*

¶ The Communist organizers, however, began to realize that if they gave too much encouragement to the most enthusiastic of their own members they were likely to find the ranks of that élite sadly depleted. A 'man on the inside' tells us the cynical result of this calculation:

'In the early days of the Spanish struggle the [Communist] Party sent many of its own members to fight . . . The leaders went out one after the other for a few months' experience. Very few lost their lives or received serious wounds . . . But the rank and file in the early days died in great numbers and set an example in heroism. Too many died, in fact, for the Party's liking. It was not intended that Party members should be slaughtered wholesale. Dead men could make no contribution to the fight for Soviet Britain. *Douglas Hyde, 'I Believed', 1951*

'So I and others doing similar work were dissuaded from sending out any more Party members. The new recruits must be non-Communists whose deaths would assist the immediate aims of the Party without jeopardizing the coming struggle for power at home.

'When cannon fodder, above all else, was needed, one Party organizer's job was to go around the Thames Embankment in London at night looking for able-bodied down-and-outs. He got them drunk and then shipped them over the Channel.

'They sobered up in Paris, were dined and primed, then made drunk again. Paralytic they went over the Pyrenees and, when next they were sober, they were already members of the British Battalion of the International Brigade.'

¶ Yet a large number of real idealists did fight in the International Brigade:

Neal Wool, 'Communism and British Intellectuals', 1959 'British volunteers in Spain totalled 2,762. Their casualties were exceptionally high: 1,762 wounded and 543 killed. About one half of those killed were members of the Communist Party of Great Britain or the Young Communist League. It is difficult to estimate the number of British intellectuals who participated in the fighting, drove ambulances, or otherwise assisted at the front. The most widely known Communist intellectuals were John Cornford, son of Francis MacDonald Cornford the Cambridge classicist and Frances Cornford the poet; David Guest son of the future Labour peer, Lord Haden-Guest; Christopher Caudwell, a brilliant young Marxist critic and poet; and Ralph Fox, the novelist and critic. All four died on the battlefield. Perhaps the greatest tragedy of the non-Communists in Spain was the death of the young poet Julian Bell, son of Clive and Vanessa Bell. Those who survived included Auden; the novelist Ralph Bates; the journalist, Claud Cockburn; George Orwell; Wogan Philipps, the painter; and Esmond and Giles Romilly, nephews of Sir Winston Churchill. Spain was the first and last crusade of the British Left-wing intellectual. Never again was such enthusiasm mobilized, nor did there exist such a firm conviction in the rightness of a cause. Disillusion had not yet sapped the idealism of the young.'

¶ That disillusion did come was largely the doing of the Russians themselves. It was not enough to be a fervent Communist; it was fatally easy to put a foot wrong:

Claud Cockburn, 'Crossing the Line', 1958 'A well-meaning man, a devoted man, wrote a piece in our paper [*The Daily Worker*] which was intended to explain to the English reader why Stalin was not a dictator in the same sense that Hitler and Mussolini were dictators . . .

190

'He was misguided enough to suggest that among the differences between a personal dictatorship and the dictatorship of the proletariat was the fact that if, for instance, our beloved leader and comrade Joseph Stalin were to pass away tomorrow, that sad event would not ruinously affect the structure and progress of the Soviet state.

'There was a father and mother of a row. Stalin, it appeared, had interpreted the statement as a direct instigation to the assassination of himself — an emphatic assertion that he was entirely expendable. For a considerable time the *Daily Worker* was banned in the Soviet Union. English enthusiasts landing at Leningrad and waving it joyously in the face of the Customs men, to show that they were absolutely on the right side, not mere capitalist sight-seers, found themselves under lock and key.'

¶ One had to be capable of doing double somersaults on a tight-rope to follow all the twists and turns of Soviet policy. On the outbreak of the Second World War —

'The [Communist] Party's Central Committee had met one day at the King Street headquarters to draw up a stirring manifesto to the British people calling upon them to sacrifice all in the great anti-fascist struggle. After hours of discussion the text was finalised. Then, unexpectedly, in walked the British representative to the Communist International whom everyone had thought was still in Moscow. *Douglas Hyde, 'I Believed', 1951*

'He took one look at the manifesto and told the leaders they would have to scrap it. It was, he said, an imperialist war. The Comintern had said so . . .

'On the morning of Sunday, June 22nd, 1941, came the bombshell, Russia after all had been attacked . . .

'After hours of discussion a statement was produced. The Party would support those who supported Russia. The entry of the Soviet Union into the war transformed it from an unjust war into a just one . . .

'We duplicated the statement as quickly as we could . . . and got our bulletin into the post in time for all the leading Party members and contacts throughout Britain to have the new Party line served up with their breakfast in the morning, before they left for the factory, mine or union office.'

¶ How was all this to be explained — or explained away?

Sir Norman Angell, 'After All', 1951 'I have continued to ask myself how it came about that the honest, idealistic, and often very learned folk who embraced Communism, above all priding themselves on their super-scientific approach, moved only by "fact", failed to foresee the one most stupendous fact which was to emerge from the Communist experiment — that the society it produced would not be free and humane, but slavish and debased ... In the flood of recantations by Communists ("The God That Failed" kind of thing) and explanations of why they changed their minds, there is no explanation of how at the beginning they could have overlooked the likelihood of their encountering along the road precisely what they did encounter.'

¶ Perhaps the most dignified and moving account of the attitude of the young idealists of the period is to be found in the first volume of John Lehmann's autobiography:

John Lehmann, 'The Whispering Gallery', 1955 'It may be difficult for anyone who was too young to experience the generation that came to manhood just at the time when the Depression of the 'thirties spread over the world, to understand how urgent our need was amongst us to break out of what we felt to be an artistic impasse, a suffocating air, and in some way in all we wrote and did help to voice the anguish of a world caught in the cogs of a pitiless economic machine, a world that demanded a drastic remedy for mass unemployment and a virile attempt to halt the forces that were making for war. We may have been wrong in many of our judgments, absurd in many of our actions; but it was impossible . . . to escape the urgency . . .

'In the very year that *New Writing* was born the Spanish Civil War had broken out, and dragged us all deeper into the morass of ideological conflict, putting to the sharpest test the idealism that the advance of fascism in Central Europe had awakened in us. Long before the Nazi–Soviet pact, the last stages of that war had seen the turning of the tide; volunteers and political workers home from Spain told stories of Communist ruthlessness, cynicism and intolerance towards minorities and minority opinion, or any opinion that did not square with the Party line, that we found it difficult to credit at first, but less and less easy to excuse as they accumulated . . .

'[George Orwell's] account of what happened in Catalonia ... broke the last resistance of many who had been desperately holding out against the shock of truth. But though truth might be unpleasant, it

192

Mr. Victor Gollancz, inventor of 'The Left Book Club'.

Intellectuals of the 'thirties: W. H. Auden, Cecil Day Lewis and Stephen Spender. This photograph, taken in 1949, is believed to be the only one of all three together.

was better than the twisted logic that condoned crimes in the name of progress and freedom; it was better late than never to realize that we had been walking beside someone whose features we had never clearly discovered until then . . . [and who] would never speak the language we recognized as our own.'

¶ Better late than never. We can leave it at that.

CHAPTER X

THE WORLD WELL LOST

At 9.25 p.m. on January 20th, 1936 the B.B.C. announced that 'the King's life is moving peacefully towards its close'. At five minutes to midnight King George V was dead. He had been much beloved and his death seemed to many to mark the end of an epoch. Men looked with high hopes to the new Monarch.

'Illustrated London News', January 25th, 1936

'In ascending the Throne, at the age of forty-one, King Edward VIII brings to his high task a unique experience of men and of the world, along with a singularly winning personality . . . Wherever he has gone, he has won all hearts by his unassuming friendliness, humour and sportsmanship. He is the first bachelor King of this country since George III, in 1760, succeeded to the Throne before his marriage. Edward VIII, has also made history, since his accession, by being the first British Sovereign to travel in an aeroplane, for on January 21st, the first day of his reign, he flew from Sandringham to London, accompanied by his brother and Heir Presumptive, the Duke of York.'

¶ The new King and his brother walked behind their father's coffin from Sandringham to Wolferton Station and from Kings Cross to Westminster. At King's Cross the Imperial Crown was placed on the coffin, and during its progress through the streets on a gun-carriage a strange thing happened. The cross on the top of the crown fell off. *Absit Omen!*

'Illustrated London News', February 1st, 1936

'Most prominent of the objects of the Regalia laid upon King George's catafalque in Westminster Hall was the splendid Imperial State Crown. Much historic interest attaches to some of the great jewels which are incorporated in it. In the centre of the cross immediately above the band is . . . the Black Prince's ruby . . . On the band

194

is set the second largest portion of the great Cullinan diamond. Finally, at the centre of the cross at the top glitters a sapphire with a very old English association. This stone is said to have been set in the coronation ring of King Edward the Confessor. During the late stages of the funeral procession which brought King George's body from King's Cross Station to Westminster Hall, it was noticed that the cross of which this sapphire is the centre was missing. In fact, it had become detached owing to the vibration of the gun-carriage on which the coffin, surmounted by the Crown, was carried. It was picked up and, after the procession had reached Westminster, duly restored.'

¶ The new King was proclaimed according to custom and, at St. James's Palace, the ceremony was watched by an unknown woman — unknown, that is, to the majority of the King's subjects. The unknown woman was Mrs. Ernest Simpson, and although she *was* unknown in England her name, and her photograph, had already figured largely in the American and European Press. Who was she, and where did she come from?

She had been born, it transpired, in Baltimore, U.S.A.

'Her geographic back-ground, of course, was quite propitious. Wallis Warfield was actually the second Baltimore girl to marry a king. The first was the celebrated Betsy Patterson, who married Jerome Bonaparte, youngest brother of Napoleon. But when Jerome was pressed to choose between the throne of Westphalia and his wife he chose, after the briefest reflection, the throne, and Betsy went back to Baltimore.

'There is, without doubt, some special quality about Baltimore girls.'

Geoffrey Bocca, 'She Might Have been Queen', 1955

¶ Her parents' circumstances at the time were not very prosperous:

'Aunt Bessie arrived early in November. Casual as she tried to be her conversation brought home to me as nothing else had done before, the lengths to which the American press had gone in its reporting of the King's interest in me. Aunt Bessie's account of some of these newspaper stories was not without its humour. My Warfield relations, she said, were not half so concerned over me as they were over the wild canards being circulated that my family had come from the wrong side of the tracks in Baltimore, that my mother had run a

Duchess of Windsor, 'The Heart Has Its Reasons', 1956

195

boarding-house. "You'd think", said Aunt Bessie with some heat, "that we'd all come right out of *Tobacco Road*." '

¶ Her father was Teackle Wallis Warfield, 'a retiring, ailing boy who worked insignificantly as a clerk in Baltimore', but the family had what are called 'good connections'.

Geoffrey Bocca,
'She Might Have
Been Queen', 1955

'Wallis's mother, like so many other mothers on the eastern seaboard of the United States, made impressive claims about her ancestry. She was born Alys Montague in Virginia, and confidently claimed ancestry back to William the Conqueror . . . Upton Sinclair, the novelist was one of Walter Warfield's cousins . . . Sinclair asserted that Wallis had Indian blood in her veins and was a descendant of Pocahontas.

'The record is at least plain on one point. Wallis came from sound, well-established American stock on both sides — on her mother's the Montagues of Virginia and from her father's side the respected Warfields of Maryland. There are several Warfields today well-known in Baltimore affairs, mostly in law and insurance, and one member of the family, Edwin Warfield, a distant uncle of Wallis's was State Governor from 1904 to 1908.'

¶ On November 8th, 1916, she was married at the Protestant Episcopal Church in Baltimore to Lieutenant Earl Winfield Spencer of the United States Navy, and five months later America was at war with Germany. The young naval officer was ordered to San Diego, California and the couple were still living there when the war ended. Curiously enough it was at a ball at San Diego in 1920 that they first set eyes on the Prince of Wales, who was on his way to Australia and New Zealand in the battleship *Renown*.

Geoffrey Bocca,
'She Might Have
Been Queen', 1955

'It was a crowded room, but no enchanted evening. There was no earthquake, no flash of lightning, no chill down the spine, no meeting of souls. It is almost impossible to imagine that Wallis, for all her ambition and will of steel, could imagine that she would ever marry this idolized Prince. At the moment she was penniless, miserably married to an honest but hard-drinking dullard, stuck in one of the most isolated corners of America.'

¶ The marriage lasted eight years. The couple were divorced in 1927.

King Edward VIII and his brothers in procession from King's Cross Station to Westminster Hall, January, 1936.

Funeral procession of King George V passing through Windsor, January, 1936.

King George V lying in state in Westminster Hall, 1936.

Wallis went to Europe with her 'Aunt Bessie' — Mrs. D. Buchanan Merryman — and in London she met Ernest Simpson whom she had already known in America. Shortly afterwards she was married to him at Chelsea Registry Office.

They lived at first at No. 12 Upper Berkeley Street, but finding this too small, soon moved to No. 5 Bryanston Court. Most of their friends were members of the American colony in London:

'In the course of her expanding relationships, Wallis became in time a particularly close friend of an American diplomat and his wife, Mr. and Mrs. Benjamin Thaw. Mrs. Thaw was formerly Consuelo Morgan, and her sisters were the two much-publicised Morgan twins, Thelma and Gloria, who became respectively Lady Furness and Mrs. Vanderbilt . . .

Geoffrey Bocca,
'She Might Have
Been Queen', 1955

'It was through Lady Furness, that the Simpsons first became good friends of the Prince though she was not responsible for the first meeting. That came about in the following way:

'The Prince, one day, was entertaining Benjamin and Consuelo Thaw at The Fort. As they were leaving, he asked them to come back to dinner. Regretfully Thaw was obliged to decline because, he explained, he and his wife had a date that evening to meet Mr. and Mrs. Ernest Simpson.

' "Bring them along", said the Prince.

'That afternoon he went to Sunningdale to have nine holes of golf with an equerry. The equerry, at the end, suggested another nine, but the Prince declined.

' "I can't", he said, "I've got some people I've never met coming to dinner. An American couple called Simpson." '

¶ The Duchess of Windsor's account of her first meeting with the Prince of Wales is rather different:

'Berny and Connie Thaw had become my close friends, and I was aware that Connie's sister, Thelma, Viscountess Furness, was greatly admired by the Prince of Wales and was widely reputed to be the object of his interest. One day in November, 1930, Connie called up in some agitation to ask my help. Her sister was having the Prince of Wales and several other guests down for a week-end's hunting at Burrough Court . . . Connie and Berny were to have been the chaperons. Unfortunately for the arrangement, Berny's mother had been

Duchess of Windsor,
'The Heart Has Its
Reasons', 1956

taken ill in Paris; and, because Berny was tied up with some business at the Embassy, Connie would have to leave for the Continent alone. Would Ernest and I take her place?'

¶ The whole arrangement was certainly peculiar. Can one chaperon a married woman in her own house? Mrs. Simpson seems to have thought it quite natural but she was alarmed as well as pleased. Would she be able to curtsy properly when the time came? However, she consented. There were 'at least thirty people' at dinner and while Thelma Furness sat, naturally, as she was the hostess, next to the Prince, the Simpsons 'were lost in the lower ranges of the spectrum of precedence'. It was nearly six months before Mrs. Simpson and the Prince met again.

This was at an afternoon reception at Thelma Furness's town house in Grosvenor Square.

Duchess of Windsor, 'The Heart Has Its Reasons', 1956 'Ernest and I were invited . . . After a while Thelma came in with the Prince . . . As he passed close by his glance happened to fall on me. He then nudged Thelma, who was standing beside him, and seemed to be asking her in a whisper, "Haven't I met that lady before?" '

¶ Different again is the account given by Lady Furness in the very frank book which she wrote in collaboration with her twin-sister Gloria Vanderbilt:

Gloria Vanderbilt and Thelma Lady Furness, 'Double Exposure', 1959 'Much has been written in many books about the famous meeting of the Prince of Wales and Mrs. Simpson, yet none of the accounts I have read is true to fact. Not even the Prince's version in his own book, *A King's Story*, is accurate. Perhaps one should understand and forgive his lapse of memory; the meeting was uneventful, and it took place a long time ago. But the claim to the dubious honour of introducing the two to each other is mine; and in the historical events that followed I was an unwilling catalytic agent.

'In the latter part of 1930, or early in 1931, when I was living at 21 Grosvenor Square, Consuelo telephoned one afternoon and asked if she could bring a friend for cocktails.

'The friend, she explained, was a young American woman married to an Englishman, Ernest Simpson. "Mrs. Simpson is fun", Consuelo said. "You will like her." And when she and Consuelo arrived later

198

in the afternoon, I found that Consuelo was right; Wallis Simpson was "fun", and I did like her . . .

'Later, Gloria arrived, bringing a few friends with her, and our gathering turned into an impromptu party. Eventually the butler came up to me to announce that the Prince had just arrived. I went to the door, "Oh, a party!" the Prince said, not too happily, as I greeted him.

' "No, darling, just a few friends", I said. "You know most of them. Consuelo, by the way, brought a friend of hers, a Mrs. Simpson." Then, repeating Consuelo's description, I added, "She seems to be fun."

'We went up to the drawing-room. The Prince immediately began a conversation with old friends. I went over to Wallis, took her to the Prince, and introduced her'.

¶ In June, 1931, Mrs. Simpson was presented at Court; Thelma Furness lent her the train and feathers she herself had worn and helped her to dress. When the Presentation was over, Mrs. Simpson went to a small party at the Furness house.

Then, about the middle of January, 1932, the Simpsons were invited to spend a week-end at Fort Belvedere. They were asked again during that year, once for tea and once for a week-end, but, early in 1933 the visits became more frequent. But, says the Duchess in her book: 'If the Prince was in any way drawn to me I was unaware of his interest. Thelma was always there.'

However, on June 19th, Mrs. Simpson's birthday, the Prince gave a party for her at Quaglino's, and soon afterwards dined at her flat. But there was still no hint that he found her anything more than 'fun'.

Various accounts have been given of what happened next. Lady Furness's will, perhaps, suffice:

'Early in January 1934, Gloria asked me to visit her. She was planning to go to California. I had not been to California for years, and we both had many friends there it would be pleasant to see again. I decided to join her in New York — then go with her.

'I spent the week-end of January 12th at the Fort . . . That Saturday the Prince went off to play golf. I had promised to pick him up. Later, on the way back from the links, I decided to broach the matter of my trip to America. "Darling," I said, "I've just had a letter from

Gloria Vanderbilt and Thelma Lady Furness, 'Double Exposure', 1959

Gloria asking me to come over for a short visit. I would very much like to go. Would you mind very much?"

'The Prince seemed surprised, "Oh, darling", he asked, "how long would you be gone?"

'I felt rather guilty, "Just five or six weeks", I announced trying to make "weeks" sound as insignificant as "days".

'His face took on a look of resignation, as if to imply that although this was not to his liking, he would say nothing that might interfere with my pleasure. "Of course, dear. Do what you want." And then he added, "But I will miss you; I will miss you very much . . ."

'Three or four days before I was to sail, I had lunch with Wallis at the Ritz. I told her of my plans, and in my exuberance I offered myself for all the usual yeoman's services. Was there anything I could do for her in America? Were there any messages I could deliver? Did she want me to bring anything back for her? She thanked me and said suddenly, "Oh, Thelma, the little man is going to be so lonely."

' "Well, dear", I answered, "you look after him for me while I'm away. See that he does not get into any mischief."

'It was later evident that Wallis took my advice all too literally. Whether or not she kept him out of mischief is a question whose answer hinges on the fine points of semantics.'

¶ Lady Furness left England on January 20th, 1934, and was back on March 22nd. Soon afterwards both she and the Simpsons were guests once more at Fort Belvedere:

Gloria Vanderbilt and Thelma Lady Furness, 'Double Exposure', 1959

'The week-end was negatively memorable. I do not remember who was there, other than the Simpsons . . . Most of Saturday passed without incident. At dinner, however, I noticed that the Prince and Wallis seemed to have little private jokes. Once he picked up a piece of salad with his fingers. Wallis playfully slapped his hand. I, so over-protective of heaven knows what, caught her eye and shook my head at her. She knew as well as everybody else that the Prince could be very friendly, but no matter how friendly, he never permitted familiarity . . .

'Wallis looked straight at me . . . That one cold, defiant stare told me the whole story . . . I left the Fort the following morning.'

¶ The road was now clear for the ripening friendship of the Prince and Mrs. Simpson, and gossip about the pair increased daily, especially in America. That acute chronicler Geoffrey Bocca has unearthed what is probably the first reference to the matter in the World Press:

'Such fun was Edward of Wales having at Cannes last week with beauteous Mrs. Wallace Wakefield (*sic*) Simpson, that he sent back to Marseilles an airplane he had ordered to take him to Paris.'

'Time Magazine', September, 1934

¶ Appearances, however, were still preserved:

'In February, 1935, the Prince went to the little Austrian resort of Kitzbühel. Mrs. Simpson was in the party frolicking with the Prince in the Alpine snows, but Mr. Simpson was not. From there the royal party, which numbered a dozen people altogether, visited Vienna and Budapest. Aunt Bessie Buchanan Merryman acted as chaperon, and Mrs. Simpson behaved so unobtrusively that there were few opportunities for serious gossip.'

Geoffrey Bocca, 'She Might Have Been Queen', 1955

¶ There were, however, those in Europe, who were only too ready to exploit the new situation:

'The Prince of Wales was very popular in Germany, and it must have seemed to the Nazis that Mrs. Simpson was a person to cultivate in order to advance their own interests. The man who came to try to perform the cultivation was Joachim von Ribbentrop, German Ambassador Extraordinary, later German Ambassador in London, later Foreign Secretary of Germany, later hanged.
'Visiting England, Ribbentrop persuaded the German Ambassador, Dr. Leopold von Hoesch to effect an introduction. Von Hoesch organized a dinner at which the Prince of Wales and Mrs. Simpson were invited. Ribbentrop was seated next to Mrs. Simpson, and pulled out all the stops of his not inconsiderable charm.'

Geoffrey Bocca, 'She Might Have Been Queen', 1955

¶ There is no evidence that Mrs. Simpson lent herself in any way to these intrigues, but she had met Ribbentrop and was friendly with the Italian ambassador Grandi. This was remembered against her in the days of the Crisis:

'One charge against Mrs. Simpson was never directly mentioned in the newspapers. But it was assiduously circulated in the clubs of the West End and the drawing-rooms of Mayfair, and thence percolated through all classes of society. Finally it was publicly ventilated by a

Warre Bradley Wells, 'Why Edward Went', 1937

Communist Member of Parliament during the debate on the Declaration of Abdication Bill.

'This charge was that Mrs. Simpson was in the pocket of Signor Grandi, the Italian Ambassador in London, that she was influencing King Edward to sympathize with Fascism abroad and pursue a Fascist policy at home.

'At that time, it must be remembered, relations between Great Britain and Italy were tense over Abyssinia.'

¶ Then, early in 1936 as we have already related, came the death of King George V and the situation was immediately transformed. The new King and Mrs. Simpson realized this and

Geoffrey Bocca, 'She Might Have Been Queen', 1955 'In private they made their plans, the object was clear, definite and admittedly remote. It was to establish Mrs. Simpson as Queen of England. No compromise was contemplated. It would be done gradually, treading carefully, a step at a time, winning bit by bit the favour of the country, the Empire, the Church, Queen Mary and Parliament. The difficulties in the way were great, but the King held the one trump card. He was the King and a Coronation was coming up; England would never get rid of her King. The first step was to make Mrs. Simpson socially acceptable. To do that he invited her and her husband to a dinner party at St. James's Palace, and on May 27th, 1936, Mrs. Simpson's name was dignified for the first time in the Court Circular. The guests were an unusual combination. They included Lord and Lady Louis Mountbatten and Lady Cunard, friends and courtiers of the King, and Mrs. Simpson; Mr. and Mrs. Stanley Baldwin; Colonel Charles Lindbergh, with his wife . . .

'The King had not told the Baldwins that Mrs. Simpson was coming. The idea was to break the barrier between Mrs. Simpson and Baldwin. It failed. They could find nothing in common . . .

'The King persisted. On July 9th, Mrs. Simpson's name appeared in the Court Circular again, very modestly and this time alone . . .

'Ernest Simpson was absent. Twelve days later on July 28th, the eighth anniversary of their marriage, he went to the Hotel de Paris in the village of Bray near Maidenhead, according to subsequent court evidence and spent the night there with a lady named Buttercup . . .

'The King then decided on a cruise, but instead of using the royal yacht, the *Victoria and Albert*, he acquired the use of the *Nahlin*, a luxury yacht owned by Lady Yule . . .

'The cruise of the *Nahlin* was a milestone pointing in many directions. It marked the high point and the end of Mrs. Simpson's reign in London. It coincided with the final break-up in the marriage between Simpson and Wallis. It precipitated the crisis which from then on progressed non-stop to the Abdication.'

¶ The King had intended to join the *Nahlin* at Venice but the Foreign Office pointed out how undesirable this would be, Mussolini having recently overrun Ethiopia and intervened in Spain, so it was decided that the yacht should await the royal party at Sibenik on the coast of Yugoslavia. With a few exceptions its members travelled on the Orient Express, breaking the journey for a short call on Prince Paul the Regent. At Sibenik a shock was awaiting Mrs. Simpson:

'Twenty thousand persons from all parts of Dalmatia dressed in their colourful native costumes swarmed around, all laughing and shouting kindly words of greeting to the British King. To my surprise, I found myself about as much the object of their attention as he was . . . That should have been a warning to David and me. It meant that our feelings had ceased to be our private secret; that they were becoming the property of the whole world . . . '

Duchess of Windsor, 'The Heart Has Its Reasons', 1956

¶ It was the same wherever they went. As far as the Continent of Europe was concerned the secret was out. It had long been out in America. Incredibly, miraculously, the Great British Public still knew nothing. Even the photographs of the cruise which appeared in the British Press were carefully selected — to show the King alone.

The King returned to England on September 14th and decided to spend the rest of the month at Balmoral. Mrs. Simpson was, of course, invited, and the King drove over from Balmoral to meet her at Aberdeen station. Unfortunately that was the very day on which he had declined to open the new buildings of Aberdeen Infirmary. He had deputed the Duke and Duchess of York to do it for him. A coincidence, but an unlucky one. It set tongues wagging.

And now the problem had to be faced of Mrs. Simpson's divorce. In the hope of avoiding publicity it was decided to have the case heard at Ipswich, instead of in London, and Mrs. Simpson had taken a villa at Felixstowe in order to obtain the necessary 'residential qualification'. It was so timed that, if a decree *nisi* were granted at

Ipswich it would be possible to have it made absolute *before* the date fixed for the Coronation. Mr. Baldwin became alarmed. He sought an interview with the King and tried to persuade him to get Mrs. Simpson to drop her petition. The King refused 'to interfere with the affairs of an individual'. But that was not the end of the matter.

It was all too likely that, if the divorce petition was carried through, the British Press would keep silence no longer — even if it were a trespass on the private affairs of the royal family. The King took precautions. He made a 'gentlemen's agreement' with the Press that the divorce proceedings should only be reported in the routine way.

¶ And so it turned out. Ipswich, to the surprise of its inhabitants, swarmed with American reporters and cameramen and the case was fully reported in the American Press. The British Press maintained its discretion. There were, however, complications:

Robert Graves and Alan Hodge, 'The Long Week-End', 1940 — 'Rumours now went round that the King was seeing more of Mrs. Simpson than was proper for a woman with a decree *nisi*, and a Common Informer complicated matters by lodging a statement which, if investigated by the King's Proctor, and proved true, would have prevented the divorce from being made absolute.'

¶ This is perhaps the most obscure and puzzling episode in the whole imbroglio:

Geoffrey Bocca, 'She Might Have been Queen,' 1955 — 'Francis Stephenson, the seventy-four-year-old solicitor's clerk had "intervened" with the King's Proctor slightly more than twenty-four hours before the Abdication, stating that he was going to show why Mrs. Simpson's divorce decree nisi should not be made absolute . . .

'The act of intervention was a little-known fact of law, yet during the Abdication crisis it had occurred to at least two people. Baldwin had warned the King that someone might take advantage of it. A week later Stephenson, coming from nowhere, known to nobody, did take advantage of it. The revelation of the power of a private citizen in a divorce case was startling.

'The British public heard, most of them for the first time, that any person can intervene in any divorce. He simply goes to the Divorce Registry at Somerset House in the Strand. He pays half a crown and states he has reason to show why a particular decree should not be made absolute. His "appearance" is noted, and notice of it sent to

204

Mr. and Mrs. Stanley Baldwin, 1935.

King Edward VIII with Mrs. Simpson at Ascot, 1935.

the solicitors of the petitioner (the petitioner in this case being Mrs. Simpson). According to law the intervener must file an affidavit within four days giving his reasons, though even if he fails to do so his "appearance" remains on the records and the divorce cannot be made absolute until it has been formally removed in court . . .

'Francis Stephenson turned overnight into a world-famous and, to some, a sinister figure. He made his "appearance" and filed his affidavit, and then when the matter came up in the Divorce Court in March 1937, he withdrew as abruptly as he had intervened . . .

'With the intervention withdrawn, the way was cleared for Mrs. Simpson to get her divorce made absolute, and the storm in the tea-cup died. Stephenson retreated into the endless jungle of London suburbia, leaving behind him two questions still not properly solved. Why did he intervene originally? and, having intervened, why did he so quietly withdraw?

'Stephenson was no ordinary crank. He had a good brain, an above-average knowledge of the law, and a self-confidence which enabled him to have his say without either losing his head or being frightened by the uproar he created.

'In the beginning he gave out a story that he was "so moved" by the King's Abdication speech that he felt he could not continue with the intervention. Later he admitted bluntly: "I withdrew because I was told to." Next the question must be asked, "By whom?"

'The answer to that is locked in the old man's mind. Stephenson, nearly ninety, and a widower, today lives in a single room in a boarding house in the wilderness of fading stucco known as Tulse Hill in South London.'

¶ Was this Mr. Baldwin's 'secret weapon', held in reserve, in case the King proved obdurate? Once the King had abdicated there was, of course, no need for it, and so Mr. Stephenson 'quietly withdrew'.

Meanwhile in America not only articles but books began to appear about 'the most famous woman in the world'.

'The most famous woman in the world today is neither a leader in public life, nor an heiress, nor a writer; not a philanthropist, a doctor, a scientist, nor a motion picture star.

Edwina H. Wilson, 'Her Name was Wallis Warfield', 1936

'Six months ago her name was comparatively unknown. Today it echoes above and below the equator — from Baltimore, Md., to the Isle of Bali, from Alaska to the Antipodes.

'She is the most romantic figure of the times, the amazing heroine of the most amazing chapter in recent history. Of international figures, she is, at once, the best known and the one known least.

'She is, of course, Mrs. Wallis Simpson, the American woman whom half the world expects to become Queen of England.

'There never has been a story like it. There never has been an individual so glamorous. Did Mrs. Simpson take tea on Sunday at Buckingham Palace? Did she drive out on Monday to go shopping? Did she really say this-and-so to the Duchess? Is it true that she wears a silver fox wrap worth $50,000? Does she, unfailingly, receive twelve dozen American Beauty roses each morning?

'Thus the tongues buzz. Thus the world wonders.'

¶ The same lively writer obviously thought that the whole thing was (almost) in the bag:

Edwina H. Wilson, 'Her Name Was Wallis Warfield', 1936

'The world asks today, "Will King Edward marry Wallis Simpson? Will she, an American-born woman, be Queen of England?"

'There is no answer until it comes from Buckingham Palace. Then America will know if Wallis Simpson is to be consort to the mightiest ruler on the earth and if she is to wear a crown. It would become her.

'For Wallis Simpson IS a queen — the queen of romance, of glamour and the unfulfilled longings of a love-starved world. She is the queenly heroine of a love story that, touching these two — Edward VIII, monarch of the British Empire, and Wallis Simpson of America — touches millions.

'A toast, America! A toast to THE QUEEN OF ROMANCE.'

¶ This jubilant attitude was not shared by those in the know in England, and Alexander Hardinge, the King's Private Secretary, thought it his duty to warn him that 'the silence of the British Press on the subject of Your Majesty's friendship with Mrs. Simpson is not going to be maintained. It is probably only a matter of days before the outburst begins. Judging by the letters from British subjects living in foreign countries where the Press has been outspoken the effect will be calamitous.' When the news did break it did so in a very curious and roundabout manner:

Sir Arnold Wilson, 'Thoughts and Talks', 1938

'At 4 p.m. on December 1st a cloud, "like a man's hand", gathered over the room in the city of Bradford in which the Right Reverend A. W. F. Blunt was addressing his Diocesan Conference. He was

206

known as a man of learning and letters, Anglo–Catholic in outlook, outspoken, but less given to intervention in secular affairs than many of his colleagues. Like the Archbishop of York he had never spoken in the House of Lords, where he might have been answered and corrected: he had no first-hand acquaintance with the King, and no ecclesiastical responsibility at the Court or in connexion with any royal residence. Whatever he said was, therefore, of necessity at second-hand; in other words he was, as indeed he proclaimed, the mouthpiece of others. A single sentence in his address, prepared, the public were given to understand, six weeks earlier, was endowed, in the light of circumstances of which, as he protested a few days later, he was wholly unaware, with high political significance. It ran as follows:

"The benefit of the King's Coronation depends, under God, upon two elements; first, on the faith, prayer and self-dedication of the King himself . . . We hope that he is aware of his need. Some of us wish he gave more positive signs of his awareness."

'The text of his sober address had been handed to the Press in advance: it was given to a small audience, very few of whom, any more than the Bishop, can have ascribed to it the significance with which it was invested, on the following day, by the *Yorkshire Post* and other provincial journals, and by the *Manchester Guardian,* whose editors simultaneously decided that the time had come when the self-imposed vow of silence, so long and so honourably observed, should be broken.'

¶ The people of Great Britain awoke suddenly to the fact that the country was faced with a 'Constitutional Crisis' of the first magnitude:

'Popular interest in the constitutional crisis was shown in various gatherings outside Buckingham Palace and the Premier's official residence . . . On December 4th, a party of workers from City offices used their lunch hour to make a demonstration of loyalty outside the Palace singing the National Anthem and "He's a Jolly Good Fellow". That night, too, there were further lively scenes, when some 300 young men and girls marched in procession from the Marble Arch and down Constitution Hill to the Palace gates, bearing a banner inscribed "Let the King know you are with him." They sang the same songs and shouted "We want Edward . . ." Another throng gathered

'Illustrated London News', December 12th, 1936

in Downing Street on Sunday, December 6th, and when the Archbishop of Canterbury left No. 10 after a visit to Mr. Baldwin, the crowd broke a police cordon and swarmed about his car, which had difficulty in moving away. A Cabinet meeting took place later. As Ministers left there were shouts from the crowd:"We want the King."'

¶ Messrs. Graves and Hodge, on whom we have called before for their apt comments, sum up the situation very neatly:

Robert Graves and Alan Hodge, 'The Long Week-End', 1940   'Most ordinary people were for the King; most important people were against him. Churchill expressed the ordinary point of view when he accused the Prime Minister in the House of betraying both the King and Parliament. The Beaverbrook Press followed the same line, its aim being as much to get rid of Baldwin as to support the King. Intrigues became complicated: it was rumoured that Beaverbrook and Churchill were pressing the King not to give way to the Cabinet. Churchill was mentioned as an alternative Prime Minister; if he were gainsaid in the Commons, it was felt, he could carry the country with him in a general election. Sixty M.P.s were supposed to have written to the King, pledging their support. Nevertheless, nobody could tell how a general election would go, nor how the Dominions would react if Churchill were successful. The risk was not run.'

¶ The idea of a morganatic marriage met with no encouragement from Mr. Baldwin. In the House of Commons, on December 4th, he made the following statement:

'Hansard', December 4th, 1936   'Suggestions have appeared in certain organs of the Press yesterday and again today, that, if the King decided to marry, his wife need not become Queen. These ideas are without foundation. There is no such thing as what is called morganatic marriage known to our law . . .

'The lady whom he marries, by the fact of her marriage to the King, necessarily becomes Queen . . . The only way in which this result could be avoided would be by legislation dealing with a particular case. His Majesty's Government are not prepared to introduce such legislation . . .'

¶ Meanwhile, Mrs. Simpson had decided that it would be best if she left the country for a time. In her own memoirs she gives us a moving

208

Newspaper placards, December, 1936,

A scene at Marble Arch, Hyde Park, London, December, 1936.

The Abdication Crisis: The Archbishop of Canterbury leaving 10 Downing Street, 1936.

account of her journey which is, unfortunately, too long to quote. We must content ourselves with a brief summary:

'The world was now watching Mrs. Simpson's dash across France to Cannes, pursued by scores of journalists and Press photographers. Hounded by these people, unable to make even a rational use of hotels on the way, at times forced to eat her meals in her car with blinds drawn, often returning on her tracks in order to escape the attentions of her pursuers, she finally arrived at the Villa Lou Viei, the home of Mr. and Mrs. Herman Rogers, American friends . . . With Mrs. Simpson travelled a Lord-in-Waiting to the King — Lord Brownlow.'

I. Lincoln White, 'The Abdication of Edward VIII', 1937

¶ For Mrs. Simpson it was an agonizing time:

'I had the sensation of sinking in quicksand . . . Despite David's reassurances, it was becoming tragically clear that the balance was tipping towards abdication . . . Ever since that awful last day at the Fort the . . . idea had been taking shape in my mind: I must wrench myself entirely out of David's life . . . I telephoned to David at the Fort to tell him of my decision and to read him the statement . . . After I finished there was a long silence. I thought that David in his anger had hung up. Then he said slowly "Go ahead, if you wish; it won't make any difference." '

Duchess of Windsor, 'The Heart Has Its Reasons', 1956

¶ Thereafter, events moved rapidly:

'Thursday, December 10th, was the climax of the constitutional crisis . . . by one o'clock the House was already fuller than even on Budget Day and at prayers no seat was vacant. The Chaplain asked God's blessing, for the last time, as we already realized, on Our Sovereign Lord King Edward . . .
'Questions to Ministers showed that the nerves of Members were on edge: they laughed at anything — or nothing, and were noisier than is their wont. At twenty minutes to four the Prime Minister, who had entered, amid applause, a few minutes earlier, left his seat and, walking to the Bar of the House, announced to the Speaker:
' "A message from the King, signed with his own hand."
'Then advancing, bowing at the gangway and again before the Mace, he handed the paper in his hand to the Clerk to pass to the

Sir Arnold Wilson, 'Thoughts and Talks', 1938

Speaker who, rising from his seat, began to read it, in a tense silence. Those Members who were wearing their silk hats bared their heads to listen to the "final and irrevocable" decision of the King to abdicate.'

¶ The same eye-witness gives us a glimps of the public reaction:

Sir Arnold Wilson, 'Thoughts and Talks', 1938 'I walked across Westminster Bridge into Southwark and went into an eating-house with a paper in my hand containing the news. A taxi driver sitting next me began to talk. "Oh dear, oh dear", he began, "to think that it should come to this after all he's done. I can't believe my eyes — but there it is — he's torn it."

' "What else could he do?" said I.

' "It's gone too far, I suppose", he replied, "but Lord, I remember seeing him in France; I've seen him a score of times on the job. I thought we were going to have such a King as never was — and now!" His distress was obvious.

' "It's his own choice and he's had plenty of time now. No one has forced it on him", I urged.

' "That's true", he assented, "I've known many a man chuck a job and his duty for a girl, that's straight, and that's what it is when all's said." '

¶ On December 11th, the Abdication Bill was passed through all its stages in a single sitting of Parliament. The procedure took two hours in the House of Commons and eight minutes in the House of Lords. Then came

'The Times', December 12th, 1936 'The last and most painful scene of the tragedy. Lord Onslow, summoning Black Rod, instructed him to let the Commons know that the Lords Commissioners desired their immediate attendance. This was quickly done, and in a few minutes the Speaker, followed by a crowd of grave-faced Ministers and members, was standing at the Bar . . . The Reading Clerk, stepping from his place to the right of the table, bowed low, spread open a vast parchment splashed with the red of the Great Seal, and slowly read out the authorisation "by the King himself, signed with his own hand" . . . The solemn words "His Majesty's Declaration of Abdication Act" rang through the silent House.

'The Reading Clerk turned and faced the Commissioners. On the other side of the table the Clerk of the Parliament also took his stand; and was required to pronounce the Royal Assent in the usual words.

He turned about and the last act of King Edward's reign was consummated with the words *"Le Roy le veult".'*

¶ At last the man who had been King Edward VIII was free to speak:

'The world was now anxiously waiting for the valedictory message *I. Lincoln White, 'The Abdication of Edward VIII', 1937* of the late King to the nation. Almost every country had made arrangements to relay the speech which was to be broadcast from a room in the Augusta Tower of Windsor Castle. Cinemas and theatres interrupted their programmes to give their patrons the opportunity to listen to the speech.

'Ten o'clock arrived. Sir John Reith, Director General of the B.B.C., announced:

' "This is Windsor Castle. His Royal Highness Prince Edward."

'Tense listeners heard a door close. Then in the well-known voice he began his last message to the people he had served:

' "At long last I am able to say a few words of my own . . .

' "You all know the reasons which have compelled me to renounce the Throne. But I want you to understand that in making up my mind I did not forget the country and the Empire which as Prince of Wales, and lately as King, I have for twenty-five years tried to serve. But you must believe me when I tell you that I have found it impossible to carry the heavy burden and responsibility and to discharge my duties as King as I would wish to do without the help and support of the woman I love.

' "But I want you to know that the decision I have made has been mine and mine alone. This was a thing I had to judge entirely for myself. The other person most nearly concerned has tried up to the last to persuade me to take a different course. I have made this, the most serious decision of my life, only upon the single thought of what would in the end be best for all.

' "This decision has been made less difficult for me by the sure knowledge that my brother, with his long training in the public affairs of this country and with his fine qualities, will be able to take my place forthwith, without interruption or injury to the life and progress of the Empire. And he has one matchless blessing, enjoyed by so many of you and not bestowed on me — a happy home with his wife and children . . .

' "And now we all have a new King. I wish him and you, his people, happiness and prosperity with all my heart. God bless you all. God save the King!"

'A moment later all the B.B.C. transmitters closed down.'

¶ And so the man who had been King went into exile:

Philip Guedalla,
'The Hundredth
Year', 1940 'The big car plunged forward through the night . . . and the slow hours passed, until his headlights swept the shuttered streets of Portsmouth. When they found the Dockyard, they went in at a gate which took them by H.M.S. *Victory*; and he passed Nelson's flagship with a lift of the hat. Then they left the car and walked about in the raw fog to find the ship that he was looking for. Not far away he recognized the looming bulk of H.M.S. *Courageous,* where he had made his little speech to cheering seamen just a month ago. A car overtook them in the Dockyard, and the Commander-in-Chief led the way to H.M.S. *Fury*. That was his destination; and as he went on board, the Admiral in tears bade him good-bye for the Navy.

'There were more leave-takings in the small cabin; and *Fury* felt her way towards the coast of France in the mid-winter fog.

* * * *

'The journey lay before him now across the Continent to Austria. He had not known for many hours that this was where he would be going. For his destination was not a matter which had engaged the attention of Ministers . . . nothing had been officially arranged for him. He was left to making his own arrangements; and something had been sketchily arranged on his behalf at a hotel in Switzerland. That was where he thought that he was bound for, as the dreadful evening opened and he drove away from Fort Belvedere for the last time. But it seemed intolerable that he should be hunted by newspaper men in a Swiss hotel, friendly voices had been busy on long distance telephones across the Continent . . . in consequence he would be going to Vienna.'

¶ At Vienna he characteristically paused to let the photographers take some pictures. 'I want you to let the photographers come along', he said. 'They have had a very tough journey and they deserve some results.'

Then he entered a car and drove to Schloss Enzerfeld, belonging to Baron Eugène de Rothschild, head of the Paris house. And there we must leave him and return to England.

212

INSTRUMENT OF ABDICATION

I, Edward the Eighth, of Great Britain, Ireland, and the British Dominions beyond the Seas, King, Emperor of India, do hereby declare My irrevocable determination to renounce the Throne for Myself and for My descendants, and My desire that effect should be given to this Instrument of Abdication immediately.

In token whereof I have hereunto set My hand this tenth day of December, nineteen hundred and thirty six, in the presence of the witnesses whose signatures are subscribed.

SIGNED AT
FORT BELVEDERE
IN THE PRESENCE
OF

The Instrument of Abdication, 1936.

Raoul Dufy—'Changing the Guard at St. James's Palace'
(Reproduced by permission of the Léfèvre Gallery).

¶ The first feeling was one of relief that the Crisis was over:

'Saturday, December 12th, was felt by many to bear the same relation to the days that went before as does Easter to Holy Week. Money flowed again, the crowds who gathered to hear the Royal Proclamation of Accession by the Officers of Arms in their tabards . . . were smiling again.

'Christmas shopping began that day in earnest. The crisis was over.'

Sir Arnold Wilson, 'Thoughts and Talks', 1938

¶ Many, however, thought that the clergy, especially the Bishops of the Established Church, might have let well alone. On Sunday, in Gloucester Cathedral, Dr. Headlam remarked that 'The King, inspired by an unlawful passion, renounced the greatest Throne the world has ever seen and the most splendid position a man could hold. Indiscretions so great that they had been notorious throughout the civilized world, cannot be held to belong merely to private life.' The Bishop of Portsmouth spoke of 'indecency and impropriety' and of 'headlong slips into the abyss of shamefulness'. Such remarks did not perhaps reach a very large audience but that night the Archbishop of Canterbury came to the microphone at Broadcasting House and said:

'It is right to be proud of the way in which the nation has stood the test. Yet let there be no boasting in our pride. Rather let us pass into humble and reverent thankfulness for this renewed token of the guidance of the nation's life by the over-ruling Providence of our God . . .

'The Times', December 15th, 1936

'Seldom, if ever, has any Sovereign been welcomed by a more enthusiastic loyalty. From God he received a high and sacred trust. Yet by his own will he has abdicated — he has surrendered the Trust. With characteristic frankness he has told us his motive. It was a craving for private happiness. Strange and sad it must be that for such a motive, however strongly it pressed upon his heart, he should have disappointed hopes so high, and abandoned a trust so great.

'Even more strange and sad it is that he should have sought his happiness in a manner inconsistent with the Christian principles of marriage, and within a social circle whose standards and ways of life are alien to all the best instincts and tradition of his people. Let those who belong to this circle know that today they stand rebuked by the judgment of the nation.'

¶ Many people thought that this was kicking a man when he was down. The witty line: 'You old Lang swine, how full of Cantuar' was repeated in the clubs. Lord Brownlow, as one of the 'circle' reflected upon, demanded an apology — and got it. Some American commentators allowed their indignation to get the better of them:

Warre Bradley Wells, 'Why Edward Went', 1937

'It was the Archbishop of Canterbury who in his disgraceful radio address, sought to convey the impression that the couple in question had been living in sin . . . When a man in his forties sets out to look for a companion in sin he seeks youth; when he selects as the object of his attentions a lady who is also in her forties it can only mean that he sees in her the possibility of a sincere and understanding friendship. With Edward VIII it was a case of "when a feller needs a friend". Surrounded by stuffed shirts who had been weaned in starched diapers, the need for a little harmless healthy laughter became a pressing spiritual necessity. Said Elsa Maxwell: "Mrs. Simpson is the only human being I know who is gay as a lark!" '

¶ The argument seems a little far-fetched. Yet, as another American wrote, a few years later:

Hugh Allen, 'Window in Provence', 1943

'Had Edward VIII elected to keep a succession of dowdy mistresses like his grandfather, Edward VII, all would have been hunkydory with the hypocritical conjurors. Instead he elected to marry the lady of his choice for what John Drinkwater called "the venerable reason that he loved her". Yet Wallis Duchess of Windsor would have shared the throne with her husband, had that been permitted, with immeasurably more grace than some of the women who have sat on that hot spot in the past . . .

'Yet at a moment when American goodwill was most important to Britain, the conjurors gave this American woman the works. "The most outrageous attack upon a woman that has ever been made in England", Mr. H. G. Wells rightly stigmatized the campaign against Mrs. Simpson, writing in the *New York American* on the Eve of King Edward's abdication.'

¶ Lloyd George, who was in Jamaica at the time, telegraphed to the man who had been created Duke of Windsor:

214

'Best Christmas greeting from an old Minister of the Crown who holds you in as high esteem as ever and regards you with deeper loyal affection, deplores the shabby treatment accorded to you, resents the mean and ungenerous attacks upon you, and regrets the loss sustained by the British Empire of a monarch who sympathised with the lowliest of his subjects.' *Hugh Allen, 'Window in Provence', 1943*

¶ To the American writer quoted above it seemed that the bombing of London was no more than England's just reward:

'According to Nostradamus, God has a special predilection for the Duke of Windsor. If that is so, it is enough for you and you. The harrowing experience which the English are undergoing partly represents the fitting of the punishment to the crime — that of thwarting a design of God with reference to the Duke. When the Eternal Justice of God has been satisfied, we may be sure He will grant to the Duke all the graces that he may need to fulfil God's plan in his regard.'

¶ We have no comment to make on this. Perhaps we should end with the words attributed to Queen Mary: 'The Yorks will do it very well.'

CHAPTER XI

TOWARDS THE BRINK

TO LIVE THROUGH what remained of the 'thirties was like sitting in a small boat rushing ever nearer and nearer to the edge of Niagara. For the moment, however, the British people were concerned with tidying up at home. The Coronation, fixed for May 1937, duly took place but it was King George VI and not King Edward VIII who was crowned. His work accomplished, Mr. Stanley Baldwin resigned at the end of the month and was created Earl Baldwin of Bewdley. Mr. Neville Chamberlain succeeded him as Prime Minister.

The political horizon was far from clear. The civil war in Spain continued and there was a new conflict between China and Japan. In Russia there was a purge of 'Trotskyists', and Marshal Tukachevsky (who had attended the Jubilee of King George V) was shot, with seven other generals. There was trouble in Palestine. Then, in March 1938, Hitler occupied Austria. The *Anschluss* of which he had dreamed since his early poverty-stricken days in Vienna was an accomplished fact. Many people in Britain became uneasy, but there was nothing they could do about it. And after all the Nazis had been accorded a tumultuous welcome by at least some of the Austrians.

One anxious voice was raised in the House of Commons. It was Winston Churchill crying 'Wolf!' again! He said:

'Hansard',
March 14th, 1938
'The gravity of the event of March 12 cannot be exaggerated. Europe is confronted with a programme of aggression, nicely calculated and timed, unfolding stage by stage, and there is only one choice open, not only to us but to other countries, either to submit like Austria, or else take effective measures while time remains to ward off the danger, and if it cannot be warded off to cope with it . . . If we go on waiting upon events, how much shall we throw away of resources

216

now available for our security and the maintenance of peace? How many friends will be alienated, how many potential allies shall we see go one by one down the grisly gulf? How many times will bluff succeed until behind bluff ever gathering forces have accumulated reality? . . . *Where are we going to be two years hence?*'

¶ The 'waiting upon events' continued, and it soon became plain what Hitler's next victim was to be. On September 17 he addressed an audience of 120,000 Storm Troopers at the November Rally. His theme was the 'atrocities' committed by the Czechs against the Germans of the Sudetenland.

Great Britain was not bound to Czechoslovakia by any formal treaty. France was, and, of course, Great Britain was in alliance with France. The Entente had received a new confirmation by the Royal Visit to Paris in July. Most people in this country were convinced that we would stand firm against any attempt to incorporate Czechoslovakia in the German Reich. But were our rulers as certain of this as the man-in-the-street?

The Times was not an official organ of the Government but, with Geoffrey Dawson as Editor, it was supposed to reflect Government policy pretty closely. It was therefore with some shock that many subscribers to 'our great national daily' opened the paper at the leader page and read these words:

'It might be worth while for the Czechoslavak Government to consider whether they should exclude altogether the project, which has found favour in some quarters, of making Czechoslovakia a more homogeneous state by the cession of that fringe of alien populations who are contiguous to the nation to which they are united by race.' *'The Times'*,
Sept. 7th, 1938

¶ This was the first hint that the Government was preparing to yield Hitler yet another point.

'The statesmen who believed the policy of "standing firm" could hold Hitler in check considered this a treacherous stab in the back. There was no doubt as to the buoying effect it had on German officialdom. Long faces became wreathed in smiles and minor Nazi leaders went about good-naturedly assuring everybody there wouldn't be a war. Dr. Dietrich, the German Press chief, explained that Hitler *Virginia Cowles*,
'Looking for
Trouble', 1941

217

didn't want a war. Then added with a sly smile, "He can get what he wants without."

'This smug conviction was widespread among the German people. The beer-gardens rang with laughter and music and everyone merrily agreed that Hitler was clever enough to score by diplomacy alone. One afternoon I climbed the hill to the old city with Bertrand de Juvenel, a French journalist. We went into a small restaurant, crowded with S.A. men, drinking beer and eating sausages and sauerkraut. Somehow it was difficult to realize that the S.A. contingents in their heavy black boots and their khaki uniforms, with the swastika pinned on the sleeve, were the ordinary citizens of Germany — the bus-drivers, the hairdressers, the garage mechanics, and small shop-keepers. Nuremberg was a holiday for them. All day long they wandered about the town visiting exhibition halls, eating enormous meals, and having snapshots taken to send home to their girls. At night they filled the cafés and were always the last to leave.

'The particular group of S.A. men in the restaurant were tall and blond with honest, scrubbed faces. There were no empty tables and they cordially invited Bertrand and myself to join them. When they asked what nationality we were and Bertrand replied that he was a Frenchman, their eyes grew wide with interest.

'The leader of the group, an older man, grasped his hand and shook it warmly; he said he had lived in France for four years. He added that the time had been spent in fighting in the war, but, nevertheless, he felt he knew the country very well indeed. No one seemed to consider the conversation tactless when he tried to recall the names of the towns he had entered; then suddenly he broke off and assured Bertrand there wouldn't be another war. He had confidence that things would be settled in a peaceful way, for no one wanted a war, least of all Hitler.

'His companions nodded in agreement, then all six raised their glasses and drank a toast to Germany, to France, and to Czecho-slovakia.'

¶ Many readers of *The Times* felt strongly about what they considered a betrayal, and its leader-writer answered them on a note of pained surprise:

'The Times',
Sept. 9th, 1938   'It is really grotesque that so much righteous indignation should be expended on the mere suggestion, which has frequently been made

in these columns before, that a revision of boundaries should not be excluded entirely from the list of possible approaches to a settlement.'

¶ These were presumably Chamberlain's sentiments, and we now know that the French agreed with him.

'I dined with a Foreign Office official the night I arrived and learned from him that it was the French who had first caved in. On the evening of September 13th, M. Daladier, alarmed by the situation, communicated with Chamberlain and announced that France was in no position to fight, imploring the British Prime Minister to leave no stone unturned to find a way out. Thirty-six hours later Chamberlain made his first trip to Berchtesgaden. You can find a subdued reference to the conversation in M. Daladier's statement to the French Chamber on October 4th in which he said he got in touch with Mr. Chamberlain on the night of September 13th-14th, and told him "how useful it would be if diplomatic démarches were superseded by personal contact between responsible men." '

Virginia Cowles, 'Looking for Trouble', 1941

¶ The next day, a startling announcement was issued from Downing Street:

'The Prime Minister has sent to the German Führer and Chancellor, through His Majesty's Ambassador in Berlin, the following message:
' "In view of increasingly critical situation, I propose to come over at once to see you with a view to trying to find peaceful solution. I propose to come across by air and am ready to start tomorrow. Please indicate earliest time at which you can see me and suggest place of meeting. Should be grateful for very early reply.
                                        Neville Chamberlain." '

'The Times', Sept. 15th, 1938

¶ The first reaction was one of relief that something, at last, was being done to stop the drift and there was a wave of admiration for the old gentleman with the umbrella who had never entered an aeroplane in his life and was now prepared to seek personal contact with Hitler in order to straighten matters out. Hitler agreed to meet the British Prime Minister at Berchtesgaden. But

'while he was flying from London to Bavaria, an event had occurred which should never have been tolerated. Konrad Henlein had proclaimed that it was no longer possible for Czechs and Sudeten Germans

Henri de Kérillis and Raymond Cartier, 'Kérillis on the Causes of the War', 1939

219

to live together in the same State, and that he therefore demanded purely and simply the return of the Sudetenland to the Reich ... A new demand, more extreme than any of the others, and almost amounting to an ultimatum, had been hurled at the head of the English Prime Minister, at the very moment when he was disembarking from the aeroplane with his head full of the love of peace and the throb of engines. Had he possessed the reflexes of a boxer, which in this age of iron are essential for the government of nations, he would have replied to the German challenge by calling on Hitler to disavow Henlein and therefore to disavow himself. And if Hitler had seen the whole British Empire climbing back into its aeroplane with its 600,000 men, its invincible fleet, its tremendous industrial resources and its immense moral and financial credit, we may be sure that he would have clutched at Mr. Chamberlain's coat tails ...

'However complex a political drama may be ... there is always one tiny segment of the clock's dial in which the decision between victory and defeat will be made. In the drama of Czechoslovakia, that tragic minute was the one in which Mr. Chamberlain agreed to converse with Hitler under the threat of Henlein's ultimatum.'

¶ Hitler made his terms known and Mr. Chamberlain returned to London. Daladier and Bonnet joined him there and agreed without discussion. By many people in England the terms were read with amazement, but *The Times* commented:

'The Times',
Sept. 20th, 1938
'The general character of the terms submitted to the Czechoslovak Government for their consideration cannot in the nature of things be expected to make a strong *prima facie* appeal to them, and least of all to President Benesh, one of the builders of the Republic in its present shape. He is invited — as is generally supposed — to agree to an alteration of frontier which will diminish the extent of his country in territory and in population, and remove the boundary in Bohemia from the tip of a range of mountains to the foothills or the plain — leaving behind moreover the elaborate line of fortifications which it has cost years of labour and millions of pounds to build. The mountain frontier is also the historic frontier of the old Bohemian Crown ... The hope of those who lay these proposals before the Czech Government will certainly be that they will leave Czechoslovakia, though smaller in size, stronger by being made more nearly homogeneous ...

Herr Joachim von Ribbentrop.

Hitler and Mussolini at Brennero station.

It may be hoped the Czech Government will come to believe that the ultimate gain will be more real than the immediate sacrifice.'

¶ That the terms submitted could not 'be expected to make a strong *prima facie* appeal' to the Czechs is a masterpiece of understatement. They saw quite plainly that they were going to be abandoned by their allies and left defenceless; but they were not to be allowed to have any say in the matter. At 5 o'clock that evening the official Ceteka Agency announced that the terms had been accepted without reservation. 'We have accepted, because we are alone.'

Even now, however, the negotiations almost broke down, for when Chamberlain met Hitler again at Godesberg, he found that the Führer had already increased his demands. He wished to carry out an immediate occupation of the territories which had been ceded to him. However, he agreed, after much argument, to a delay of six days.

Mussolini telephoned to Hitler proposing a conference of the four great Powers in order to arrive at a peaceful solution of the Czecho-slovakian dispute. It was agreed that the representatives of Germany, Italy, France and Great Britain should meet at Munich.

Chamberlain at least had a great send-off:

'The Prime Minister's departure for the Munich conference was marked by a public demonstration of his Cabinet's good wishes which was without precedent. Unknown to him, some sixteen Ministers had agreed among themselves to give him a united send-off from Heston, as a gesture of appreciation of his efforts for peace. The Prime Minister's pleasure at this was evident. Ministers and their wives crowded round him, patting him on the shoulder; there were warm handshakes; and a great cheer was given as Mr. Chamberlain walked towards the aeroplane. Besides members of the Cabinet were the High Commissioners for Canada, Australia and Eire and many members of the Diplomatic Corps, including the French Ambassador and the German Chargé d'Affaires. Immediately after the Prime Minister had exchanged greetings with his colleagues, Count Grandi, the Italian Ambassador, came up to offer his sincere wishes for success.' *'Illustrated London News', Oct. 8th, 1938*

¶ *The Times* continued to take a line which can only be described as self-righteous:

'Justice does not become injustice because a dictator demands it. There is nothing sacrosanct about the present frontiers of Czecho- *'The Times', Sept. 22nd, 1938* slovakia. They were drawn twenty years ago; and they were drawn wrongly in the opinion of many well qualified to judge . . . Mr. Chamberlain deserves the thanks not of this country alone for having averted, so far, the immediate danger of war.'

¶ However, in the same issue *one* voice was raised in protest:

'The Times',
Sept. 22nd, 1938

'Sir.—The emotions of the country have seldom been so deeply stirred as by what is called "the betrayal" of Czechoslovakia . . . The proposal to have Czechoslovakia "neutralized", disarmed, and then guaranteed by her principal enemies, with England and France playing the same protecting role as at present, is not calculated to inspire confidence . . .

'During this summer I have spoken with people belonging to almost every country in Central and Eastern Europe. With scarcely an exception they all spoke of Germany with dread and dislike, and of England with sympathy; but they added, "How can we trust England? What has happened to the Armenians, the Abyssinians, the Chinese, and other members of the League?" . . . I do not say that the charges implied in these questions are justified, but they are made, and will now be made with redoubled force. Surely the world can be shown that at some point somewhere Great Britain will keep her covenants and protect those who trust in her.

Yours obediently
Gilbert Murray.'

¶ *The Times* continued to believe that all was well, and even that Chamberlain had 'won over' Hitler himself:

'The Times',
Sept. 28th, 1938

'He has captured the imagination of the people of Germany, who in welcoming him have found an opportunity for pacific demonstration that their own political system does not give. More than this he has inspired in the mind of the German Chancellor a personal trust that Herr Hitler has conceded to no other democratic statesman . . . On this trust . . . the main hope of peace continues to depend. That it will be reinforced by a full measure of his fellow countrymen's confidence, expressed through Parliament, is not to be doubted.'

¶ When Daladier, returning from Munich, arrived over Le Bourget airport and saw enormous crowds waiting for him, he was alarmed.

222

Did they mean to lynch him? On the contrary, they greeted him with shouts and tears of joy. He was, for the moment, the most popular man in France.

'In France, the first reaction to Munich was a tremendous relief. This is undoubtedly very human and understandable. Our people had been living under the threat of war. Every one of us had tried to envisage the horrors which seemed to be in store for us, and it is not surprising that Daladier was cheered at Le Bourget and on the boulevards . . . *Henri de Kérillis and Raymond Cartier, 'Kérillis on the Causes of the War', 1939*

'He called the Deputies and the Senators for the 5th October to demand their ratification of the treaty. . . It was a strange session. He entered the Chamber symbolic of all his own weaknesses and mistakes, of his lack of initiative after the 21st May, his reluctance to support England, his cardinal error of proposing the Berchtesgaden journey, and his dilatoriness as far as French national defence was concerned. Yet he was acclaimed as Clemenceau had been when he entered the same hall on the 11th November, 1918, bringing victory and the return of Alsace to France . . . the Deputies had every right to prefer Munich to a war. But they had no right to rise to their feet and give a five minutes' ovation to the messenger of a treaty which had dismembered a friendly nation . . . Munich was ratified by 535 votes to 73. The French Parliament had made its choice.'

¶ The British Prime Minister also returned in triumph.

'Chamberlain returned to England. At Heston, where he landed, he waved the joint declaration which he had got Hitler to sign, and read it to the crowd of notables and others who welcomed him. As his car drove through cheering crowds from the airport, he said to Halifax, sitting beside him, "All this will be over in three months"; but from the windows of Downing Street he waved his piece of paper again and used these words, "This is the second time in our history that there has come back from Germany to Downing Street peace with honour. I believe it is peace in our time." ' *Winston S. Churchill, 'The Second World War', 1948*

¶ Not *everybody* agreed. Duff Cooper resigned from the Government and Churchill issued a stern warning to the Press:

'The partition of Czechoslovakia under pressure from England and France amounts to the complete surrender of the Western Democracies *'The Times', Sept. 1st, 1938*

223

to the Nazi threat of force. Such a collapse will bring peace or security neither to England nor to France. On the contrary, it will place these two nations in an ever weaker and more dangerous situation. The mere neutralization of Czechoslovakia means the liberation of twenty-five German divisions, which will threaten the Western front . . . It is not Czechoslovakia alone which is menaced, but also the freedom and the democracy of all nations. The belief that security can be obtained by throwing a small State to the wolves is a fatal delusion. The war potential of Germany will increase in a short time more rapidly than it will be possible for France and Great Britain to complete the measures necessary for their defence.'

¶ But for most people it was 'Peace in our time.'

Virginia Cowles,
'Looking for
Trouble', 1941

'I watched a girl in a scarlet taffeta dress and a young man in tails whirl round the Ritz ballroom so fast they looked like a red and black top. I was at a dinner party, sitting next to Alfred Duff Cooper who, two weeks before, had resigned from the British Cabinet. Earlier in the evening he had said to me: "It was 'peace with honour' that I couldn't stomach. If he'd come back from Munich saying, 'peace with terrible, unmitigated, unparalleled dishonour', perhaps I would have stayed. But peace with *honour*."

'The girl in the scarlet taffeta dress wasn't bothering herself about honour or dishonour, and neither were the other couples on the dance floor, from the look of them. Peace was the important thing. Once more the music was playing and Mr. Chamberlain was the hero of the day. Business firms advertised their gratitude in the newspapers; shops displayed Chamberlain dolls and sugar umbrellas; and in Scandinavia there was a movement to present the British leader with a trout stream. Only a few people like Duff Cooper shook sad and sceptical heads over "peace in our time" and stared gloomily into the future. When the girl in the scarlet taffeta dress spun past us, Duff Cooper said: "I wonder where that couple will be a year from today!" '

¶ What did the Czechs think about it? The same acute observer, who had actually seen the German troops moving in to take over the ceded territories, tells us:

Virginia Cowles,
'Looking for
Trouble', 1941

'Two miles outside Carlsbad a small group of Czech soldiers had drawn up alongside the road where the new frontier began. They stopped our car and one of them asked us, curiously, what the

224

celebration was like. He listened quietly, then remarked in German: "I suppose you'll be leaving Czechoslovakia soon. Are you going to France?" Geoffrey nodded and the soldier said: "When you get there, you can tell them for us that one day they will look across that Maginot line of theirs and ask, 'Where are those two million Czechs?' And we won't exist. They will fight alone."

'We drove the rest of the way to Prague in silence.

*   *   *   *

'Sidelight for America: a few days after the Munich agreement, Jan Masaryk, the Czech minister in London and son of Thomas Masaryk, the founder of Czechoslovakia, was walking through Hyde Park when Joseph Kennedy, the American Ambassador, drove past him. The car stopped and Kennedy called out:

' "Hi! there, Jan. Want a lift?"
'Jan got into the car and Kennedy slapped him on the back.
' "Oh, boy! Isn't it wonderful!"
' "What is?" asked Jan.
' "Munich, of course. Now I can get to Palm Beach, after all!" '

¶ 'Munich' was to have been the 'final settlement', but, unfortunately, Germany and Italy had other views. In Rome, Signor V. Gayda, who was usually regarded as Mussolini's mouthpiece, wrote:

'The Czechoslovakian affair is simply one danger to European peace the less. Many other important problems, involving moral and political injustices either recent or of long standing, give Italy and Germany good cause for regarding the present situation with mistrust.'

'Giornale d'Italia', Oct. 2nd, 1938

¶ And then, a week later, Hitler spoke at Saarbrücken.

'The extreme pessimists expected at least a few words of appease- ment, while the extreme optimists were hoping for a regular peace plan . . . But in fact the Führer refused to satisfy these hopes . . . His speech was fierce and intransigent. Mussolini was described as the only true friend of Germany, and the sole initiator of the Munich Agreement. Mr. Chamberlain and M. Daladier had not even the distinction of being mentioned by name. On the other hand, French and British political institutions received a full measure of violent

Henri de Kérillis and Raymond Cartier, 'Kérillis on the Causes of the War', 1939

P

criticism, and the leading members of the British opposition, Duff Cooper, Eden and Churchill, were the objects of outrageous personal attacks. "Since they may return to power, and a world war may break out, Germany refuses to disarm." This was the substance of what Hitler said . . . This threatening speech from Saarbrücken was a rude shock to post-Munich rejoicing. Nevertheless, some Frenchmen were so resolutely blind that they actually congratulated themselves on the fact that France had not received much mention. These unfortunate individuals quite failed to understand that the Führer's outburst had been a direct result of the lengthy foreign affairs debate at Westminster, and that his comparative neglect of France had simply been an expression of thanks to MM. Daladier and Bonnet for having stifled discussion in the Palais Bourbon. They failed to arrive at the obvious conclusion that in future the only way to avoid German abuse would be to tremble and hold our tongues.'

¶ On 8th November, Hitler, in a speech at Munich, demanded the return of 'the Colonies which were stolen from us on pretexts which were entirely contrary to the principles of justice. Apart from this question, Germany has no further demands on France and England.' Once again the French might congratulate themselves for the former German Colonies had passed to England. But now Italy also raised her voice:

Henri de Kérillis and Raymond Cartier, 'Kérillis on the Causes of the War', 1939 'On the 30th November, the very day when France was indulging in the luxury of a General Strike, Count Ciano was making an *exposé* of Italian foreign policy in the Chamber. It was the usual happy coincidence! The Duce was in the Chamber too, with his eyes fixed on his son-in-law. This ministerial *exposé* had nothing particularly remarkable in it, but at the close of Count Ciano's speech, the Deputies rose to their feet like a well-drilled regiment. Prolonged shouts echoed through the hall. "Tunisia! Tunisia! Corsica! Djibouti! Savoy!" '

¶ Still the democracies continued to hope and, early in December, 1938, Ribbentrop travelled to Paris and with Georges Bonnet signed a Franco-German Peace Pact. They signed with golden pens. Perhaps they were symbolical of the money which Germany had already spent in purchasing the support of an influential portion of the French Press.

More significant were the proposals for a formal alliance between Germany and Italy. Ciano notes:

'January 4, 1939. Conversation with Grandi [Italian Ambassador to the Court of St. James] . . . I gave him a rather vague idea of our future alliance with Germany in order to get his reaction. He has declared himself in favour and does not believe that there will be very serious repercussions in British circles . . . Von Ribbentrop has sent me the text of the Pact, as well as the secret military conventions.' *Ciano's 'Diary', 1947*

¶ Perhaps Chamberlain had wind of this. At all events, early in January he decided to visit Mussolini. Ciano regarded the expedition with some amusement:

'January 7, 1939. Prepared a moderate toast for the coming of Chamberlain. I do not believe the situation calls for or will permit the expenditure of too many idle words . . . *Ciano's 'Diary', 1947*

'January 11, 1939. Arrival of Chamberlain. Essentially the visit was kept in a minor key, since both the Duce and myself are doubtful about its utility. The welcome of the crowd was good, particularly in the middle-class section of the city, where the old man with the umbrella is very popular. The welcome was colder on the outskirts, where the workers are less emotional. Chamberlain, however, is very happy over the reception . . .

'6 p.m.: Conference at the Palazzo Venezia. The recorded conversations gave an impression of tiredness. The matters which were discussed were not particularly important, and both parties betrayed their mental reservations. Today's conversation has been exploratory. Effective contact has not been made. How far apart we are from these people! It is another world. We were talking about it after dinner with the Duce, gathered together in a corner of the room. "These men are not made of the same stuff", he was saying, "as the Francis Drakes and the other magnificent adventurers who created the empire. These, after all, are the tired sons of a long line of rich men, and they will lose their empire" . . .

'January 12, 1938. Conference at the Palazzo Chigi with Lord Halifax . . . The recorded discussion of the afternoon was characterized by the profound uneasiness which dominates the British attitude to Germany. German rearmament weighs on them like lead . . . This sombre preoccupation of theirs has convinced me more and

227

more of the necessity of the Triple Alliance. Having in our hands such an instrument we could get whatever we want. The British do not want to fight. They try to draw back as slowly as possible, but they do not want to fight . . . Our conversations with the British have ended. Nothing was accomplished. I have telephoned von Ribbentrop that the visit was a fiasco ("big lemonade"), absolutely innocuous, and I thanked him for the attitude of the German press . . .

'January 14, 1939. I accompanied the Duce to the station on Chamberlain's departure . . . The leave-taking was brief but cordial. Chamberlain kept repeating his thanks for the treatment that was accorded him during his stay in Italy.

'Chamberlain's eyes filled with tears when the train started and his countrymen began singing "For He's a Jolly Good Fellow". "What is this little song?" the Duce asked Grandi.'

¶ Every well-meaning gesture made by Chamberlain was misunderstood, or laughed at and exploited.

Ciano's 'Diary',
1947

'January 27, 1939. Lord Perth has submitted for our approval the outline of the speech which Chamberlain will make before the House of Commons, in order that we may suggest changes if necessary. The Duce approved it and commented: "I believe this is the first time that the head of the British Government has submitted to a foreign government the outline of one of his speeches. It's a bad sign for them" . . .

'March 23, 1939. Chamberlain has sent a letter to the Duce. He expresses his concern over the international situation and asks the Duce's help in re-establishing mutual trust and ensuring the continuance of peace. Mussolini will answer after striking at Albania. The letter strengthens his decision to act because in it he finds another proof of the inertia of the democracies.'

¶ In England the 'Left' was now thoroughly alarmed. Those who made up its strength blamed Chamberlain for yielding to Hitler, yet they were still opposed to conscription and critical of rearmament. The Pacifist wing adopted the attitude that since *anything* was preferable to war, the proper action was to give Hitler everything he wanted. Perhaps — one day — he would be satisfied:

C. E. M. Joad,
'Why War?', 1939

'If Hitler absorbs all the territories with the desire for which he is

228

'I believe it is peace in our time.' Chamberlain on his return from Munich.

Professor Joad.

credited, one of two things may well happen: (*a*) he will suffer from indigestion and become indisposed for further assimilation — it is not, after all, a foregone conclusion that all South-eastern Europe will lie easily on his stomach; or (*b*) he will digest and be quieted. Germany, in other words, will become a sated power, and, with satiety, may once again be prepared to show symptoms of humanity and to settle down into moderately decent behaviour. After all, hunger and humiliation were the causes that produced Hitler. When both causes have disappeared, their effects may disappear too. Even if Hitler remains, it is not inconceivable that he should himself begin to behave. Kemal Ataturk, once an aggressive dictator, became by a similar process, a quiet one. Admittedly, to allow Hitler to take what he wants may, in the long run, involve a smaller British Empire, but a British Empire maintained intact in all its present bulk may be a factor making not for but against world peace.'

❡ Armaments, he argued, were worse than useless, and he brought up the old Pacifist chestnut about Denmark.

'It is sometimes maintained that the security of the Scandinavian countries is dependent upon the power and protection of France and England, especially England. It is only, it is said, because they know the English to be strong and know, too, that the English would come to their defence if they were attacked, that the Danes feel comparatively secure against attack. I doubt this, and I doubt whether the statesmen of these Scandinavian countries believe it. I have already referred to the remark of the President of the Norwegian Parliament, to the effect that Mr. Chamberlain would not afford the expense of an aeroplane trip to Berlin in order to save Norway. No, it is not upon the problematic support of England and France that the comparative security of the Scandinavian countries rests. It is upon their own defencelessness. Being weak, they do not provoke fear and they are not, therefore, regarded with hostility; nor would the conquest of those who are not in a position to defend themselves confer prestige upon their conquerors.' *C. E. M. Joad, 'Why War?', 1939*

❡ And if they were, after all, invaded, what then? The man who had persuaded the Oxford Union that it would under no circumstances fight for its King and Country, was convinced that, even so, all would be for the best, so long as nobody resisted the invader:

C. E. M. Joad,
'Why War?', 1939 'If the Belgian Government had cared for the happiness and prosperity of the Belgian people, it would have let the Germans through in 1914 without resisting them. China, had she been wise, would not have sought to check Japan by force of arms — for a non-resisting China could absorb the Japanese, as she has absorbed so many of her "conquerors" in the past. Melancholy as the fate of the Czechs has been, it would have been worse if war had been declared and Czechoslovakia become the cockpit of Europe. After a few weeks a large part of Prague would have been destroyed, thousands of Czechs would have been killed, thousands more maimed and wounded. Men would have seen their sweethearts gassed and burnt; women would have mourned their dead husbands and watched their children being dismembered. There would have been semi-starvation as there was later in Government Spain, and, when winter came in in earnest, with temperatures ranging below zero, as they did in December, undernourished bodies would have been exposed to the full rigours of the cold. Today — I am writing in the week before Christmas — I am told, there is prosperity in Prague; unemployment has diminished; shops are doing a roaring trade; everywhere there are parties and Christmas reunions of happy families.'

¶ It is a pity that Professor Joad, with all his gifts, did not have the gift of prophecy.

Virginia Cowles,
'Looking for
Trouble', 1941 'On March 15th, 1939, Hitler's troops marched into Prague. That date will go down in history as the date when England woke up. Sugar umbrellas disappeared from shop windows and Mr. Chamberlain asked angrily: "Is this an attempt to dominate the world by force?" . . . From then on the nation prepared for war.

'Many foreign observers did not understand the change that swept the country. Some had associated the policy of appeasement with a "ruling class" of England, which, they claimed, had grown so effete that it was willing to drive a bargain with Nazi Germany to preserve peace (and property) at any cost . . . Cynics were bewildered by the sudden swing-over. When Chamberlain signed the Munich agreement they took it to mean that Great Britain had washed her hands of Europe and surrendered her long overlordship. They failed to understand that the Chamberlain Government was not compromising from fear, but from a genuine belief in Germany's capacity to prove herself a good neighbour.'

230

¶ Britain was now prepared to fight but at what a disadvantage! Few people, except Churchill, yet realized exactly what had been given away at Munich.

'The subjugation of Czechoslovakia robbed the Allies of the Czech Army of twenty-one regular divisions, fifteen or sixteen second-line divisions already mobilised, and also their mountain fortress line, which in the days of Munich had required the deployment of thirty German divisions or the main strength of the mobile and fully trained German Army. According to Generals Halder and Jodl, there were but thirteen German divisions, of which only five were composed of first-line troops, left in the West at the time of the Munich arrangement. We certainly suffered a loss through the fall of Czechoslovakia equivalent to some thirty-five divisions. Besides this the Skoda works, the second most important arsenal in Central Europe, the production of which between August 1938 and September 1939 was in itself nearly equal to the actual output of British arms factories in that period, was made to change sides adversely.'

Winston S. Churchill, 'The Second World War', 1948

¶ In spite of everything most people in France and England were still hoping for peace, and believing that it might still be preserved:

'Right up to the last moment the astrologers were prophesying "No war". Right up to the last moment the dress-designers were saying the same thing, in their own language, and saying it with even more conviction . . . Fashion is never arbitrary. It has its roots in . . . the Collective Unconscious, and the hopes and fears of a whole society are reflected in the cut of a dress. In the clothes of the 'thirties there was an element of true prophecy and an element of sheer wishful thinking, and as we came nearer and nearer to the edge of the precipice Fashion had to choose. It chose wishful thinking . . . The broad outlines of development were plain. We were ready for a new Paternalism. Society was about to set hard. The age of economic licence, general promiscuity and female emancipation was over. Tight-lacing could not long be delayed . . . The principal fashion houses [in Paris] seem to have been unanimous in their determination to bring in tight-lacing, real tight-lacing in the spring of 1939 . . .

James Laver, 'Taste and Fashion', 1945

'The advertisers hastened to join in the dance. "Wasp waists are here!" they clamoured . . . As summer drew to an end the manufacturers were promising woman "an old-fashioned, boned, laced corset, made by modern magic, light and persuasive as a whisper". "Control it with corsets", they cried. "Where there's a will there's a waist!"

'[The corset and] the bunched or "peasant" skirt . . . both pointed from different angles at a new conception of woman, at the end of the woman-as-comrade ideal which had reigned ever since the emancipation of the First World War. Perhaps it is hardly necessary to add that the peasant skirt in question was an *Austrian* peasant skirt. It was the faint but unmistakable echo of Hitler's "Kirche, Kinder, Küche!" '

¶ It became obvious that Hitler was now casting his eye on Poland.

Winston S. Churchill, 'The Second World War', 1948
'The time had come when the last illusions of the British Government had been dispelled. The Cabinet was at length convinced that Nazi Germany meant war, and the Prime Minister offered guarantees and contracted alliances in every direction still open, regardless of whether we could give any effective help to the countries concerned. To the Polish guarantee was added a Greek and Roumanian guarantee, and to these an alliance with Turkey . . .

'Addressing the Reichstag on April 28 [Hitler] said: "Since England today, both through the Press and officially, upholds the view that Germany should be opposed in all circumstances, and confirms this by the policy of encirclement known to us, the basis of the [Anglo-German] Naval Treaty has been removed . . ."

'In the same speech Hitler also denounced the German-Polish Non-Aggression Pact . . .

'The British Government had to consider urgently the practical implications of the guarantees given to Poland and to Roumania. Neither set of assurances had any military value except within the framework of a general agreement with Russia. It was therefore with this object that talks at last began in Moscow on April 15 between the British Ambassador and M. Litvinov . . . On April 16 [the Russians] made a formal offer, the text of which was not published, for the creation of a united front of mutual assistance between Great Britain, France, and the U.S.S.R. The three Powers, with Poland added if possible, were furthermore to guarantee those States in Central and Eastern Europe which lay under the menace of German aggression . . . [but] Poland, Roumania, Finland, and the three Baltic States did not know whether it was German aggression or Russian rescue that they dreaded more. It was this hideous choice that paralysed British and French policy . . .

'It is not even now possible to fix the moment when Stalin definitely abandoned all intention of working with the Western Democracies and considered coming to terms with Hitler . . . On May 3 an official communiqué from Moscow announced that M. Litvinov had been released from the office of Foreign Commissar at his request and that his duties would be assumed by the Premier, M. Molotov . . .

'The dismissal of Litvinov marked the end of an epoch . . . The Jew Litvinov was gone, and Hitler's dominant prejudice placated. From that moment the German Government ceased to define its foreign policy as anti-Bolshevism, and turned its abuse upon the "pluto-Democracies". . . From the moment when Molotov became Foreign Commissar he pursued the policy of an arrangement with Germany at the expense of Poland . . .

'A renewed effort to come to an arrangement with Soviet Russia was made by the British and French Governments. It was decided to send a special envoy to Moscow. Mr. Eden, who had made useful contacts with Stalin some years before, volunteered to go. This generous offer was declined by the Prime Minister. Instead, on June 12 Mr. Strang, an able official but without any special standing outside the Foreign Office, was entrusted with this momentous mission . . . In any case all was now too late . . . On the evening of August 19 Stalin announced to the Politburo his intention to sign a pact with Germany. On August 22 Marshal Voroshilov was not to be found by the Allied missions until the evening. He then said to the head of the French Mission: ". . . The French and English Governments have now dragged out the political and military discussions too long. For that reason the possibility is not to be excluded that certain political events may take place . . ."

'The next day Ribbentrop arrived in Moscow.'

¶ The Russo-German Pact was signed on August 22nd, and it seemed that war was now inevitable. Chamberlain made one more effort to avert it. He sent a personal letter to Hitler:

'Your Excellency,

'Your Excellency will have already heard of certain measures taken by His Majesty's Government, and announced in the Press and on the wireless this morning.

'The steps have, in the opinion of His Majesty's Government, been rendered necessary by the military movements which have been reported from Germany, and by the fact *that apparently the announcement of a German-Soviet Agreement is taken in some quarters in Berlin to indicate that intervention by Great Britain on behalf of Poland is no longer a contingency that need be reckoned with.* No greater mistake could be made. Whatever may prove to be the nature of the German-Soviet Agreement, it cannot alter Great Britain's obligation to Poland which His Majesty's Government have stated in public repeatedly and plainly, and which they are determined to fulfil.

'It has been alleged that, if His Majesty's Government had made their position more clear in 1914, the great catastrophe would have been avoided. Whether or not there is any force in that allegation, His Majesty's Government are resolved *that on this occasion there shall be no such tragic misunderstanding.*

'If the case should arise, *they are resolved, and prepared, to employ without delay all the forces at their command, and it is impossible to foresee the end of hostilities once engaged. It would be a dangerous illusion to think that, if war once starts, it will come to any early end.* . .

Yours sincerely,

Neville Chamberlain.'

When this despatch was handed to the Führer by Sir Neville Henderson on the afternoon of August 23rd, Hitler went up in smoke. Indeed he became so angry that he let slip one incautious, and revealing phrase. He said he preferred to make war at 50 rather than at the age of 55 or 60. He was already determined on war.

Still, in Chamberlain's letter, he saw something which he thought he could turn to his advantage. Chamberlain had proposed a 'truce'. Hitler immediately got in touch with Mussolini and suggested that he should prepare a trap. On August 31st a message was handed by Count Ciano to the British and French Ambassadors in Rome. It read:

'Signor Mussolini offers, if France and England agree, to invite Germany to a conference to be held on September 5th, at which the present difficulties arising from the Treaty of Versailles would be examined.'

This was the sort of manoevre in which the Duce delighted, for

'Signor Mussolini knew that at dawn on the following day (September 1st) the German troops would penetrate into Poland, and would already have seized upon sureties there, the result being that Hitler would already be in part possession when the Berlin Government was *officially* informed of the acceptance or refusal of the Chancelleries of London and Paris.'

Elie J. Bois, 'Truth on the Tragedy of France', 1941

¶ This was a brilliant stroke. If they agreed, the scene was set for another Munich. If they refused, they could be blamed for starting the war.

This time Chamberlain was not to be taken in. He said in the House of Commons, on September 2nd:

'I confess that in the present case I should have to be convinced of the good faith of the other side in any action which they took before I could regard the proposition which has been made as one to which we could expect a reasonable chance of a successful issue. . .

'Hansard', Sept. 2nd, 1939

'While appreciating the efforts of the Italian Government, His Majesty's Government, for their part, would find it impossible to take part in a conference while Poland is being subjected to invasion, her towns are under bombardment and Dantzig is being made the subject of a unilateral settlement by force. His Majesty's Government will, as stated yesterday, be bound to take action unless the German forces are withdrawn from Polish territory. . .

'If the German Government should agree to withdraw their forces, then His Majesty's Government would be willing to regard the position as being the same as it was before the German forces crossed the Polish frontier.'

¶ This was to go to the very limit of concession, for Polish soldiers had already been killed and Polish cities bombed. The British Government instructed its Ambassador to present its ultimatum to Germany at 8 o'clock on the morning of September 3rd and to request a reply before noon.

There was no reply. On Sunday morning, September 3rd, crowds gathered in Downing Street and Whitehall and heard, through the loud speakers, Chamberlain's Declaration of War. A moment later the sirens screamed. It was a false alarm, but it added its own dramatic touch to that tense moment of history. The hectic, frivolous, frustrated, puzzled, frantic period of 'Between the Wars' had come to an end.

Neville Chamberlain at the Back Door of 10 Downing Street.

INDEX